Tourists, Tourism and the Good Life

Routledge Advances in Tourism

EDITED BY STEPHEN PAGE, *University of Stirling, Scotland*

Tourists, Tourism and the Good Life

Philip Pearce, Sebastian Filep and Glenn Ross

Routledge
Taylor & Francis Group
New York   London

First published 2011
by Routledge
270 Madison Avenue, New York, NY 10016

Simultaneously published in the UK
by Routledge
2 Park Square, Milton Park, Abingdon, Oxon OX14 4RN

Routledge is an imprint of the Taylor & Francis Group, an informa business

Typeset in Sabon by IBT Global.

Library of Congress Cataloging-in-Publication Data
Pearce, Philip L.
    Tourists, tourism and the good life / by Philip Pearce, Sebastian Filep and Glenn Ross.
        p. cm. — (Routledge advances in tourism ; v.20)
    Includes bibliographical references and index.
    1. Tourism—Psychological aspects.   I. Filep, Sebastian.   II. Ross, Glenn F.
III. Title.
G155.A1P3624 2010
306.4'819—dc22
2010006198

ISBN13: 978-0-415-99329-6 (hbk)
ISBN13: 978-0-203-84586-8 (ebk)

Contents

Figures

Tables

Preface and Acknowledgments

Most of us at least at some stage of our lives ponder over the following questions: Am I leading a good life at the moment? How could I make my life better in the future? Or later in our lives we ask ourselves: Have I led a good life and how did I define it? The special interest in this book is on the role of the tourism context in promoting the positive experiences that lead to a good life: positive emotions, engagement and meaning. Like our pondering over the good life, tourist trips can be conceived in terms of time: we anticipate positive emotions at destinations, we value being immediately satisfied and engaged at the places we visit, and we reflect back on our holidays and sometimes gain wisdom and meaning from them.

The chapters in this volume plot a pathway to understanding this very important human desire to lead a good life in the context of being a tourist and in other contexts relevant to the world of tourism. The book represents the efforts of three academics, two of whom have detailed research backgrounds in psychology and tourism, one of whom has recently completed his doctorate work on the topic. The two core aims of the book are to: 1) offer a resource of new methodological and conceptual tools for scholars and students; and 2) to orient the audience to a fresh awareness of the value of well-being ideas from positive psychology and the research field's role in understanding the good life.

A somewhat unusual feature of this book is the integrating part introductions which present lead-in comments. These are contextual statements raising issues in the whole area defined by the part titles: "Principally About Individuals" (Part I) and "Individuals and Tourism Contexts" (Part II). Chapter 1 is also preceded by its own introduction. The introductions place all the specific chapters in a context. It is recognised that a book of this sort needed this "glue" to make it a coherent and complete statement while further recognising that all topics could not be covered. The three authors worked closely and tried to achieve stylistic consistency as much as possible while completing the chapter contributions.

Professional assistance of several people is highly appreciated. From James Cook University, we would like to thank Mrs. Robyn Yesberg for her cheerfulness and administrative assistance. From Victoria University, we would like to thank Professor Margaret Deery for her encouragement of this book initiative and the Centre for Tourism and Services Research staff for their advice and administrative support.

We hope you'll enjoy our small contribution to the good life!

Philip Pearce, Sebastian Filep and Glenn Ross
Australia, 2010

Introduction

It is appropriate at the start of this book to introduce Generation T. Who belongs to this newly designated group? In answering the question, readers do not have to recall their birth dates or formative years but instead should reflect on the educational routes which have prepared them to read this book. The defining feature of Generation T membership is an education about tourism, tourists and related topics, which is multidisciplinary, phenomenon centred and often ahistorical. If the educational route taken has been a combined pathway mixing subjects and courses in the social sciences as well as business and marketing and also includes various liberal options then an individual belongs to the Generation T (a short description for a tourism-focussed education). If readers have studied a single discipline as a major focus of undergraduate or first-degree education—effectively a three- to four-year concentration on one way of viewing the world—then the Generation T label does not apply. Generation T membership is growing and individuals in the cohort are successfully inhabiting the academic corridors of the world's universities and research centres which contribute to the analysis and teaching of tourism.

There are strengths and limitations in the preparation of Generation T members as researchers and educators. From a positive perspective, Generation T can combine their ready access to the world's published material with the shifting dynamics of the tourism sector to establish a productive, contemporary and broad outlook. Nevertheless, an enduring difficulty can be a modest basis on which to interrogate new patterns of thought, most especially when these concepts and ideas derive from a long established discipline such as psychology, sociology, economics or anthropology.

The purpose of Chapter 1 in this volume is to provide an accessible overview of the disciplinary biography in psychology. It is hoped that by providing this background an effective and informed use of the positive psychology ideas which underpin this volume can be employed in many kinds of tourism studies. The focus is on the core psychology ideas used throughout the chapters in this book. For a reader already familiar with the intricate history of psychology, it will appear as an abbreviated account of a long journey. It may also be viewed as idiosyncratic as its purpose is to prepare for an understanding of the roots of positive psychology rather than to record all the historical pathways. To assist readers to check the approach taken to the research provided in Chapter 1, there are some publications and Internet resources which might be particularly helpful, particularly those of the American Psychological Association (http://www.apa.org/) and the British Psychological Society (http://www.bps.org.uk/). These sources are usefully supplemented by popular books written by well-credentialed scholars such as the work of Furnham (2008) and Diener and Biswas-Diener (2008).

There are wider implications generated by the kind of review undertaken in Chapter 1 which repay some contemplation and reflection. These implications can be summarised with an alliterative trio of terms: productivity, politics and parasitism. The contrasting terms are quality, anarchy and symbiosis. The ideas constitute potential chapters in themselves, but in this context it can be simply observed that contemporary scholars are under political pressure to be productive and produce an array of publications for their careers and the status of their institutions. These pressures can result in the rapid borrowing of fashionable ideas, a form of parasitic plundering of the work of other areas. The responses to such pressures are understandable and much of the work produced in this way is still of high quality. Nevertheless, a close reading of the origin of the ideas and an effort to be anarchic in the sense of taking the time to independently assess the value and roots of the concepts offer the potential for exchange and symbiosis which reaches beyond some present achievements. Many of the historical figures in psychology discussed in Chapter 1 were colourful and independent figures finding their own way to lead the good life and flourish. If after completing this review the reader is stimulated to attack some of the original works, then there is the prospect of some surprisingly rich rewards and scholarly insights.

1 Scholarship in Psychology and Tourism

It is the intention of this book to contribute some novel and stimulating ideas to the study of tourism. These fresh ideas derive essentially from the work of positive psychology in the last decade. The area of tourism study of specific interest is the happiness and well-being of those undertaking or shaping tourism. The stated aim of making a novel contribution is ambitious, possibly even arrogant. It is necessary therefore to acknowledge immediately the considerable efforts of previous scholars in the fields of activity which are of chief concern. These fields are broadly but not exclusively the science of psychology and the developing study of the phenomenon of tourism and well-being. As Gould (2004) reveals, contemporary researchers should reflect seriously on their relationships with previous studies. Too strong a preoccupation with the efforts of previous researchers can cast one into the role of a latter-day gold miner who is left picking over the tailings of a well-worked field for something new to say. Yet again, insufficient efforts to note what others have contributed can amount to the reinventing of wheels, surely a rather circular affair.

The problem of one's relationship to previous study is particularly significant in a book where the implicit theme is "The Good Life" and the subthemes are happiness and well-being. Most attention will be given in this chapter, and indeed in the whole of the book, to the application of the efforts of positive psychology researchers. Nevertheless, for over two thousand years religious and humanities scholars have also considered how to live well and be happy. Such work can scarcely be ignored. Possibly the phrase Sir Isaac Newton used in a letter to his fellow physicist Hooke can be employed: "If I have seen further it is by standing on the shoulders of giants" (Gould 2004: 70). Merton (1965) reports that this was not a new phrase and its artistic representation is depicted in the twelfth-century Chartres Cathedral, where New Testament scholars are portrayed as dwarfs neatly astride the shoulders of much larger Old Testament prophets. While the authors are happy to conceive of themselves as gnomish academic dwarfs, the ensuing question is on whose shoulders are we standing? As an answer, we see ourselves perched on the back of previous work on the psychology of happiness while resting some weight on select concerns in tourism study. In essence, then, this volume amounts to a respectful but purposeful foray into the contemporary scholarly understanding of how people come to be happy and content, most especially in tourism settings. This chapter provides the context for the contribution and attempts to respect and learn from much previous analyses of human behaviour both in general and as specifically displayed through tourism.

It is important to provide one small note of preparation for reading this chapter. Not every contributor to the history of psychology whose work is mentioned is referenced in terms of their specific studies being cited. The interest in many formative figures is much more in their dominant ideas and overall contributions to a disciplinary history. To cite all or even select works from many such contributors would reduce the following pages to a spaghetti of names and dates. Nevertheless, acknowledgment of key sources and review material is made on a regular basis. For historical figures, birth and death dates are provided to place their work in a time frame but for contemporary figures this practice is not pursued.

PSYCHOLOGICAL FOUNDATIONS

As many psychology undergraduate students rapidly discover, popular views of psychology tend to misrepresent the focus of the discipline in the twenty-first century.

The public stereotype of the psychologist often confuses the psychologist and the psychiatrist and to the extent that the television and film media portray psychologists at work, it is the clinician, the ever popular mind reader and the criminal profiler who feature most strongly. The experimental researcher, the cognitive scientist and the statistician are marginal characters in the public image. Becher and Trowler (2003) suggest that a discipline or area of study can be understood more formally through a number of pathways. One can, for example, track dominant themes and people in the evolution of the study area. Since our interest is in a contemporary shift in the way psychologists orient themselves to public life, this thematic and historical approach will be our first endeavour in this book.

Edmund Boring, in his massive 777-page history of experimental psychology completed in 1950, observed "a psychological sophistication that contains no component of historical orientation seems to me to be no sophistication at all" (1950: ix). Boring also made the astute observation that the present changes the past or at least affects those parts of the historical record which authors seek to emphasise. At the outset of the review process in this chapter it can be clearly acknowledged that the following overview does indeed favour "presentism", a term which specifies that the historical review is distorted towards those aspects of the past which are of greater interest to contemporary concerns (Pickren, 2007). In particular, it will be suggested that an understanding of the different kinds of psychology in both the nineteenth and twentieth century assists powerfully in defining the current approaches in positive psychology.

The landmark topics which stand out in the history of psychology and which need consideration as a context for applying contemporary work to tourism include empiricism, positivism, hedonism, dynamic motivation, attitudes, values, phenomenology, the experimental method and the application of evolutionary theory. In order to present these concepts and approaches to studying human well-being, it is possible to propose and report on a set of hypothetical events. In keeping with the spirit of the times in which the study of psychology evolved, the first event can be depicted as a "parlour game" where one is restricted to inviting three guests for a dinner conversation. The specific restriction is that they have to be the great psychologists of their era and the initial invitation is to those born in the first half of the nineteenth century. Wilhelm Wundt (1832–1920), the person responsible for the first planned psychology laboratory, is in attendance, together with William James (1842–1910), America's foremost founding psychologist from Harvard. They are joined by Francis Galton (1822–1911), the British polymath who is independently wealthy and whose family is linked to that other prodigy of the age, Charles Darwin (1809–1882). At the turn of the twentieth century their conversation would undoubtedly have been lively since James was known to have complained that Wundt was so prolific that even when his ideas were dissected each fragment would regrow and he would write another book on that topic (Boring, 1950: 346).

Wundt's conversation initially focuses on the value of the experimental method as it has been applied at his Leipzig laboratory from the late 1870s. Wundt argues in his thorough and erudite German way that the experimental method is not suitable for all of the topics of interest to psychology, but its application is leading to insights into sensation and perception beyond the reach of the previous armchair philosophers. Wundt is on sound ground here because, in addition to his experimental approach to the elements of sensation and perception, he is in the middle of writing his *Volkerpsychologie* (*Folk Psychology*), a ten volume (1905–1920) history of man which he sees as the other route to studying psychology and most especially the higher order processes. On this point, James and Wundt can be seen to agree, for while James too has experimental rooms at Harvard he is not inclined to use them. He is more attracted to dealing with problems of consciousness, emotion and religious experience at a philosophical and cultural history level. James claims that consciousness contains knowledge and meaning not just sense data and that emotions are intimately linked to the person's perceptions of their own bodily changes. This perspective is still current and remains relevant to understanding the context-dependent nature of emotional responses in any situation including tourism settings.

Francis Galton is hardly a passive participant in the conversation and the extent of his work enables him to make several kinds of conversational contributions. Whereas Galton understands Wundt's quest to isolate the elements of sensation and perception and establish lawful generalisations applicable to all people, his own interests lie more in the products and outcomes of human capacity. Consistent with Britain's status in the world at the time, Galton asserts the value of understanding the ways in which the intelligence and the capacity of his countrymen and his country may be further improved. He explains his quest to establish the nature of individual differences and argues for the value of constructing tests and measures to describe statistically the distributions of talent and ability in the community. He is Darwin's half cousin and the controversial evolutionary theory of his relative informs much of his interest in the genetic inheritance of abilities. James and Galton chat comfortably, united by an interest in the higher mental processes and the pragmatic value of the developing field of psychology. Wundt is not alienated from the conversation but sees a prime role for the purer form of study linking physiology and philosophy. In the seeds of these conversations we have the beginnings of the distinctions between applied and fundamental work in psychology, the nascent emergence of different methods for undertaking the exploration of human capacity and even the founding of testing procedures that will lead to the ability to describe markets and group differences.

Other conversations are needed to develop the review of the issues and concepts in the field. Our next soiree brings together figures born in the second half of the nineteenth century. The gathering is a little larger because the study of psychology expands in the three principal locations—in Germany following Wundt, in Britain following Galton and especially in the United States following James and a wide band of other scholars. Our principal invited guests this time are Sigmund Freud (1856–1939), John C. Watson (1878–1958) and Kurt Lewin (1890–1947). Others drop by and the guest list records the attendance of William McDougall (1871–1938), Granville Stanley Hall (1844–1924), Hermann Ebbinghaus (1850–1909), Edward Titchener (1867–1927), some learning theorists, young psychoanalysts, educational psychologists and gestalt enthusiasts. All of these attendees provide snippets of interesting conversation.

The differences in perspective at this fresh gathering are palpable. G. S. Hall and Ebbinghaus, the two oldest members of the gathering, report the successful application of the experimental method to topics of broader social and psychological concern. In Hall's case he has applied the questionnaire technique, derived in part from Galton's work, to a detailed study of adolescence and he has amassed much statistical information. Like his educational psychology colleague John Dewey (1859–1952), he is effectively developing the groundwork for a functional approach to psychology where the questions to be asked are oriented to the use of the ideas as opposed to an inherent interest in the structure of thought. Ebbinghaus, too, fits broadly into this approach. He has studied memory with meticulous and inventive experimental procedures and is formulating important ideas about contiguity and repetition as frames for understanding this higher order mental process. Titchener leaves the gathering early because he is disillusioned with this new functional and useful kind of psychology, preferring to remain true to the Wundtian tradition (in which he trained) of trying to understand the human mind at an abstract rather than an applied level. For William McDougall, the Englishman who has migrated to the United States, there is no such conflict. He describes the ideas informing his now very popular first ever textbook of social psychology. His approach is in accord with some recent experimental research on teams and competition and McDougall envisages an important future for the study of social behaviours. In his view it will be a future independent of sociology. In this new social psychology the individuals responding to their social worlds are the objects of interest rather than the analysis of the structure of society which looks at social behaviour from a more molar view. In McDougall's scheme to explain rather than just describe social behaviour, he suggests the use of the term *purposive psychology* and list numerous needs which drive behaviour. After a period of neglect, the topic of motivation or, in more philosophical terms will or volition, reappears in the psychology conversation and is addressed here most directly through McDougall. There is another voice in the meeting which is about to take the gathering by storm and rebuild the concept of motivation from an altogether different perspective. The voice belongs to the Austrian Sigmund Freud.

Freud's complex scheme for understanding damaged individuals takes the listeners on a long historical journey linked to the topic of hedonism. Freud, like McDougall, is concerned with motivation but he suggests that there are deeper and less obvious motives to be considered. The notion that there are elemental, possibly unconscious, forces guiding human conduct has a long history and Freud's creative and often original perspective on these motivational themes is of interest to any researcher looking at pleasure, play and psychology. Freud says that his pleasure principle or libido is the driving factor motivating all individuals. The excesses which would result in a constant lust for pleasure, as represented by the libido, are subdued by a monitoring psychological counterweight, the censorious superego. The outcome of their warring control of the individual's desires results in varying levels of personal control depending on the individual's life experiences and the resolution of key childhood issues. The importance of pleasure as a prime mover for social life is not unfamiliar to the gathered assembly. It is also a key concept in many popular views of what constitutes the good life (Diener and Biswas Diener, 2008: 244). Freud's idea is a recasting of the concept of hedonism, which has a long philosophical and political lineage (Grayling, 2005). The founding figures here were the Greek scholars Aristoppos and Epicurus, who claimed that the highest purpose of life was an active devotion to pleasure. At core, hedonism proposes that individuals seek to maximise their pleasure and avoid pain. Immediate pleasure and gratification when enjoyed without any view of their consequences tend in the end, however, to let people down. Whereas continuous sensory indulgence, even licentiousness might appeal—a position adopted by the Greek writer Aristippos—a slightly longer term view recognises that such a set of actions quickly results in conflict with others. The ensuing interpersonal conflict can be painful. Some of the key writers in English philosophy and early political thought, such as Locke, Mill and Bentham, built their analyses on hedonism. It is conceived here as the optimal ratio of pleasure to pain or, more colloquially, the best deal to be had in terms of both immediate gratification and longer term gratification. The discipline of economics, itself built on the work of Adam Smith, is underpinned by just such a view of humanity as driven by hedonistic self-interest (Gould, 2004). In the economics case, the necessary social condition to enable the self-interest to be expressed is defined as free trade. This kind of calculus, where the happiest communities were viewed as those achieving the greatest good for the greatest number, was most clearly expressed in the work of Jeremy Bentham. His approach is expressed in the concept of utilitarianism, although Bentham had a slightly grander vision of the greatest good than hedonism alone can provide.

The remarks Freud makes about pleasure are then less of a surprise than the other parts of his system which addresses the development of personalities. Theories of motivation and personality development tend to have deficit, balance or energy models as their underlying force. Freud reveals that his defining energy force is the libido, a kind of surging current of power that develops in childhood and needs correct management at oral, anal and genital stages of development. The mismanagement of desires built around these key childhood experiences can leave the individual with strong phase-linked characteristics in adult life such as the love of talking and eating deriving from inadequate or excessive oral stimulation.

The gathering of psychology scholars is both intrigued and dismayed by Freud's ideas. J. B. Watson and Thorndike both contend that Freud, in giving power to the superego, places too much emphasis on the individual's view of future consequences, something with which they are not at all comfortable. The prevailing tradition in animal and human behaviour studies is based much more on the individual's reactions to past consequences. Other younger psychoanalysts, as well as the broader community, murmur discontentedly at the periphery when the most sexually charged notions of the Freudian system are mentioned. Like Darwin before him, Freud's views are readily mocked, with his view of personality later to be depicted as the outcome of brawls between a maiden aunt and a sex-craved monkey (Kelly, 1955).

Freud's perspective undoubtedly reintroduces motivation to the psychology conversation. Kurt Lewin tackles many of the same topics but with a more experimental mind-set and a less clinical orientation. While Freud forces the audience to think about the past stages of their development, Lewin makes immediate tensions the driving force of life. For Lewin, objects in the individual's life space have positive or negative attracting power, a term he calls valences. Lewin accounts for people's lives and actions in terms of field theory. This is a psychological field in that the conditions and goals are as they are perceived. Lewin notes that he seeks to understand individuals through all of the particulars of the forces and interrelationships in which they are involved. The discharge of tension when a goal is reached resets the force field until new tensions are generated by the passage of time or the actions of others. Lewin informs the listening gathering that recent studies with children's play and with the challenge of leaving an activity unfinished are vindicating his approach of conceptualising behaviour in terms of tension levels, valences and the actual life space in which the individual is embedded at the immediate point where we are studying the behaviour.

Lewin's ideas about driving tensions resonate with the approach to human needs to be found in the work of Henry Murray. It is Murray who makes the concept of needs accessible to scientific study with a tight definition which sees needs as direction-giving forces terminated only by achieving specific end states. Murray provides a compelling case that social and cultural needs must accompany biological needs to account properly for human conduct.

Watson and Thorndike, powerful figures of their age, argue for the value of the tradition of behaviourism which they represent. In their view, the understanding of behaviour is best approached by avoiding the nebulous world of the mind, force fields and needs, and it is through concentrating on what people do and how they are rewarded or punished that we will best build a study of people's well-being. Their work is at the core of the field of learning at the time. A young B. F. Skinner is in the wings of this conversation and he will push these ideas to their limits in the coming decades.

There are other conversations taking place at the same time as these key figures describe their distinctive kinds of psychology. The dominant theme in these somewhat parallel interchanges is the growing usefulness of psychology and its emerging practical and professional applications. In particular, the interests are in clinical work, counselling psychology and educational applications. These interests will have a major role in shaping the directions of the whole discipline for the rest of the century, but it is the advent of World War Two and its consequences which thrust these practitioners into prominence (Pickren, 2007).

A final assembly of key players and interested parties needs to be included in our overview of the history of psychology scholarship. This time the gathering is very large and like a mass rally has many segments scarcely in touch with one another. World War Two has had many effects on the assembled psychologists. German psychology has altogether lost its prominence, with key figures either having emigrated due to Nazi persecution or personal distaste with the Nazi regime. Both American and British psychologists have been involved in the war effort with notable contributions on personnel selection, code-breaking, the analysis of propaganda, soldiers' welfare and postwar counselling (Furnham, 2009). B. F. Skinner, taking up the leadership of the behaviourists group, focusses the attention of scores of followers globally on the topic of learning, especially as understood through reinforcement principles derived principally from studies of white rats. Behaviour modification, built on these reinforcement principles, becomes an important topic inside and outside the laboratory and fuels the growth and power of the professional psychologists who now are more concerned with application of ideas than their development (Lovett, 2006; Pickren, 2007).

A different kind of conversation can be heard in another part of the crowd. Here there are some key figures opposing the dictates of behaviourism. Tolman, himself once a behaviourist, is speculating that his maze-running rats do indeed develop a memory; in effect a cognitive map of where they are going. This is a view in contrast to the prevailing behaviourist thinking that there are simply sequences of learned reflexes guiding action. Tolman's initial reactionary thoughts have some parallels with the ideas of Piaget, whose astute and empirical observation of his own children's behaviour has led him to propose innate cognitive structures shaping intellectual growth. Noam Chomsky, later famous as a public intellectual and political commentator, agrees with Piaget in the sense that his own studies of language argue for the need for deep structures of readiness to learn languages. In Chomsky's considered view, simple iterative stimulus–response links are inadequate explanations. Bartlett and later Broadbent, both from Cambridge in the United Kingdom, add that their work on memory and information processing also utilises organising schema of the mind. This kind of thinking is crystallised in the 1966 publication by Neisser and defined as *Cognitive Psychology.* Many powerful figures are drawn into the cognitive psychology conversation, and studies of thinking by Bruner, decision making by Janis are further topics of interest. The Nobel Prize–winning efforts of Simon on information processing and systems, and later again Tversky and Kahnemann on the biases in human judgment, are all a part of this strong tradition.

Some pivotal research directions for leisure and tourism interest are established because of the growing respectability and achievements in understanding mental processes and building models about cognitive functioning. Ellen Langer establishes that individuals tend to be in one of two cognitive processing states—they are either mindful or mindless. Being mindful means reacting to new situations in an active sense whereas mindlessness involves a more passive following of existing and tried routines. Mindfulness is induced by humour, novelty surprise and mindlessness by boredom, familiar situations and information perceived to be irrelevant. The positive outcomes of mindfulness have been shown to be enhanced memory for information, a sense of control and even longevity. Her work summarised most recently in the 2009 book *Counterclockwise,* where she depicts her studies as researching the psychology of possibility is an important link between the core traditions of cognitive research and a contemporary application with a positive framework (Langer, 2009). The early studies of Martin Seligman on learned helplessness and then later learned optimism are allied to this mindfulness work. Seligman's role as a leading figure in the genesis of positive psychology emphasises the importance of this tradition of cognitive styles and processes in underpinning new traditions in the field.

Another enabling program of work for the development of studies in positive psychology originates in the specification of a tightly argued model of attitudes. The work, originally conceived by Fishbein and Ajzen in the 1970s and developed further by Ajzen, is known as the theory of reasoned application, which transmutes into the theory of planned behaviour. The importance of the theory of planned behaviour can be described as its valuable role in integrating the long tradition of attitude research and measurement already mentioned in the work of the earliest psychologists. The ability to assess attitudes within a conceptual scheme which gives weight to behavioural intentions, the value of others' opinions and one's own perceived competency to control the behaviour—all key elements of the theory of planned behaviour—have been and remain fundamental in considering attitudes towards well-being and happiness.

The resurgence of cognition as a key and acceptable topic of research attention also paves the way for another topic, that of emotion or more broadly affect, to be raised in the conversation. The differences between the terms *emotion* and *affect* warrant a specific introduction. *Emotion* is now widely regarded as the more specific of the two terms and is usually linked with a reaction to a defined object, event or experience (Frederickson, 2001). The reactions of interest here include physiological responses such as heart-rate increases or pupil dilation but also include relatively uncontrolled but widely recognised facial expressions, as well as a linked set of subjective feelings and thoughts. Further, emotion is often seen as shorter in duration than the more general term of *affect* and is subdivided into more classes or distinct categories. Typical emotions include well-known experiences such as fear, disgust and surprise. By way of contrast, affect is seen as summarising those feelings which are consciously accessible and which focus principally on general ongoing subjective experience. Mood, a topic of interest in this volume, is usefully seen as a part of affect since mostly people are able to inform others of their mood and their immediate sense of well-being. While the behaviourists scorned the issue of emotion and the dangers of anthropocentrism were an ever present concern to animal psychologists, Darwin's early treatise on emotions in man and animals was now reread and studies of the affective mental processes emerged. Some of this work was based in detailed studies of the brain and the work of Thomson and Penfold provides powerful evidence locating emotional reactions in the limbic system (Ekman and Davidson 1994; Rosenberg, 1998). The topic of emotional reactions and feeling states, like many other topics in these long-running psychology conversations, will be reconsidered at various points in this chapter and in this volume.

The clinical and counselling emphasis in psychology results in the development of a range of therapies and conceptualisations about human functioning. A loose collection of people sometimes described as the third force (behaviourists and cognitive psychologists occupying the other two positions) share some approaches to the tasks of repairing and developing human potential. The two most prominent figures in this third force are Carl Rogers and Abraham Maslow. Also known as the founders of the humanistic psychology movement, these individuals owe more to the insights of William James and Kurt Lewin than to their more immediate learning theory and experimentally oriented contemporaries. Importantly for the present interests in the history of psychology, Maslow and, slightly later, Rogers introduce a positive tone into the conversation. Basing some of his work on the lives of the very successful people rather than damaged individuals, Maslow discusses a hierarchical model of human motivation representing the striving towards a pinnacle of deep personal well-being. The work will become very well known in undergraduate textbooks on management and introductory psychology but this popularisation omits much of the subtlety of Maslow's assessments. Maslow's hierarchy of needs does not, as many think, involve a staged deterministic model of personal growth but rather describes a pattern of motivational forces. The pre-eminence of any pattern and a concentration on one set of motives is influenced by a Lewin-like consideration of the person's life space and situational context. The borrowing from Maslow in the tourism and general management literature is important for this volume and will be considered further in documenting the rise of tourism scholarship. Again, the specific heritage of positive psychology is addressed here with the work of Csikszentmihalyi on the topic of flow which also derives from the humanistic tradition. This work will feature again at multiple points in this volume.

The social psychologists, often a small gathering at earlier meetings, gain a new prominence in the conversations of the 1960s and 1970s as their leading figures respond to the times and tackle topics of mounting public relevance. In Britain, the German émigré Himmelweit is one of the first eminent women in the field and produces much work on the social attitudes towards television. Peter Warr develops some of the foundation studies on psychology at work and prefigures numerous interests in attitude assessment related to management. Michael Argyle at Oxford writes prolifically and has an influence on many doctoral students through his work on nonverbal behaviour, social skills, then relationships and finally happiness. There is a laboratory and experimental orientation in Argyle's early social skills work and a continuing rigorous use of evidence in the other topics he covers. A similar comment can be made about Henri Tajfel, who is concerned with the anatomy of group membership. His Bristol group become some of the first to emphasise identity and provide a link to the politics of ethnicity. The North American social psychologists too address contemporary topics, with Solomon Asch working on conformity, Stanley Milgram conducting a set of famous experiments on obedience, Phillip Zimbardo simulating and studying prison behaviour and John Darley and Bibb Latane experimenting with public responsiveness and helping. Titchener might not have approved of the breadth of all of these topics, but possibly he would not have been too disturbed by the experimental and quasi-experimental rigour which informed the work. There is a widespread use of control groups and experimental groups. There is often the elimination of alternative explanations through controlling contexts and conditions. Multiple statistical procedures are used to substantiate the significance of the observed contrasts. The broad conversation may be about topics of public interest but the in-house talk is about clever research designs, sample selection, statistical assumptions and probability values. The topics are of broad social interest but they are closely dissected with traditional psychological techniques. The implications for the foundation of positive psychology are perhaps less direct here, but the more general spirit of inquiring into significant social topics is fertile ground for happiness studies.

The fragmentation of the contemporary gathering offers opportunities to hear other conversations of interest. One group of psychologists has identified the physical environment as a topic of concern and, temporarily ignoring Lewin's psychological space, they discuss the physical spaces and realities in which everyday life operates. This group, which has been operating since the 1970s, is known as environmental psychology. Initially somewhat deterministic in their view of how the physical setting influences behaviour, the discussion turns in time to a more constructivist position in which people's interpretation of the setting guides action. Like some of the first post–World War Two social psychology research, much of the early work in environmental psychology relies on the efforts of other psychologists who have made advances in assessing attitudes. Terence Lee and David Canter are strong British contributors to the conversation. They assert the value of seeing that users of environments categorise and describe their use of places in socio-spatial schema which may not reflect the way designers and architects think and plan settings. The North American contributions are also well defined. Repeating the themes of their textbooks, Harold Proshansky and colleagues, Amos Rapaport and then the Kaplans all agree that environmental psychology is a separate area of study from the interests of geographers. For the environmental psychologist, people and their perceptions and behaviours are of central interest in any setting rather than the way space shapes experience. This group of psychologists expands the conversation and applications of psychology to people's behaviour in built and natural settings and provides a glimmer of an interest in the topic of tourism. The notion that there are happy places, or at least places seen as highly desirable for migration and often leisure, represents one small strand in the evaluation work of environmental psychology. The leisure and tourism interest is strengthened when Mehrabian and Russell discuss their assessment tools and measures to examine the emotional character of places. Like their social psychology neighbours, there is no abandonment of highly empirical and often positivist works in this conversation.

It is worth eavesdropping on one further little gathering. In most previous groups the behaviours of interest have been those of middle-class Americans or perhaps more generously the affluent citizens of the Western world. The cross-cultural psychologists have a different focus. Towards the end of the twentieth century international and ethnic differences are no longer of minor interest to the world of research. Richard Nisbett, for example, is able to discuss his book on the geography of thought. He suggests that the original psychological pursuit of universal ways in which the mind works now needs to be reframed. In this view, the legacy of cultural evolution and local experience must be incorporated into understanding cognitive functioning. There have been voices expressing these kinds of views for thirty to forty years but the anthropologists and sociologists have had much to say on cultural variability at the international scale and it has not always been easy for the psychologists to be heard. This topic will resurface when the topic of tourism scholarship and cultural interaction is reviewed in a subsequent section.

Another and larger part of the crowd is somewhat less interested in the nuances of academic psychology and seeks instead to claim a professional territory for their discipline area. The topic of conversation here is how to be a successful practitioner. The interest is what kind of education is needed to be effective as a professional rather than becoming an academic researcher or scientist. In stating their position for professional education, the practising psychologists draw analogies with the high-status fields of medicine and law, which also prepare people to practise rather than to research. The conversation is pressing as psychiatry, moving away from the ideas of Freud, has evolved into a biomedical science, thus restricting the area of expertise in which psychologists may operate. The construction and control of the use of psychological and diagnostic tests form an important platform for this professionalization. The founding contributions of Galton, then Cattell, followed by Hans Eysenck, are all important in developing the array of tests which come into vogue. Particularly in the United States the case for a focussed professional education is won and clinical programs come to be important in many universities (Pickren, 2007). Quite quickly this part of the crowd swells. The professional employment of psychologists and their majority membership in associations sees a split between the researchers and those treating those who are troubled. There will be replays of this issue of applied versus basic studies in subsequent discussions of tourism scholarship.

These conversations and contributions have taken us to the start of the current century. It is a momentous restart for the concerns of this book.

Martin Seligman, in a 1999 presidential address to the American Psychological Association and subsequently in a special edition of the journal *American Psychologist*, suggests a new direction to supplement previous concerns. The direction is to consider human well-being and happiness by analysing and researching the positive components of human existence. The direction is given the label positive psychology. Psychology, the 120-year-old science, is finally about to focus more directly on the Good Life.

Positive psychology is best described as a supplement to rather than being opposed to general or clinical psychology. Seligman and colleagues argue that much previous work on human behaviour has focussed on the problematic side of human affairs. Positive psychologists do not intend to supplant this work but aim instead to provide a fuller picture of human conduct (Gable and Haidt, 2005). Scholars working in this field still see themselves as psychologists rather than necessarily using the label *positive psychologists*. They are consistently keen to avoid the perspective that their interest area is faddish, inconsequential and incompatible with sound empirical inquiry (Linley et al., 2006). The term *happiness* is central to positive psychology but is considered by the founding researchers to be scientifically unwieldy (Seligman, 2002). Instead, the concept of happiness is viewed as a guiding concern, analogous to a general term like *depression*, and is considered more precisely as consisting of three domains. First, there is a focus on hedonic or pleasure-based happiness with the concept applying to the past, the present and the near future. There is a concern too with engaged or eudaimonic happiness where this expression applies to the development of character strengths and participation in a meaningful life. There is a third but less developed domain which is how institutions and organisations may serve happiness and well-being.

It is valuable to gather together the key concepts from our consideration of scholarship in psychology and to see how this new endeavour of positive psychology is aligned to or is at odds with previous concerns. In order to make sense of the approaches adopted by positive psychology, its orientation to key topics of psychology's past need to be established. Particular topics to assist with this placement include hedonism, empiricism, positivism, phenomenology and introspection, dynamic motivation, emotion and the experimental method. Following the themes of more recent psychology conversations, the roles of positive psychology in relation to professional practice, as well as its possible links to social, environmental and cross-cultural study, also deserve attention.

Hedonism has already been briefly outlined. It was noted that hedonism proposes that individuals seek to maximise their pleasure typically through sensory enjoyment. In the least sophisticated version, this is effectively licentious indulgence. By way of contrast, the hedonism which has come to be associated with the Greek philosopher Epicurus is more cultivated. Here hedonism or Epicureanism involves a knowledgeable enjoyment of food, wine, music and sensual rather than sensuous experiences. Hedonism has frequently been seen as anti-intellectual, though others have suggested that our intelligence is a "distillation of our senses" and to deny our sensory pleasures is to deny life (Rolls, 1984: 156–157). This acknowledgment of the healthy qualities of sensory satisfaction is essentially Freudian with the caveat that excessive childhood indulgences can create unbalanced adult behaviours. Positive psychologists have embraced the view that pleasure can derive from immediate, remembered or anticipated sensory experiences, and a basic platform in their construction of happiness is hedonistic pleasure (Ryan and Deci, 2001). Importantly, there is no evaluative appraisal in this categorisation, although there is a clear statement that there are other pathways to well-being in addition to these hedonistic routes. Hedonistic and sensory pleasures have a strong neural basis with direct links to memory and emotion through the limbic system. Certain aspects of hedonistic behaviour, notably eating, drinking and sexual activity, appear to be quite well explained by the traditional behaviourist tools of schedules of reinforcement. Partial reinforcement, for example, appeals as an explanation of the persistence of attempted sexual behaviours, whereas interval- or time-based reinforcement schedules fit with the consumption of food. More contemporary evolutionary psychology perspectives conceptualise some hedonistic behaviours as functional in the broader sense of individual and species survival. In the applications of positive psychology concepts of happiness to tourism study, the further treatment of hedonism, emotion and sensory experiences will be an important point of reference for our analyses and research directions.

Empiricism, positivism and research methods are topics which can be tackled together when reviewing the status and position of positive psychology. Empiricism provides the key point of differentiation between philosophical and literary treatments of the topics of happiness and well-being and the attempts by positive psychologists to consider these human concerns. While philosophers and humanities scholars use logic, insight and narrative to argue for or present their perspective, psychologists are thoroughly empirically grounded in the sense of bringing evidence to bear on the discussion. The nature of the evidence has been persistently dominated by the experimental method as the conversations reviewed in this chapter have revealed (cf. Goodwin, 2005). In the last two decades, though, there has been something of a relaxation of the laboratory-based protocols for admitting evidence to the discussion and both more qualitative forms of inquiry, and nonexperimental assessments involving survey and interview work have become more permissible and common (Marchel and Owens, 2007).

Positivism is a term linked to discussions of research methods and has acquired some strong pejorative overtones (McCarthy, 1981; Outhwaite, 2000). It is of immediate importance here to specify that apart from sharing some common syllables, positive psychology and positivism are separate entities. Positivism originated as a philosophical movement at the end of the nineteenth century and expressed the view that the methods of natural science, particularly experimentation, should be applied to the study of human behaviour. It follows that this is associated with the belief that all facets of human behaviour could be quantified and in fact operated according to a set of yet-to-be-discovered laws. A further and much criticised point is that scientific inquiry is value free and that what ought to be done operates in a different sphere to the world of the scientist. Positive psychology is partially positivist in its scientific orientation and its attempts to measure abstract concepts such as happiness and well-being, but few sophisticated researchers in the field would hold the view that law-like regularities of behaviour can be established. Instead, an appreciation of context and constraining variables which limit the application of any developing conceptual schemes are now much more widespread. Additionally, few positive psychologists of the current century would ascribe to a view that scientific study is not enmeshed in cultural values and connected to researchers' values in some ways. The prominence of these contextual considerations owes much to or at the very least is very consistent with Lewin's formulation of valences and life spaces.

Phenomenology and introspection represent different but equally challenging points of reference for positive psychology. The challenge arising from introspection is inherently about how the results and applications of this new genre of psychology research will be received in the wider community. Not surprisingly, perhaps, Boring (1950) devoted little space in his history of experimental psychology to introspection, which is best understood as the systematic observation of one's own mind. As a research method, its limitations, particularly the distortions occasioned by repeated practice of the activity, were seen by the experimentalists as negating its value, and it has been cast aside as a blind alley in the evolution of psychology (Gomm, 2004; Furnham, 2006). Nevertheless, positive psychologists write about and present data pertaining to people's conscious experiences of happiness, emotions and well-being. Additionally, they sometimes write in journals and publication outlets where the readers have no such history of questioning the value of introspection. The current work is thus exposed to subjective evaluations, the basis of which is the audience's own personalised introspective accounts. One consequence of this clashing of methods of understanding has resulted in some public scorn of the studies of happiness, most notably by journalists. If, for example, the positive psychology studies demonstrate that money is not related in a neat linear fashion to happiness, it is easy for the cynic to mock the findings citing personal experience built on introspection and random case studies to debunk the research effort.

The topic of phenomenology presents a related challenge to positive psychologists. A distinction is necessary between the use of this concept in the history of psychology and its sociological and philosophical incarnation in the works of Husserl and others. In the psychology conversations already considered, the group of researchers known as the Gestaltists were present but their views not heard in any detail. Gestaltists are the group of psychology scholars where the term *phenomenology* has a special meaning in the discipline. The Gestaltists, in common with many other early psychologists, studied perception, but they brought to this topic the notion that there are phenomena which cannot be understood by breaking them into parts. The ideas derive from the earlier thinking of Brentano, who, for example, distinguished between red things (seeing elements) and seeing red (combining elements to see an overview based on multiple inputs). The holistic emphasis aspect of the gestalt approach to the world has a modern consequence and implication. The relevance to our concerns in positive psychology and its application to tourism is that some complex phenomenon may need to be treated in multiple ways and from different perspectives to acquire an adequate view of their meaning. Love, romance, contentment and ecstasy may need to be approached not just by their constitutive elements but need to be treated in the original holistic phenomenological sense by making sure emergent properties of the parts are not neglected.

One topic, that of the relevance of evolutionary theory, straddles the eras of psychology's past and its present. Galton's links with Darwin have already been considered. The further development of testing for intelligence and aptitude in particular have always owed a certain allegiance to Darwin. The specific purpose of intelligence testing has often been to assess, select and reward individuals with socially useful characteristics which were assumed to be underpinned by genetic determinants. The distortions of this purpose, either through morally dubious political agendas in the name of social Darwinism or, more simply, through the poor interpretation of what the tests were measuring, has been a key debate amongst both educational psychologists and other scientists (Dawkins, 2009).

Evolutionary theory has had strong influences on psychological thinking in several other ways. The pragmatism or functionalism of American psychology was due in large measure to researchers and analysts contemplating the question what is the purpose of behaviour? and further what is the purpose of studying this topic? The American answer to the latter question consisted essentially of seeking to help others, and this theme spearheaded the strong growth of professional activity throughout the United States. In social psychology circles, too, evolutionary theory offered some answers to some of the immediately puzzling problems of altruism since individuals are not directly rewarded for altruistic acts and may even be punished for their helpful responses to others. The wider view of social networks and gene pool preservation offered by evolutionary theory explanations, while not always accepted, have become a part of the framework for interpreting much social behaviour. The most specific application of this approach to the interests in positive psychology lies in the adaptive value of emotions and emotional expression. This was of course a topic which Darwin himself considered (Darwin, 1872). The positive psychology assessment of positive emotions reaches beyond asserting that they are simply linked to well-being either as causes or outcomes of that happiness. In addition, the approach emphasises that positive emotions predispose people to collect more and different kinds of information about their setting. In turn, this broadens and builds people's resilience and capacities (Fredrickson, 1998, 2001; Fredrickson and Losada, 2005). In essence, this amounts to establishing their functional and evolutionary value.

The links between positive psychology and the fields of social psychology, environmental psychology and cross-cultural psychology are indistinct. While the content matter and the areas of interest of psychologists in these subareas are all compatible with the reach of positive psychology concerns, it is more the case that the ideas have slowly been incorporated into existing research efforts rather than providing dramatic new emphases. By way of contrast, the positive psychology effort has recently become very devoted to assessing positive interventions, and in so doing it seeks to supplement the major clinical applications of the discipline (Seligman et al., 2005).

TOURISM SCHOLARSHIP

The scholarly style of tourism as an area of social science endeavour also needs to be explained since any attempt to graft one area of interest onto another requires an understanding of the prevailing compatibility of host and donor. The phenomenon of tourism has a long history, but it is only in the latter half of the twentieth century that it has become a truly large-scale global presence. Nearly 800 million people crossing international borders annually have to be of some academic and psychological interest, particularly when the general intent of most is to enjoy themselves and be happy (UNWTO, 2009). While there have been instances of sporadic social commentary about tourism from its earliest days—Pliny the Younger, Adam Smith and Mark Twain all made wry and amusing observations about those who travelled—empirical approaches emerged mostly after World War Two (Young, 1973). Pimlott, for example, contributed an impressive survey and analysis of *The Englishman's Holiday* in 1947. In the 1950s a number of French scholars explored the changing character of destinations in France due to tourism (Nash, 2007). Perhaps more importantly key figures in geography, sociology, anthropology and leisure in and around this period provided studies which anticipated tourism analysis or developed specific tools for that analysis. Important figures in this list included Christaller discussing peripheries, Huizinga writing about play and leisure, Simmel and Schuetz separately considering the role of the stranger and Goffman dissecting social encounters and formulating the backstage–frontstage distinction. Other figures of influence included Neulinger on leisure, Durkheim on alienation and Turner on phases of experience. It is perhaps notable here that there are no immediate psychology figures whose work influenced the earliest tourism researchers. This matter will be considered more fully presently.

In the preceding abbreviated listing of anticipatory studies it would be appropriate to suggest that none of these authors or their contemporaries focussed most of their work on tourism. A similar comment can be made about most of the sociologists and anthropologists who participated more directly in the early construction of tourism study. For example, tourism was initially an incidental interest for Cohen and an accidental interest area for Nash, while van den Berghe reports taking a crooked path to the study of tourists, first by ignoring them and then by being intellectually challenged by their influence (Cohen, 2004; Nash, 2007; van den Berghe, 1994). A pivotal gathering of those interested in the sociological and anthropological dimensions of tourism took place at an American Anthropological Association meeting in Mexico in 1974. The results of the discussion later produced a book edited by Valene Smith entitled *Hosts and Guests*, which helped define and build interests in the noneconomic dimensions of tourism study.

Two major figures are of special note in stimulating a widespread interest in the social science dimensions of tourism study. One primary figure of interest is Dean MacCannell, who has worked variously in the academic ranks of landscape architects and planners as well as in departments of rural sociology and environmental design. MacCannell has links to both anthropological and sociological traditions and in his multiple books analysing symbolism, staging and authenticity he fundamentally directs attention to the "search for who we are and how we fit into the world" (MacCannell, 2007: 150). This suggested touristic quest has generated much interest and reinterpretation. Erik Cohen, one of the leading commentators on MacCannell's work, is a second powerful figure of influence. In addition to incisive commentary on other people's work, Cohen has made an independent and productive contribution to tourism study largely through a qualitative sociological lens. In his long list of publications, Cohen has confronted theoretical and definitional struggles in tourism and dealt with such content areas as tourism crime, prostitution, guided tours, attractions, backpackers, cultures in contact and sustainability.

Tourism scholarship built around social and cultural issues has at least one notable sibling. Studies of the business of tourism were conceived in a different way and have their own growth pattern. In Britain, in particular, but globally to some extent, the economic analysis of tourism initially dominated the business and applied interests in the topic area. Formative studies in this area included the work on multipliers by Brian Archer and forecasting studies by Stephen Witt and colleagues. The notion that destinations have a life cycle, conceived by the geographer Richard Butler, fits well into business analyses of locations and sits alongside a suite of marketing, strategy and management applications. In Europe and Britain the business-oriented tourism studies departments have tended to be an expansion of earlier hospitality departments or hotel schools. By way of contrast, the sociological, anthropological or cultural studies interest groups tend not to be linked to business colleges and not to have hospitality academics as co-workers (Tribe, 1997).

In the United States the origins of business-based studies have a slightly different growth pattern. McIntosh (1992) reports that the development of tourism education and research was linked to the land-grant universities of the Midwest. The founding mission of these institutions was to provide advice to agriculture and industry for the expanding economy of the country in the nineteenth century. In time, the agriculture emphasis broadened to include food production and its delivery as well as recreational use of land. As a part of this community responsibility, many universities in the United States had extension officers who delivered the findings of research to their communities. It was as an extension officer in business and tourism that Robert McIntosh at Michigan State University put together the very first courses in tourism education. By 1969 there were full tourism courses at the university and in 1972 he co-authored the first tourism text (the revised editions still keep coming in the twenty-first century).

There are several ways of summarising these different emphases in the building of tourism scholarship. Jafari (1990, 2005) has offered an overview of these traditions; first of all with a four-platform approach and more recently with the identification of a fifth area of emerging work. The first of Jafari's four platforms was the advocacy approach, which described largely economic work advocating the importance of tourism and indeed trying to boost the sector. A second and subsequent platform, largely the work of the sociologists, anthropologists and geographers already reviewed, was referred to as the cautionary grouping since in many but not all instances these academic voices identified some of the problems and changes tourism and tourists generated. A minor amount of work was assigned to an adaptancy platform representing a smaller group of more evenhanded contributions. Jafari himself became an advocate for the fourth platform, the knowledge-based approach. Jafari's own work in editing a leading journal, *The Annals of Tourism Research*, for over thirty years stands as a testimony to his commitment to that cause. Self-evidently the knowledge-based platform was reserved for thoroughgoing academic studies of tourism. The authors of work falling into this platform were more concerned with building an understanding of processes and outcomes and less concerned with arguing for a position or political goal. In 2005 Jafari added a fifth grouping—the public platform—where he noted the need for an emerging cache of work seeking to address public policy issues with a research-informed approach. This fifth grouping may be seen to be partly influenced by global concerns about sustainable tourism and its place in sustainable development.

In a somewhat simpler but readily understood analysis of tourism's research traditions, Tribe (1997) suggested a T1 and T2 approach. Under the first label he included all the business management and applied work while the second designation was the umbrella label for liberal arts, humanities and broader social science concerns. It was noted that these traditions tended to have somewhat different methods and epistemologies. Ryan (2005), in his analysis of publishing in tourism, supports this diversity of methods and effectively suggests that there is a mindful eclecticism when editors and reviewers assess the research approaches underlying tourism research manuscripts. More recently, John Tribe's work with Irena Ateljevic and others promoting the value of thinking about tourism from a critical point of view might be seen as a T3—a new holistic approach appraising all ongoing work. It can be noted that the critical position often singles out the T1-style studies for closest scrutiny and asks valuable questions about the inherent values involved when tourism research seeks principally to support business (Ateljevic, 2009; Tribe, 2008, 2009).

A particular feature of tourism study is its content focus (Pearce, 2004). This is manifested in multiple ways and a few typical examples can briefly illustrate the range of material on offer. There are publications on types of tourism products (religious sites, cultural places, national parks, ecotourism destinations, ski fields, museums, cruise ships, festivals), on specialist tourism markets (honeymooners, bird watchers, backpackers, seniors, Japanese), on tourism regions (tourism in China, in the Caribbean, in Latin America) and on tourism infrastructure (hotels and resorts, airlines, theme parks, visitor centres). The emergence of some of these topic-oriented concerns and publications is important to this volume. Most notably the recent writing on tourists' health and wellness in spa tourism and medical interventions is of special concern. This area has seen a rise of interest in the marketplace and a surge of academic analysis (Bushell and Sheldon, 2009; Erfurt-Cooper and Cooper, 2009; Hall and Brown, 2006). A specific chapter of this volume will assess the ongoing contributions in the context of the positive psychology insights.

The selection of topics of interest is of course only one part of the research process. It is the expressed intention of this book to consider new ideas and underlying conceptual schemes to add insight to the area of the Good Life, happiness and well-being in tourism. As a consequence, the issue of existing conceptual and theoretical models in tourism study needs to be addressed. For some, theory in tourism, or the lack of such theory, is almost a depressing topic, and it has been argued that tourism researchers have failed in this domain (cf. Aramberri, 2001; Rojek and Urry, 1997). It is possible that this kind of concern stems from a demanding conception of what a theory is or can be. Gergen (1983) suggests that two kinds of theories exist; the first organises ideas within a discipline or a subset of that discipline while the second is larger in its reach and flows into the broader intellectual life of the community. Psychoanalytic theory, evolutionary theory and social exchange theory are examples of the second category.

The distinction between the notion of theory and subsidiary terms is important. At core, a theory sets out assumptions, integrates information, specifies the links among key driving factors and predicts new outcomes (Blalock, 1967; Dawkins, 2009). The manner in which driving forces and outcomes are related may be expressed mathematically or in terms of clearly stated links, chains or sequences. From these considerations it can be suggested that the existence of theory in tourism is unlikely and the term is probably overused. There are few instances where tourism studies addressing a large part of the phenomenon set out assumptions and then state propositions which are mathematically expressed or clearly linked in sequential chains. There are fewer instances still where there is accumulated evidence providing support for a well-organised hierarchy of testable hypotheses. A more pragmatic approach, in keeping with the diversity of topics studied in the area and the levels at which those topics are investigated, is to look for insightful conceptual schemes. These research-guiding devices may be seen as a component part of fully fledged theories, the component which specifies the relationships among key concepts (Greene, 1994). The very term *concept* is also quite valuable in tourism study because it offers the promise of sorting and organising much descriptive material.

These considerations set the context for the transfer and interaction between the field of tourism study and positive psychology. Tourism study, it is being suggested, offers opportunities to develop conceptual schemes around component parts of its content-based study areas. In the past there has been a tradition of the scholarly reapplication of conceptual schemes and models from other fields. Sometimes the approaches have been simply transferred, whereas on other occasions they have been embellished and reworked to good effect. For example, Butler's depiction of stages of growth in tourism areas is a relocated discipline-specific application of the business product life cycle (Butler, 2006). McCannell's authenticity deliberations depend heavily on the sociological work of Goffman's front- and backstage framework (Goffman, 1959; MacCannell, 2007). In the field of tourist motivation, Plog's psychocentric allocentric model has much in common with Eysenck's personality scales, whereas Pearce's travel career patterns are built in part on Maslow's hierarchy of needs (Hsu and Huang, 2008; Maslow, 1954; Pearce, 2005; Ryan 1998). The prospect of unearthing new linkages of importance from the positive psychology developments is a driving force behind this book and some possibilities are discussed in the final section of this chapter.

LINKING FIELDS OF STUDY

The dominant concerns of positive psychology can be summarised as follows. There is a particular concern with the broad conception and component parts of happiness, especially through an understanding of hedonistic happiness and eudaimonic happiness where the latter emphasises the development of valued personal qualities. The development of a comprehensive scheme to categorise these eudaimonic interest areas is a special contribution with the potential for broad application. There is an explicit interest in positive emotions and their value, particularly in terms of the evolutionary significance of the "broaden and build" approach. An emphasis on positive interventions to improve people's well-being is a further area of interest. And finally, but not unimportantly for this volume, there is a stated but not particularly well realised goal of trying to understand the character and influence of positive institutions and contexts. The prevailing methods to research these topics include the construction and use of standardised tests, experimental testing of groups and the associated evaluation of contrasting performances. There are also numerous studies of attitudes and an acceptance of the value of self-reports (Diener and Bewas-Diener, 2008). The purpose of positive psychology is both professional in the sense of following the North American functional tradition of attempting to improve individual well-being, but it is also theoretical in terms of fostering streams of research which explore fundamental issues in human functioning. The roots of positive psychology are deep and much of the current work builds on the 130 years of psychology's disciplinary debates and achievements, most notably in the areas of empirical foundations, methods of study, understanding of attitudes, affect, cognition, testing procedures and a balance between holistic and atomistic study. Many of links to tourism research which can be developed in and beyond this volume can be captured by considering ten key areas of application. These can be itemised as follows.

1   Anticipating Experiences

A renewed focus on the hedonic and sensory experiences which people expect to make them happy can be suggested because of the linking of positive psychology interests and tourism study. The emphases here are on expanding and improving on standard expectation questions and seeking ideal, acceptable and probable interpretations from travellers. A special research interest is suggested in the desired tangible components of the holiday which are seen as happiness generating and fulfilling. Such lines of work develop from Mehrabian and Russell's analysis of the emotional and sensory feel of places and specifically explore multisensory elements—epitomised, for example, by the appeal of warm sun on one's face or sand between the toes. Other new directions could involve the applications of Langer's work on the psychology of possibility, which emphasises that people should avoid being trapped by premature commitment to the way things have to be.

2   On-site Experiences

Close attention can also be suggested to what writers in the experience economy literature term the *experiential promise* (Schmitt, 2003). This interest directs attention to what the customer or traveller actually feels and experiences, always appreciating that this may not actually be what they hoped for or anticipated (de Botton, 2002). The positive psychology contribution to this interest lies in the application of the scales and testing instruments constructed to assess ongoing and just completed experiences. The conceptual contribution of flow as discussed by Csikszentmihalyi (1990) is a key positive psychology contribution to this area of interest. In the tourism context, the application of these ideas can be in many contexts and examples in this volume will consider visitors' immediate reactions to cultural attractions.

3   Reflections on Pleasure

Hedonic pleasure in Seligman and Csikszentmihalyi's account of happiness is often reflective. This point of view is entirely consistent with well-recognised phases of the leisure and tourism experience (Clawson and Knetsch, 1966), and it directs researchers to the analysis of post-travel talk and more generally travel writing as sources of information. Studies of tourist satisfaction fall within the ambit of this reflective process and the benefits of widening the array of measures and approaches to post-experience appraisals are becoming increasingly apparent as social communication technologies prosper. More specifically, visitors' reflections can often be accessed from the increasingly popular Web-based travel stories. They can also be obtained by asking respondents to identify their best and worst experiences in a critical-incident approach or by discussing travel experiences in detailed interviews (Phillimore and Goodson, 2004; Pritchard and Havitz, 2006; Woodside et al., 2007). This kind of material and work will be illustrated in later chapters of this volume.

4   Building Personal Qualities

A fuller consideration of the building of personal qualities and values gained through the travel experience is a further area for development. Peterson and Seligman (2004), for example, have identified such character strengths as love of learning, appreciation of beauty, creativity, teamwork, bravery, persistence, kindness, forgiveness, humour, zest, vitality and open-mindedness. These character strengths were derived from multiple studies and a broad international review of philosophies and cultural contexts. Whereas this is a not a full listing of all the character strengths identified by the positive psychology researchers, it can be suggested that attributes like this could serve as guiding elements when assessing the value and outcomes of travel experiences. Pearce and Foster (2007), in their work on the "University of Travel", have demonstrated that some of these qualities are seen as being enhanced by travellers themselves. This is a beginning to a wider view of the benefits and outcomes of the cumulative effects of tourist experiences.

5   Power of Emotions

Fredrickson (2001), a leading figure in positive psychology, proposed a specific theoretical model to understand the special effects of positive emotions. The approach which was identified previously and is particularly relevant to thinking about the benefits of tourism experiences is labelled the "Broaden and Build" theory of positive emotions. The approach suggests that a set of positive emotions such as contentment, joy, pride and interest, while being separate and distinct, share a common potential to grow human capacity. Being joyful and contented are not only hedonistic states valued in themselves but they are also enriching conditions which predispose people to seek more information, reach out to others, better understand the world and foster resilience in difficult times. Viewed in this way, emotions are not some peripheral component of tourism study but key processes to be understood in terms of both visitor well-being and the likely behaviour of visitors towards others. It is an area deserving of much more research attention and some small steps towards this goal are considered in subsequent chapters.

6   Relationships in Context

De Botton (2009) makes the observation "We cannot enjoy palm trees and azure pools if a relationship to which we are committed has abruptly revealed itself to be suffused with incomprehension and resentment" (2009: 41). The importance of relationships to happiness and well-being generally has been a key social and positive psychological interest for some time (Argyle, 1999; Argyle and Henderson, 1985). It has been little explored in tourism research, though Pearce and Maoz (2008) note its importance to the holiday plans and experiences of backpackers. There is therefore room for much work on the development of relationships and the conditions and circumstances for love rather than the current concerns with only the sexual exploitation components of tourists' behaviour (Bauer and McKercher, 2003). Much more exploration of relationships would appear to be well justified and not just for tourists themselves but for those who interact with tourists in a range of service settings and attractions. At core, the proposed relationship work is two directional because it also suggests a fuller consideration of the emotional, aesthetic and performative labour required of both employees and visitors (Bryman, 2004).

7   Patterns of Motivation

The history of psychology reviewed in this chapter has included a discussion of the fluctuating emphasis on the topic of motivation. Positive psychologists are prepared to accept a teleological and future-oriented view of motivation but essentially build on Maslow's formulation and accept a patterned rather than a single or dominant trait approach to the topic (Ryan and Deci, 2000). The challenge for tourism researchers interested in motivation is to trace how motivation changes with experience and further how current accounts of traveller motivation might be linked to the hedonistic and eudaimonic goals underlying happiness. This challenge represents a stimulating new assignment for the area of tourist motivation study and is line with the goals of this volume in creating new research directions to add integration and understanding across fields of inquiry.

8 Positive Individual Interventions

The rising professionalism in psychology in the last half of the twentieth century has also penetrated the work and goals of positive psychology researchers. In short, many aim to be useful and offer guidance to others as to how to live. This can be a contentious and problematic perspective for the pure researcher and some qualms about such an approach to psychology stems back to its earliest years. In the contemporary world, as any bookshop devotee knows, there is no shortage of self-help and personal-improvement books. Similar kinds of advice are emerging in tourism with codes of conduct and rising social pressure to be a good, intelligent or ethical tourist (Horne, 1992; Swarbrooke, 1999). Butcher (2009) sees a danger in any kind of moralising arising from tourism research and provides a staunch defence of the invisible hand of development. This debate is alive and very current with replies to Butcher and the wider growth of responsibility in consumer behaviour, what Goleman refers to as ecological intelligence, providing a strong case for individuals to change their perspectives and behaviours (Ateljevic 2009; Goleman, 2009; Smith, 2009a). A consideration of the individual ethical issues and the role of research in providing informed choices will be a theme of several chapters in this volume.

9 Positive Institutions

A stated aim in the development of positive psychology involves the consideration of institutions and frameworks which assist happiness. This is a challenging realm for psychologists, who are mostly used to working with individuals rather than organisational structures. The possibilities would appear to be greatest in assessing the fit between the goals of the organisation and the individuals' motivational patterns and character strengths. Tourism is missing from these positive psychology considerations and applications. And yet, tourism is arguably "one of the largest self initiated commercial interventions to create happiness on the entire planet" (Pearce, 2009: 39). A closer look at the measurement approaches of positive psychology might assist in determining how better links or indeed, at this stage, some links can be created. A lead can be taken here from the work in leisure studies assessing enjoyment and commitment (Stebbins, 2004) and documenting and recommending the use of humour and fun at work as suggested by a number of management advisers (Lundin et al., 2000). The value of universities as positive institutions will be discussed in one chapter of this volume together with a consideration of tourism's further potential to promote well-being.

10   Ethical Tourism Development

The debate about individual development and moralising tourism has already been considered at the individual level. There is also the larger scale of this conversation when the corporate social responsibility of tourism businesses is considered. In academic tourism circles and sometimes within government departments, there are often strong statements made about the obligations of tourism. These obligations are expressed in such terms as "tourism businesses should" or "tourism managers must" or "the responsibility of the tourism industry is . . ." Unfortunately, such broad appeals to corporate social responsibility are often not communicated to the right people or even if they are heard they are not acted upon. The difficulties here lie in the different cultures and realities which separate those who preach and advocate action and those who are trying to earn money from their actions (Fennell, 2009). The problem is not without signs of change as the entrepreneur Richard Branson reports in highlighting Virgin's efforts to improve social benefits across a number of fronts (Branson, 2009). While there are well-advanced conversations about the changing values of select groups across the globe (Ateljevic, 2009), as Wheeller reminds tourism researchers it is still money "which makes the world go round" (2009: 207). One of the chapters in this volume will explore in further detail ethical perspectives in tourism while further work will focus on materialism as a driving force shaping social status and perceptions of self-worth.

The previous efforts of scholars in psychology and tourism have been considerable. This chapter has acknowledged and explained some of these debts. For the contributors to this volume and hopefully for those who read it, there is also a contemporary responsibility to not just stand on the shoulders of the giants but to reach out towards new knowledge to create better lives.

Part I

Principally About Individuals

In the planning of this volume it was decided that some organising statements could usefully be included to orient the reader to two main parts of the work. The parts were designated, somewhat prematurely, as principally about tourists and then as predominantly concerned with tourism. Each contains three chapters. In introducing these parts, and indeed in tourism generally, a simple dichotomy between dealing with tourists and dealing with tourism is difficult to uphold. Tourism is of course a social business, entirely dependent on the interaction among a variety of people for its multiple shapes and destiny. Nevertheless, there remains some value in a book of this kind with its diversity of ideas to provide some structure and a sense of anticipation as to what follows.

A more sophisticated version of the tourists-tourism dichotomy as it applies to the following chapters is one where in the first part the interest is principally the experiences of individuals where that experience is interesting for its own sake. The individual experience focus may have some relevance for the businesses which are in the tourism sector. The first part consists of three chapters broadly dealing with ethics, a sense of time and satisfaction, and this material will be set in context in due course. These concepts are defined and considered both for tourists and for members of the communities which tourists visit. The second part sees a slight shift in emphasis. Since the present volume lies within and builds on foundations in psychology, there is a continuing emphasis on individuals in these three chapters. On this occasion, however, the relevance to the people and organisations conducting tourism operations and who plan for the development and change in tourism destinations is a little more direct. The chapters deal with values and materialism as related to tourism consumption, the character strengths of tourism entrepreneurs especially those with a lifestyle orientation and tourist motivation as studied in the context of spa and wellness.

A road map or an organising system to place the concepts in this first part in a context requires a brief overview of the material covered as well as some key ideas left untouched and offering additional locational cues. The chapter offerings start with the treatment of the key role peak or leading tourist experiences play in contributing to deep feelings of satisfaction and well-being. It addresses indirectly what Wordsworth once called "spots in time", existential or transcendent moments associated with visiting places when living the good life is an embodied, spontaneous and conscious altering experience (de Botton, 2002). The chapter explores the application of the positive psychology notion of flow to this material and additionally considers a tourism context, that of visiting cultural heritage sites, where the extension of the flow research can be applied. The following chapter deals with the value of individuals adopting a balanced time perspective to their reflections on the quality of their lives. Reminiscence as well as engaged involvement in the present both have roles to play in serving well-being. The conception of time in this chapter is explored by focusing on older residents who live in communities where the presence of tourists and tourism is substantial. In particular the value of interventions conducted in a quasi clinical tradition which might assist residents to cope with the tourism presence is considered.

A third chapter in this part deals directly with ethics and derives its ideas and approaches from Aristotle's views on the good life and the expression of these foundation ideas in the concepts of happiness developed in positive psychology. It emphasises again the development of individual experience particularly as key character strengths such as resilience, stress management and wisdom develop in tourism-linked contexts such as volunteering, and tourism sector employment.

An overview of these contributions identifies a range of processes and capacities operating in individuals who are in tourist roles or affected by tourist roles. What is missing from these chapters and what other kinds of work could be developed in the future to extend the boundaries of the studies undertaken here?

The key and related literature which is not addressed by these chapters is the broad array of material concerning the quality of life of countries and communities. The differentiation between the existing chapters and these quality of life studies helps locate the present work at a particular or scale of concern. The larger quality-of -life framework sees an interest in the development of well-being for whole communities and thus embraces notions of multiple forms of capital—financial, social, physical, ecological and individual (Costanza et al., 2007). It is these broad concerns which have expanded traditional notions of development beyond a narrow economic focus and oriented assessments of national well-being to using indices of happiness and social progress (Sen, 2000). These larger welfare concerns are not the level at which this volume and these chapters are conceived. Some studies in the tourism context have already developed components of this broader welfare interest (Hall and Brown, 2006). Instead, the present chapters offer more searching and some novel routes to explore human capital and individual functioning, potentially augmenting and possibly replacing some of the other self-report tools currently in use.

This context provides a way to read these next three chapters—they share an ideological position that there is more work to be done to understand thoroughly the positive development of human capacity and its assessment when trying to pinpoint pathways to a good life. Attention to the many ideas and conceptual schemes the chapters offer can act as a toolkit for researchers as well as a helping formulate a way to promote the well-being of a range of tourism-connected stakeholders.

2 Flow and Tourist Satisfaction

This chapter firstly critically considers some ways tourist satisfaction has been understood and measured. Secondly, it presents an approach from positive psychology as an alternative way of understanding and evaluating aspects of satisfaction. This alternative approach adds to the already established and widely used approaches in tourism management. The positive psychology approach is the flow-state approach. The state of flow is the experience associated with engaging one's highest strengths and talents to meet just-doable challenges. When a person is in flow, everything comes together for him/her and the person is totally involved in the activity at hand (Csikszentmihalyi, 1975, 1990).

While the state has been used in the past to conceptualise tourist satisfaction (Han, Um and Mills, 2005; Ryan, 1995), flow-state methods and approaches were typically beyond the scope of these previous analyses. The third and final part of this chapter reviews flow-state assessment techniques and then discusses in detail a research study in which flow questions were added to an on-site satisfaction interview. It is argued that flow is particularly useful in uncovering immediate, momentary satisfaction—a satisfaction type which has been neglected in previous research.

TOURIST SATISFACTION APPROACHES

While acknowledging that the list of satisfaction topics and measurement approaches presented here may not be exhaustive, the list broadly builds on the classifications provided by Ryan (1995) and Pearce's (2005) earlier review of tourist satisfaction. Three approaches to tourist satisfaction are discussed: the dominant, expectations approaches; the qualitative, Nordic approaches and those that can be collectively labelled experience approaches. More attention is given to the discussion of these experience approaches as they are relatively new and/or unorthodox, yet relevant to the analysis of flow. Links to loyalty, however, as a concept related to satisfaction are not drawn in these analyses.

EXPECTATIONS APPROACHES

This tradition defines tourist satisfaction as the degree to which a tourist's assessment of the attributes of a destination exceeds expectations (Tribe and Snaith, 1998). In other words, consumer's dissatisfaction and satisfaction is a function of disconfirmation arising from discrepancies between prior expectations and actual performance (Oliver, 1980). In lay terms, if destination attributes are equal to or better than expected, the tourist is left satisfied; if, on the other hand, destination attributes do not match the level of expectations, the tourist is not satisfied. This school of thought, which commonly equates tourists to consumers and thus tourist satisfaction to service satisfaction, has dominated the way satisfaction has been conceptualised in tourism (Pearce, 2005). Specific models based on this school of thought as classified by Truong (2005) include, but are not limited to: SERVQUAL, SERVPERF, IPA and HOLSAT.

The SERVQUAL (Service Quality) model is entirely based on the above-mentioned disconfirmation paradigm by Oliver (1980). SERVQUAL is therefore a discrepancy model which basically assumes that consumer satisfaction is measured as difference between expected provision and actual provision (Parasuraman, Zeithaml and Berry, 1988; Truong, 2005). In SERVQUAL, destination attributes are absolutes and satisfaction is measured as difference between an ideal and actual state, typically through questionnaires (Ryan, 1995). The questionnaires, commonly consisting of Likert scales, typically require respondents to rank their expectations and judge the performance of their service on a seven-point scale (Teas, 1993). The scales measure five underlying dimensions of service quality, consisting of: tangibles, reliability, responsiveness, assurance and empathy (Parasuraman et al., 1988). Due to the ease and efficiency of data collection and the straightforward nature of the questions, the SERVQUAL scales are commonly used in the tourism industry and in academic tourist satisfaction research. A variation of SERVQUAL is SERVPERF, which is a performance-based model that better reflects long-term service quality attitudes in cross-sectional studies (Cronin and Taylor, 1994) and is more construct-valid and efficient than SERVQUAL (Crossley and Xu, 1996). Essentially, however, SERVPERF is also based on the expectations—performance analysis.

The third expectations-based approach is Importance-Performance Analysis (IPA). In a seminal marketing paper, Martilla and James (1977) explain that IPA is an easily applied technique for measuring attribute importance and performance. IPA suggests that consumer satisfaction is a function of both expectations related to specific important service attributes and judgments of attribute performance (Martilla and James, 1977). Importance and performance ratings can be obtained for various service attributes through questionnaires and the results can be plotted on an IPA grid. In this grid there is a performance axis and an importance axis. The attribute ratings are then plotted on these axes based on performance (from fair to excellent) and importance (from slightly important to extremely important) (Hudson and Shephard, 1998; Martilla and James, 1977). The real benefit of IPA is that it is simple to use. Tourism managers can identify areas where services need to be improved without employing complex statistical skills (Truong, 2005).

The last of the major expectations approaches is the HOLSAT (Holiday Satisfaction) model, devised and developed by Tribe and Snaith (1998). It is also a "gap" model as the other approaches, but explicitly focuses on tourism services. The model "compares the performance of a wide range of holiday attributes against a holidaymaker's expectations as a means of evaluating satisfaction with a particular holiday destination or experience" (Truong, 2005: 229). The attributes are grouped into five categories: attractions, activities, accessibility, accommodation and amenity (Tribe and Snaith, 1998). It focuses less on performance alone than SERVPERF (Cronin and Taylor, 1994) and more on the relationship between performance and prior expectations. It also does not focus on performance in relation to importance (IPA; Truong, 2005) or performance related to best absolute quality (SERVQUAL; Parasuraman et al., 1988). It therefore overcomes the concept of absolute values of satisfaction and addresses the multidimensional nature of consumer satisfaction with a holiday (Tribe and Snaith, 1998).

The expectations approaches and measures of tourist satisfaction have, however, received significant negative criticism. Empirical studies have shown that SERVQUAL fails to exhibit construct validity and that there is conceptual confusion about the interchangeability of the terms *service quality* and *satisfaction* (Brown, Churchill and Peter, 1993; Childress and Crompton, 1997; Teas, 1993; Truong, 2005). SERVPERF aims to give a full picture of satisfaction in the context of a price-based strategy, but not in the context of performance alone (Tribe and Snaith, 1998). IPA lacks statistical significance testing ability and the technique is not intended to provide thorough information to managers (Hudson and Shephard, 1998). The HOLSAT questionnaire instrument does not include general questions and open questions and hence has limited ability to gain rich information. The model also requires further testing with large samples to achieve reliable results and interpretations (Tribe and Snaith, 1998; Truong, 2002, 2005).

There are more serious problems with the expectations approaches to tourist satisfaction. The appropriateness of tying expectations to the construct of satisfaction has been questioned. In particular, it has been noted that expectations can change, that they can be superficial and uncertain, that tourists may not occasionally have expectations about their holiday and that expectations can be inflated to preserve ego (Babakus and Boller, 1992; Crompton and Love, 1995; Mazurksy, 1989; Pearce, 1988; Ryan, 1995). Additionally, these expectations assessments typically originate from applied disciplines, such as marketing and management (Pearce,

2005; Ryan, 1995). Tourism, however, may not only be viewed as a service, but as a social force (Higgins-Desbiolles, 2005) or as an experience (Tosun, Pinat-Temizkan, Timothy and Fyall, 2007). As such, tourist satisfaction should also not be viewed exclusively through the business and consumer lens (Martilla and James, 1977; Parasurman et al., 1988). In this context, critics have argued that a greater array of methodological tools is necessary to understand the complexity of tourist satisfaction, in particular its affective dimension (Barsky and Nash, 2002; Pearce, 2005).

NORDIC APPROACHES

As an alternative way of studying and measuring tourist satisfaction, a Scandinavian or Nordic school of thought has also formed (Kozak, 2001; Pearce, 2005). This approach is exemplified by some not-so-recent works on participants in guided tours (Hughes, 1991), marine tourists (Greenwood and Moscardo, 1999), rural travellers (Black and Rutledge, 1996) and birdwatchers (Applegate and Clarke, 1987). This smaller school of thought avoids the expectations emphasis and includes performance-only measures of tourist satisfaction (Crompton and Love, 1995; Prakash, 1984). Satisfaction is commonly evaluated through cross-section surveys (Kozak, 2001). Crompton and Love (1995) showed that the performance-only measures were superior to expectations-based approaches in measuring satisfaction at tourist festivals.

The key disadvantage of the Nordic approaches, however, is the following: "at core, Nordic approaches to satisfaction are pragmatic and consistent with the definition of satisfaction as a post hoc attitude" (Pearce, 2005: 172). In other words, the approaches are reflective and thus cannot adequately evaluate near immediate conscious experiences. These are experiences of the present moment (James, 1890) and include the flow of perceptions, purposeful thoughts, fragmentary images, bodily sensations or emotions (Pope and Singer, 1978) which form part of tourist's satisfaction levels during an on-site visit. Mannell and Iso-Ahola (1987) emphasise that both post hoc and immediate conscious satisfaction are relevant to tourist and leisure experiences. Yet the measurements of tourist satisfaction in tourism studies have focused mainly on the former (Pearce, 2005).

Therefore, to overcome the issues of operationalisation and measurement which evidently abound in the tourist satisfaction literature (Noe, 1999), experience approaches to the conceptualisation and assessment of tourist satisfaction have emerged in tourism, leisure and allied social science specialisms.

EXPERIENCE APPROACHES

Tourism can be defined by its focus on the production of experiences (Prentice, Witt and Hamer, 1998), and experiences have for a long time been a central concept in tourism research (Pine and Gilmore, 1999; Stamboulis and Skayannis, 2003; Uriely, 2005). Experience can be understood in affective as well as in cognitive terms. That is, as any sensation or knowledge acquisition resulting from a person's participation in an activity. Although the research on tourist experiences is not always linked to tourist satisfaction (Uriely, 2005), experience concepts and empirical assessments of these concepts may improve the operationalisation and measurement of the complex satisfaction construct. The following experience approaches broadly correspond to the array of related concepts mentioned by Moscardo (2009a) in her analysis of tourist experiences. Slow time, aesthetic experience and restoration have been added to this collection of experiences approaches.

1 Mindfulness

Mindfulness, as it is known in psychology, is:

> A flexible, cognitive state that results from drawing novel distinctions about the situation and environment. When one is mindful, one is actively engaged in the present and sensitive to both context and perspective. The mindful condition is both the result of, and the continuing cause of, actively noticing new things. (Carson and Langer, 2006: 29–30)

This construct is the opposite of mindlessness, which is a state in which one is oblivious to context or perspective and in which one has a limited ability to reconsider or reinterpret information (Djikic and Langer, 2007; Swanson and Ramiller, 2004).

The link between satisfaction and mindfulness has been acknowledged (Moscardo, 2009a). The theory has been applied in various tourism contexts and the evidence has frequently shown that mindfulness is associated with a range of positive outcomes. Some of these outcomes are: more effective learning, better mental and physical health, positive evaluations of experiences and positive affective responses to different situations (Carson and Langer, 2006; Houston and Turner, 2007). On the contrary, mindlessness is more commonly associated with feelings of helplessness, boredom, frustration and incompetence (Carson and Langer, 2006).

There are also linkages between mindfulness and the creation of meaning. A key feature of mindfulness, according to Moscardo (2009a), is the processing of new information and creation of new ways of looking at the world, both of which are prerequisites for the creation of new meanings of that world. Indeed, Houston and Turner point out: "Mindfulness is a process through which meaning is given to outcomes" (2007: 139).

In tourism studies, researchers have employed both quantitative and qualitative approaches to evaluate mindfulness (Moscardo, 2009a). A discussion of these methods is beyond the scope of this analysis. The contexts have included: interpretation (Moscardo, Ballantyne and Hughes, 2007), wildlife-based tourism situations (Woods and Moscardo, 2003), natural environments (Moscardo and Woods, 1998) and built tourist attractions (Benckendorff, Moscardo and Murphy, 2006).

2   Existential Authenticity

Mindfulness is a precursor for authentic experiences of self (Carson and Langer, 2006; Kim and Jamal, 2007). These authentic experiences of self resemble the concept of existential authenticity. Steiner and Reisinger (2006) point out that authenticity is a blurry concept in tourism studies because it has been perceived in two general ways: as realness of artifacts or events (MacCannell, 1976) or as a human attribute signifying being one's true self or being true to one's nature (Steiner and Reisinger, 2006). Existential authenticity refers to the second interpretation and is the essence of human individuality. It is, for instance, about the mutually exhilarating feeling of hosts and tourists when they feel special while dancing together but not about a forced smile of airline personnel or travel agents (Hochschild, 1983). This genuine and satisfactory experience makes a person feel human and happy (Hegel, 1977; Heidegger, 1996; Kant, 1929). Existential authenticity is challenging to empirical study in tourism (Wang, 1999), but phenomenological, qualitative methods seem most appropriate (Cohen, 1988). These include long, in-depth interviews or written narratives about holiday experiences (Reid, Flowers and Larkin, 2005).

3   Tourist Moment

Tied in with the notion of existential authenticity is the experience satisfaction concept of tourist moment. Hom Cary (2004) points out that "it is Wang's rethinking of MacCannellian authenticity, and his subsequent formulation of existential authenticity, that comes closest to the tourist moment" (p. 63). Hom Cary (2004) refers to the citation from Daniel (1996) describing the tourist moment and the state of existential authenticity through dance:

> For many tourists, the dance becomes their entire world at that particular moment. Time and tensions are suspended. The discrepancies of the real world are postponed ... Tourism, in moments of dance performance, opens the door to a liminal world that gives relief from day-to-day, ordinary tensions, and, for Cuban dancers and dancing tourists particularly, permits indulgence in near ecstatic experiences. (Daniel, 1996: 789).

Hom Cary therefore defines the tourist moment as the heightened experience—a confluence of authenticity, history and culture that surpasses the tourist perception of herself or himself as a tourist. Of course, tourist moments can also be dull, painful, highly frustrating and entirely negative (Hom Cary, 2004), but these moments are not the focus of attention for tourism researchers who are focused on understanding satisfaction in depth as opposed to dissatisfaction.

Hom Cary suggests that these special and highly satisfactory tourist moments can best be evaluated through narratives. The narratives could feature in travel journal entries, diaries, postcards or conversations. Researchers could interpret the tourists' narratives to better understand the tourist moments and hence tourist satisfaction. Another concept loosely tied to these considerations of satisfaction is slow travel.

4 Slow Travel and Slow Food

Slow travel is type of travel where tourists experience a deeper understanding of a place by staying in that place for longer periods of time than mass tourists and avoiding long day trips. This type of travel could involve staying in a vacation rental for a week and attempting to live like a local (such as shopping at local stores, going to the same coffee shop every morning or taking the time to see attractions that are in the vicinity of the vacation home) (Slow Travel Web site, 2008). Stories or narratives are ways of studying satisfaction through the concept of slow travel. In her examination of slow forms of travel as holiday experiences, Dickinson (2007) examined the stories people tell about their travel. Findings from Dickinson's research suggest that these travellers typically engage more deeply with places and people and that slow travel experiences can be constructed very positively. Slow travel is thus a useful experience concept for analysing tourist satisfaction at an in-depth, personal level.

An aligned construct is the notion of slow food in hospitality research (Bratec, 2008). Slow food in the context of satisfaction is about slowly savouring and enjoying food and respecting the effort and time involved in turning it into a delicious meal. The slow food therefore does not only feed people's bodies but also their minds, as Miele and Murdoch (2002) argue. The slow food has therefore been linked to personal satisfaction and mental rejuvenation (Bratec, 2008). In a context of Slovenian gastronomy, hour-long, in-depth interviews were combined with observational work to assess the concept of slow food in selected restaurants around the country. The results showed that slow-food experiences were generally very positive and enriching to the participants.

5 Aesthetic Experience

A different tourist satisfaction experience approach is an application of aesthetic experience, which has been used in visitor studies and museum research (Csikszentmihalyi and Robinson, 1990). The concept, however, originates from the work of a German philosopher, Alexander Baumgarten, who arguably first used the term *aesthetic experience* in *Reflections on Poetry* (1936, first published 1735). Baumgarten argued that reason articulates a set of rules within which the mind can operate, but that humans also have another way of understanding reality: "an experience of blinding intuition, a sense of certainty and completeness as convincing as any reason provides" (Csikszentmihalyi and Robinson, 1990: 10). It is this second way of seeing reality that resembles aesthetic experience.

Beardsley (1982) lists five basic dimensions of the aesthetic experience:

1. Object focus (attention is fixed on intentional field)
2. Felt freedom (release from concerns about past and future)
3. Detached affect (objects of interest are set at a distance emotionally)
4. Active discovery (active exercise of powers to meet environmental challenges)
5. Wholeness (a sense of personal integration and self expansion).

Csikszentmihalyi and Robinson point out that the state is inherently pleasurable. The experience is thus clearly linked with satisfaction. Aesthetic experience, just like slow travel, is typically assessed qualitatively. Csikszentmihalyi and Robinson, for instance, conducted long in-depth interviews with art museum professionals to evaluate the nature and conditions of the aesthetic experience in a museum context.

6   Mental restoration

Mental restoration is an additional experience-related tourist satisfaction approach (Packer, 2008). Four conditions form part of the mental restoration process: fascination (being engaged without effort); being away (physically and mentally removed from one's everyday environment); the perception of "extent" (the environment has significant content and structure to occupy the mind for an extended period) and compatibility (providing a good fit with one's purposes and inclinations) (Kaplan and Kaplan, 1989).

The name itself and the dimensions suggest that restoration is a satisfying state. The four restorative factors have been most commonly found in natural environments (Packer, 2008). There is evidence, however, that indoor, educational leisure settings, such as museums, also possess restorative elements (Kaplan, Bardwell and Slakter, 1993). Similar to the presence of the aesthetic experience in Csikszentmihalyi and Robinson's study, Kaplan et al. (1993) found that many museum visitors had a restorative experience during their visit. In this restoration study, focus groups were used to find out if visitors raised any of the themes theoretically related to the mental restoration concept. The researchers found evidence of all the four dimensions and two conditions they identified as outcomes: a peaceful, positive, calm state; and engagement in reflection (Packer, 2008). The focus-group method was shown to be a useful technique of soliciting satisfaction data.

7 Flow

Lastly, flow can be added to the list of these relatively recent, experiential conceptualisations of satisfaction. With the exception of mindfulness, flow seems to have the most developed methodology out of the just discussed experience approaches. Yet, unlike mindfulness, it has received limited attention in tourism research and only marginal consideration in leisure research (Cohen, forthcoming; Han, Um and Mills, 2005; Ryan, 1995). In the following discussion, the concept is further defined and linked to tourist satisfaction.

As stated earlier, flow is a highly engaging state and, axiomatically, a deeply satisfying state (Jackson and Eklund, 2004). The flow theory originates from Csikszentmihalyi's (1975) work in psychology. In this seminal work, experiences of visual artists were examined. Csikszentmihalyi (1975) was interested in trying to understand how artists got cognitively involved in their paintings and the feelings of joy and pleasure which they had during their engaging experiences. He later identified nine core features or dimensions of such flow states (Csikszentmihalyi, 1990):

1. Challenge-skill balance (there is a match between perceived skills and challenges)
2. Action-awareness merging (deep involvement leads to automaticity and spontaneity; there is no awareness of self as separate from the actions one is performing)
3. Clear goals (there is a strong sense of what one is going to do)
4. Unambiguous feedback (clear and immediate feedback that the person is doing his/her activity well and is succeeding in his/her goal)
5. Concentration on task (total concentration on the task at hand)
6. Sense of control (sense of exercising control without actively trying to be in control)
7. Loss of self-consciousness (concern for the self disappears and the person becomes one with the activity)
8. Time transformation (time disorientation or a loss of time awareness)
9. Autotelic experience (an intrinsically rewarding experience involving a sense of deep enjoyment).

The dimensions have been linked to the dimensions of the aesthetic experience. Csikszentmihalyi and Robinson argued that the concepts of flow and the aesthetic experience describe a very similar state of mind. They suggested that (a) the flow dimension of merging of action and awareness resembles Beardsley's (1982) object focus; (b) the time transformation from flow is similar to felt freedom; (c) the loss of self-consciousness is comparable to detached affect; (d) the challenge-skills balance and the sense of control resemble active discovery; and (e) the clear goals and unambiguous feedback dimension link with the concept of wholeness. These links are important because they suggest that the flow concept could be applied to visual tourist experiences.

There are arguably also linkages to the mental restoration criteria, although works that directly link the two concepts seem to be missing. Finally, the flow state has also been linked to the mindfulness concept, as its cognitive dimensions (such as challenge-skill balance or concentration on task) resemble the cognitive state of mindfulness (Moscardo, 2009a).

Csikszentmihalyi's (1975) work on flow theory is seminal because there has been a proliferation of studies which have applied the model and/or proven the existence of the dimensions in various contexts. The theory has therefore been explored in music, games, religious rituals and other creative activities (Csikszentmihalyi, 1999), in various sports (Jackson and Eklund, 2002; Jackson and Eklund, 2004; Jackson and Marsh, 1996; Phillips, 2005), in passive activities such as chess and more active ones like dancing (Jackson and Eklund, 2004) and in work settings, particularly reading and writing contexts (Csikszentmihalyi and LeFevre, 1989; Seligman and Csikszentmihalyi, 2000). Works exploring relationships between flow and tourist activities, however, are infrequent (Han, Um and Mills, 2005; Ryan, 1995).

Despite this scarcity, relationships between this engaging state and tourist satisfaction have been established more than a decade ago (Ryan, 1995). Ryan discussed the application of the theory to whitewater rafting tourist experiences. He presented the model as a lens through which tourist satisfaction can be conceptualised. Nevertheless, a discussion of flow-state methodology and its usefulness in measuring tourist satisfaction (Csikszentmihalyi, 1990; Csikszentmihalyi and LeFevre, 1989; Jackson, 1992) was beyond the scope of this analysis.

Conceptually, therefore, the flow state relates to tourist satisfaction. The following section describes flow in the context of recent tourism methodological debates and explains how this fulfilling state can be measured.

METHODOLOGICAL DEBATES, CRITICAL REALISM AND FLOW-STATE METHODOLOGY

Methodological Debates

In a 1999 paper, Small commented that the tourism literature revealed that debate about tourism research methodologies and methods is not high on the agenda of tourism authors. Among the few authors who raised methodological concerns were Dann, Nash and Pearce (1988), who commented that "new research methods in tourism as a whole have not been high in the publication stakes" (p. 419) and Walle (1997), who claimed that there was a need for tourism scholarship to expand its toolkit and embrace a greater plethora of techniques.

The opposite seems to be the case today. A critical tourism research block has flourished with its innovative research methodologies in tourism studies (Ateljevic, Pritchard and Morgan, 2007). In the tourist behavior field (Pearce, 2005) there are calls for greater diversity in measuring complex phenomena, such as motivation and satisfaction (Dann and Phillips, 2001). Perhaps the reason for these increased calls for methodological creativity is that published tourism research is commonly seen as methodologically deficient when compared to other academic disciplines (Ryan, 2005).

The new era of tourism research could indeed be seen as an era of creativity. There are many recent examples of fresh methodological approaches in tourism. Aligned with the new approaches is an ongoing critique of the dominance of positivism.

The dominance of positivism in tourism research is widely recognised (Walle, 1997). Walle points out that both qualitative and quantitative approaches are generally regarded as useful in social sciences. In tourism, however, since the time when tourism has formed as academic specialism, there has been a focus on research from practical disciplines (such as management and marketing) and an emphasis from traditional disciplines, such as sociology or psychology, to transform theoretical knowledge in practical ways (Walle, 1997). In such an environment, dominated by management imperatives, qualitative research, characterised by rich and complex information about relatively few subjects (Veal, 2005), was seen as inferior to quantitative research. In relation to the hospitality industry, Lewis, Chambers and Chacko therefore point out that the purpose of qualitative research is to "provide information for further development of quantitative research" (1995: 171).

The reality is a lot more complex. Lowych, van Langenhave, and Bollaert (1992) and Walle (1997) point out that a major drawback of quantitative methods is that it is asking the researcher to refrain from using insight, intuition and other nonrigorous knowledge. This drawback is especially problematic in tourism research because tourism is a complex social phenomenon (Dann and Phillips, 2001). Tourism researchers, managers and others who study tourism and require diverse evidence and information on complex aspects of tourist behavior may find it challenging to get adequate answers using predominantly quantitative techniques.

This challenge particularly applies to tourist motivation and tourist satisfaction research (Dann and Phillips, 2001; Pearce, 2005). In relation to tourist motivation research, Dann and Phillips state:

> should one desire to go beyond a close-ended, standardised checklist of items prepared by the investigator to more open-ended and unclassified

issues raised by the research subjects, a more qualitative, multimedia approach becomes necessary. (2001: 251)

They then refer to qualitative research which explored travel brochures (Dann, 1996; Selwyn, 1996), videos (Hanefors and Larsson, 1993), guidebooks or tourist maps (Seaton, 1994) to understand travel motivation. Similarly, satisfaction scales typically cannot capture the complexity and subtleties of the tourist experience. Dann and Phillips (2001) point out that the commonly used scales cannot capture ambivalence, confusion or unease, all of which are concepts relevant to tourist satisfaction or dissatisfaction.

Nevertheless, positivism and quantitative methods should not be over-enthusiastically dismissed as not useful to tourist satisfaction and behaviour research. Regardless of the fact that it is fashionable to do so (Aramberri, 2001; Franklin and Crang, 2001; Nash, 2001; Tribe, 2008), a simplistic rejection of positivism would be somewhat naive. Quantitative, empirical evidence is well worth collecting even if it does not apply to every research problem, and there is a role for generalisations about tourist behaviour even if they are not law-like. It is also not suggested here that positivist methods are necessarily uncreative. Quantitative methods from positive psychology, such as positive emotion scales (Fredrickson, 2001), measures of optimism (Peterson, 2000) and character strengths inventories (Seligman and Peterson, 2003) might assist tourist satisfaction measurements by helping social scientists to better understand aspects of tourist behaviour.

Critical Realism and Flow-State Methodology

This notion of methodological plurality fits well under the critical realist methodological paradigm (Downward and Mearman, 2004). While acknowledging the roles of perception and cognition, critical realism maintains that a mind-independent reality could exist (Lopez and Potter, 2001). The term was coined by an American philosopher, Sellars (1916), in his attempt to mediate between direct realism and idealism by saying that the objects of perception are neither objects themselves nor simply ideas (Drake, Pratt, Rogers, Santayana, Sellars, Strong and Lovejoy, 1920). In a methodological sense, this philosophy argues that a particular problem can be studied and/or solved through both positivist and relativist methods (Groff, 2004), as is commonly the case in triangulation (Veal, 2005). Groff (2004) argues that strict relativism as well as strict positivism are problematic. In strict relativism, as all beliefs about the world are equally valid, no claims can be challenged on cognitive or epistemic grounds. On the contrary, in strict positivism the alleged truth is always obtainable.

In the tourism field, prolific works from the critical realist paradigm are studies conducted by Alison Gill, mainly in the area of community development and planning issues in tourist environments (Gill, 2000, 2004; Gill and Reed, 1997). In the tourist behaviour literature there is little specific mention of critical realism (Botterill, 2007), although there are calls for greater triangulation in research. Flow-state methodology seems to be another appropriate example of the critical realist approach. Flow-state methods are typically flow-state scales (FSS) and dispositional flow-state scales (DFS) (Jackson and Eklund, 2004), flow in-depth interviews (Csikszentmihalyi, 1975; Jackson, 1996) or experience sampling methods (ESM) (Csikszentmihalyi and LeFevre, 1989) resembling the eclectic plethora suggested by critical realism. Each of the methods has its advantages and disadvantages and each is very new to tourist behaviour research (Filep, 2007). The real benefit of the flow-state methods is that they can be used to evaluate immediate conscious as well as post hoc satisfaction (Mannell and Iso-Ahola, 1987) and cognitive as well as affective dimensions of satisfaction (Csikszentmihalyi, 1990; Ryan, 1995), hence overcoming some of the disadvantages of the Nordic and the Expectations approaches. The flow-state methods do not however have to be used in isolation to the more traditional satisfaction measures.

MEASURING FLOW

Perhaps the most common technique for evaluating flow is ESM (Schimmack, 2003). Signalling devices are used in ESM research and frequently involve electronic personal data assistants (PDAs) which are given to study participants. Respondents are signalled at random times during their experiences and then asked to respond to questions related to their feelings and thoughts during their experiences (Scollon, Kim-Prieto and Diener, 2003). At a first glimpse, therefore, the most appropriate approach for studying flow at tourist sites would appear to be the ESM technique. This method allows the researcher to delve into respondents' momentary reactions and hence analyse their experiences from up close. ESM allows data results to be transferred onto a disc and immediately analysed without the need for transcribing.

A close look at ESM, however, suggests otherwise. Stewart and Hull (1996) emphasise two major limitations of the ESM measure: alteration of experience and lack of compliance with the self-administration. The authors suggest that "invasiveness to the on-site experience is higher with *in situ* compared to traditional methods" (1996: 15) and thus more likely to alter experience. Using a signalling device during a site visit may detract tourists from their experiences and could alter their perceptions.

Respondents may also not be willing to use the PDAs. A tourist may not respond when signalled or may not answer each item on the questionnaire. In a seminal ESM compliance study, Hormuth (1986) found that more than 95% of participants responded to signals. However, the percentage of participants doing so within 5 minutes was as low as 60% in one population and around 80% in another. This finding suggests some tourist groups may not be willing to input information on a PDA when instructed to do so. This lack of compliance may especially be prevalent with highly enjoyable experiences.

The use of flow scales, on the other hand, may be less problematic. FSS and DFS scales, respectively, assess flow experiences within an event and the dispositional tendency to experience flow in an activity (Jackson and Eklund, 2002, 2004; Jackson and Marsh, 1996). The scales are based on the general ESM principle of measuring reactions to an experience or an activity. However, they have an advantage of being designed in a way that allows respondents to fill them out immediately after their experience as opposed to during the experience (Jackson and Eklund, 2004). Hence, no signalling device is necessary and the problem of the alteration of the experience may be minimised. Compliance may also be greater than with a traditional ESM approach. Visitors could be asked to fill out the scales in front of researchers following their site visit, possibly increasing the chances of participation. The FSS and DFS scales have been validated and used in sport settings, but have not been applied to more passive activities such as on-site visits. They can, however, be adapted to tourism contexts and the modified version of an FSS survey form is currently being refined. The DFS version is similar, but the questions are presented in a different tense. The modified scales have received approval by the scale founders (Jackson and Eklund, 2004).

Another useful method is the interview method with flow questions. In this type of interview, respondents are typically asked to describe an experience that stands out as being better than average in an activity in which they normally participate (Jackson, 1992, 1996).The interviewees are then given three quotes to orient their attention to flow. More specific questions about the dimensions of flow can then be asked. The interviews permit a detailed evaluation of experiences. They are designed in a way that allows respondents to comment on experiences immediately after their visit (within the first 10 minutes). The interviews therefore avoid the problem of alteration of experience while almost avoiding recall bias. Research compliance could also be greater, as face-to-face interviews and small incentives may increase the chances of respondents agreeing to participate. The following section describes a research study on tourist satisfaction which employed face-to-face in-depth interviews with flow questions.

INTRODUCTION TO THE STUDY

The aim of the study was to identify immediate conscious satisfaction themes from on-site experiences. The psychological analysis of immediate satisfaction was conducted by Filep in the Spanish towns of Salamanca, Logroño, Madrid, Granada and Barcelona in June 2007 at cultural heritage sites. Questions on flow were integrated into the interview template. The sample was a group of twenty Australian study-abroad university students (ten females and ten males). The students were on a study-abroad year in Spain as part of their University of Technology, Sydney degree. The research was conducted at seven cultural heritage sites. The cultural heritage sites were not selected randomly. They had to be located in towns where the students were based. The sites had to be relatively unknown to the students so that their immediate conscious experiences were not biased by previous experiences or knowledge. In addition to these criteria, buildings with diverse architectural styles were selected (gothic, baroque, art nouveau). Very large sites had to have clearly distinguishable sections (such as an entrance, corridor or main section) so that the study could be restricted to one area. The interviewer has been to all the sites in the past and this knowledge was useful in setting up the procedures for the study.

Cultural characteristics of the heritage sites, the students' profiles and background and the social environment, however, were not the focus of the investigation. While other studies may focus on evaluating research respondents in more detail or evaluate places where research studies are conducted, this study focused on evaluating cognitive and affective psychological states. The aim was to delve into minds of tourists to understand satisfaction from a micro, positive psychology perspective. The rationale for this focus is that detailed psychological, and almost clinical, analyses of how tourists think and feel while they experience something are very few in tourism studies.

The students were asked to meet the researcher at the seven sites. They were then instructed to engage in sightseeing, preferably alone. If they insisted on being part of a group, they were asked to keep their conversations to a minimum so they would not influence each other's perceptions of experiences. Groups of more than two were not allowed. The author (interviewer) met the students immediately after the on-site experiences and the interviews began within 10 minutes of the site visit.

THE INTERVIEW METHOD

The interview questions were strongly grounded in the tourist satisfaction literature. The purpose was not to ascertain whether the participants experienced flow at the sites. Rather, it was to use the flow model (and related satisfaction concepts) to uncover a fresh layer of satisfaction and, therefore, identify immediate conscious satisfaction themes. Because of this focus, the questions were based on Jackson's (1996) suggestions for conducting in-depth flow interviews as well as Ryan's (1995) tourist satisfaction themes. Three general questions about life in Spain were first asked to ascertain the respondents' general state of mind at the time of research. Thus, if the students were dissatisfied with their life in Spain and were not interested in the Spanish cultural heritage, their responses could have been affected by this negative or apathetic state of mind. The opposite could be argued for those who were generally positive about their study-abroad experience and who were highly engaged in learning about the Spanish culture and history. Other questions in the interview template were linked to Ryan's (1995) satisfaction themes of mindfulness, psychological risk and stress and the flow dimensions. So the core questions in the interview template comprised of general contextual questions, flow questions and other satisfaction questions.

The respondents were, however, probed beyond the core questions. The questions merely served as a rough interviewing guide. Each interview was semi-structured and lasted for approximately 30 minutes. The interviews were audio recorded; they were entirely voluntary and conducted with the students' consent at a nearby venue.

ANALYSIS

Interpretive phenomenological analysis (IPA) was used to evaluate the interviews. Reid, Flowers and Larkin point out that "understanding experience is the very bread and butter of psychology, and interpretive phenomenological analysis offers psychologists the opportunity to learn from the insights of the experts—research participants themselves" (2005: 20). The technique aims to capture and explore meanings that participants assign to their experiences (Smith, 1996). IPA is an inductive process which does not test hypothesis and where prior assumptions are avoided (Smith, 2004). Therefore, while the construction of the interview questions was based on the flow theory and the tourist satisfaction literature, no hypotheses were tested and assumptions about the way satisfaction might be experienced by the participants were avoided.

This technique was the most appropriate method for several reasons. IPA is commonly used to analyse lived experiences with a subjective and reflective process of interpretation (Reid et al., 2005). The spontaneous nature of on-site experiences fits this criterion. Secondly, the technique is particularly suited for researching concepts where much of theoretical structure is lacking (as with immediate conscious tourist experiences).

Lastly, IPA is gaining increasing popularity in qualitative positive psychology works. Reid et al. (2005) also argue that there is scope for IPA research to move beyond applications in problem behaviours and for participants to be given a chance to talk about their strengths, well-being and quality of life which fits the broad premises of positive psychology (Seligman and Csikszentmihalyi, 2000).

Following the IPA framework, the interview analysis was based on the substantial verbatim excerpts from the data. The technique challenges the traditional linear relationship between numbers of participants and value of research (Reid et al., 2005). Instead, idiographic focus is retained with the average number of subjects normally involved in IPA research being fifteen (Smith, 2004). The sample of twenty in this study is somewhat higher because the interviews typically did not exceed 30 minutes instead of more common hour-long discussions (Smith 2004; Reid et al., 2005).

Works employing IPA commonly require more than one researcher for transcription coding (Lyons and Coyle, 2007). This procedure ensures acceptable congruence in findings. In this case, the completed transcripts were given to two qualified colleagues with knowledge of IPA research procedures. The colleagues independently coded the interviews without reference to each other's coding sets. In line with IPA principles, the coded themes were then discussed. The themes that overlapped were agreed on and differences were debated until a final set emerged.

The emphasis on congruence in findings instead of reliability is deliberate. Considering that, in IPA studies, the researcher is inevitably involved in research (through interviewing and probing, observing and/or participating), the traditional criteria that aim to eliminate 'bias' are inappropriate. Instead, a set of alternative evaluation criteria are proposed for good IPA research (Elliot, Fischer and Rennie, 1999; Yardley, 2000). These are sensitivity to context; commitment and rigour; transparency and coherence; and impact and importance (Yardley, 2000). In this immediate satisfaction study, effort was made to adhere to these core tenants of good qualitative IPA research, despite the lesser focus on the context and the research setting than in a more standard IPA study.

Storey (2007) suggests the following key stages for conducting interpretive phenomenological analysis:

1. initial readings of the transcripts;
2. identifying and labeling themes;
3. linking themes; and
4. producing a summary table of themes with illustrative quotations.

While not strictly prescriptive, this broad IPA framework provided a useful basis for analysing the in-depth interviews. The analysis of the results therefore follows these stages.

1   Initial Readings

This is typically the most overwhelming and the most challenging part of the IPA analysis. The process consists of investigators skimming the transcribed text to try to make some sense of it (Storey, 2007). The aim is to get an overall feel for the data by reading and rereading the transcripts. The investigator is commonly presented with a mass of interview data and it can seem an impossible task to find coherent meaning in the transcripts (Coyle and Olsen, 2005). The presence of seemingly haphazard and incoherent data was also a key feature in the initial readings of these interviews. It was evident that the students found it challenging to articulate their feelings and thoughts despite probing by the interviewer and comparisons to previous immediate conscious experiences. While the interview template was structured, not every respondent spent the same amount of time on each question. The articulation difficulties and the uneven attention to different aspects of the interview therefore made the initial readings of the transcripts a challenging process for all the coders.

Presence of additional issues or themes raised by the students further added to the complexity of the data. Balance had to be made by ensuring that the issues specified in the interview template were covered but also to allow the students the freedom to raise issues that were relevant to their immediate conscious satisfaction but which were not considered when the template was compiled. For example, at the cathedral in Salamanca, both Peter and Kristen voiced highly negative views about the role of the Catholic Church in Spain. As the study was a psychological evaluation of immediate experiences, such issues about the symbolism of the sites in the Spanish society were seen as less relevant to the research question. These sociological and cultural issues were therefore not specifically addressed by the interview questions. Yet, as the respondents' strong opinions have affected their immediate conscious satisfaction at the cathedral, Kristen and Peter were not interrupted:

> "It's amazing, inspiring, but I couldn't help thinking that Catholic church has so much money, so many people are starving and it's kind of just a sign of imperialism. They've got stuff about El Sid who killed so many people. It's all about the Catholic Church taking over Spain, kicking out everyone else."—Kristen

> "It sort of sickens me that they spent so much money, they put in so much effort into the façade of the church as opposed to actually

helping people out. That's what really bothered me. Also, in context,
when I'm in there I think of the Spanish inquisition. That church might
have been used to, like, torture people. It sort of sickens me. And the
fact that people still have so much pride in it. I dunno, it doesn't sit
well with me . . ."—Peter

The presence of these additional themes has further complicated the initial
readings. One of the biggest threats of inappropriate initial reading is over
identification or negative disidentification with the respondents. Storey warns:

> . . . an over-identification with an interviewee on the basis of shared or
> analogous experiences may lead the analyst to force the data to con-
> form to his/her experiences or a negative dis identification with the
> interviewee can make it difficult to empathise with the interviewee and
> thus attain the sort of 'insider' perspective on the research topic to
> which IPA aspires. (2007: 54)

To minimise this risk, the coders worked independently but jointly discussed
their rationale for thinking about aspects of the text before agreeing on common threads. As such, if one of the coders was also negative towards the
Spanish church, he or she may have struggled to flesh out any immediate satisfaction themes from Kristen's and Peter's interviews. That is why the discussion between the researchers was so valuable in this initial analysis phase.

So despite the articulation problems, the uneven attention to the questions by the respondents, the additional issues raised and the potential for
identification or negative disidentification, an overall immediate conscious
satisfaction feature was identified. This feature is that immediate satisfaction was conceived by the group as a cognitive as well as an affective state.
In other words, for the students, the immediate conscious satisfaction is a
mental state which includes both pleasurable feelings as well as engaging
and satisfying thoughts about what is being experienced. This conceptualisation is somewhat logical and fits the immediate conscious experience
definition by Pope and Singer (1978). Yet, much of the tourist satisfaction
literature conceptualises satisfaction in almost entirely cognitive terms con-
veniently ignoring this other, more spontaneous, affective aspect.

So once it was established in the initial readings that the immediate conscious satisfaction for the students is indeed a cognitive-affective mixed state,
more specific identification and labeling of these themes could follow.

2   Identifying and labelling themes

It was mentioned earlier that IPA is an inductive approach with a phenomenological commitment and that there is an inherent risk of overemphasising
interpretive aspects of texts and overwriting people's subjectivity with certain theories. This overemphasis was not present in this analysis. Although

the flow theory informed the analysis together with the other tourist satisfaction themes, testing the flow theory was not the objective. A priori theoretically committed approach in IPA normally involves choosing a single theory in advance, but using it to inform rather than drive the analysis (that is, no attempt is made on testing the theory) (Coyle and Rafalin, 2000; Turner and Coyle, 2000). By using the flow theory to inform and not drive the analysis, the risk of overusing the theory was reduced. The cognitive-affective themes could, however, be identified and labelled as either flow themes, other satisfaction themes (i.e. non flow themes) or contextual themes (based on the general questions). Some of the nine dimensions of flow were clearly identifiable in the interviews and it was hence appropriate to highlight the positive psychology contribution in fleshing out the immediate satisfaction.

The following themes were identified by coding assistants (shown in Tables 2.1 and 2.2).

Table 2.1   Coder 1 Set—Immediate On-Site Satisfaction Themes

Flow	Other satisfaction themes	Contextual information
time transformation	no crowding and no photos	language ability
total concentration	pleasant temperature (not hot or cold)	inability to communicate/ express oneself
challenge-skills balance	relaxation/calm/ peacefulness	homesickness
action awareness merging	absorption	ability to live away from home
autotelic events	curiosity	experience something different
clear goals	interaction/engagement	career development
loss of self-consciousness	focus	new perspectives
	excitement/ stimulation	living without friends or family
	no interruptions from other people	wanting to be like a local
	no tourists	wanting to get by (difficulty in day-to-day tasks)
	discovery (unexpected events)	
	learning	
	daydreaming and imagination	
	respect for local culture	

Table 2.2 Coder 2 Set—Immediate On-Site Satisfaction Themes

Flow	Other satisfaction themes	Contextual information
time transformation	crowds	language problems
total concentration	temperature (pleasant or unpleasant)	cultural immersion/wanting to fit in
action awareness merging	relaxation	satisfaction with time in the country
autotelic events	interest	novel environment
	aesthetics	loneliness
	interaction	self-discovery
	excitement	cultural comparison
	solitary experience	ups and downs
	tranquillity	independence
	contentment	
	discovery	
	calm	
	learning	
	freedom	
	lighting	
	personal experiences	
	association (historical, present day)	

3 Linking Themes

Following the formal identification and labelling of this cognitive-affective mix, connections between different themes and different coding sets were identified. This linking process ensured that the themes from coder 1 and coder 2 sets could be integrated with a less formal and methodical draft labelling by the principal researcher. The coders discussed in detail the initial labelling and identification. Some of the themes were eliminated as they formed a larger theme or were only identified by one coder on one or two occasions. Other themes were grouped to form new labels.

The rationale for grouping and final labelling was in many cases supported by relevant literature. For example, the other satisfaction themes of interest and learning from coder 2's set and the themes of absorption, curiosity, interaction/engagement and learning from coder 1's set were grouped into a single theme of mindfulness. The concept of mindfulness, as indicated in the review of experience satisfaction approaches, neatly incorporates all of these subthemes. This is a "flexible, cognitive state that results from drawing novel distinctions about the situation and environment" (Carson and Langer, 2006: 29). Mindfulness is therefore about interest, absorption, curiosity, interaction/engagement and learning (Moscardo, 1996). Similarly, the contextual information themes of ups and downs, cultural comparison, cultural immersion/wanting to fit in and language problems (coder 2) and the themes of language ability, inability to communicate/express oneself, wanting to get by (difficulty in day-to-day tasks), homesickness, living without friends or family (coder 1) all point to Oberg's (1960) elements of culture shock (physical, orientation, cultural components, daily hassles). Oberg defines culture shock as a term that describes difficulties of operating in a foreign culture. These difficulties were common for the students yet did not seem to affect their immediate conscious satisfaction. One of the clearest accounts of culture shock was given by Maria, yet her experience at the cathedral in Salamanca was highly fulfilling. The theoretical concept of culture shock, however, was regarded as too broad by the coders and was hence divided into three contextual final themes: wanting to fit in/ learn about the culture, language challenges and loneliness. The remaining contextual and other satisfaction themes from the initial coding sets were also discussed and grouped to form a final set.

The flow themes were not grouped. Instead, overlaps were discussed and commonly agreed on. Two flow themes, however, were omitted from the final set: clear goals and action-awareness merging. The clear goals dimension was discovered on one occasion in one of the interviews and by one coder. It was agreed that this does not warrant its inclusion in the final group of themes because the flow dimension does not adequately represent the immediate conscious satisfaction of the student group. The action awareness merging dimension was identified by both coder 1 and 2 but also did not feature prominently (it was uncovered in two separate interviews on one occasion). The action-awareness merging label was used for the following quotes:

> "And it's kind of like, there were heaps of people there. It was hot there in this crappy little demountable cube thing, but because the stuff I was seeing was so intense and so visual, you didn't notice anything at all."

> "You do focus on yourself, you don't hear anything cause you're just sort of looking."

After a discussion with the coders, it was agreed that the quotes actually more appropriately represent the other satisfaction theme of object focus and not the action-awareness merging theme.

Following this initial labeling and linking of the themes, a final set representing the immediate conscious tourist satisfaction of the students emerged. It was finally possible to provide illustrative examples from the in-depth interviews for each of the cognitive- affective themes as they were not changed further. Connections, however, between the final flow themes and the final other satisfaction themes were drawn to show that aspects of flow are distinct but complementary elements of the overall immediate satisfaction mix.

4   Summary of Core Themes with Illustrative Examples

In line with the IPA procedures noted by Storey (2007), illustrative quotes are provided here under each main final satisfaction theme. Contextual themes are discussed as one whole single theme because they are not part of the immediate satisfaction mix. As with some other IPA analyses (Smith, 1996, 2004; Reid et al., 2005) and in a similar manner to Uriely and Belhassen's (2005) phenomenological investigation of drugs in tourist experiences, a frequency table of the main themes was not developed. Considering the sample of twenty students and the exploratory approach to this study, statements such as "50% of respondents or 10 out 20 students mentioned mindfulness" are therefore not used in this section.

The students' immediate conscious satisfaction is presented in Figure 2.1.

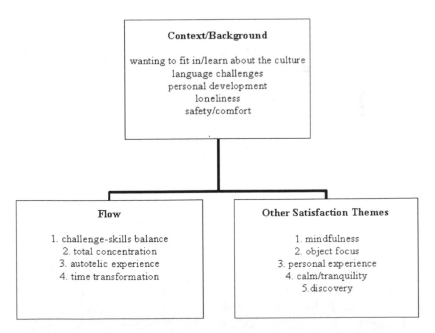

Figure 2.1   Core contextual and immediate conscious satisfaction themes.

CHALLENGE-SKILLS BALANCE AND MINDFULNESS

These two themes are expressed in a similar manner by the students. It was mentioned in the literature review that mindfulness is similar to the flow dimension of challenge-skills balance. This is because both of the concepts describe a state in which a tourist actively processes what he or she is observing and commonly learns from this experience. This is how Gareth described his mindful experience at the St Paul's hospital in Barcelona:

> *"The sounds and the site were very relaxing but at the same time your mind's working and thinking about the history of the place and the purpose—why it was built the way it was. There's a lot of religious symbols and those sorts of things you take in more. It's not the same as the beach where you just escape and relax, the atmosphere is such that you have to be more involved."*

Catherine also described her state of mindfulness at the exhibition in Logroño's church:

> *"We just sort of had a look at the ones (the exhibits) we liked and read a bit about the artist and passed the exhibits we weren't interested in."*

Even June, who had a rather ordinary experience at the Saint Paul's Hospital in Barcelona, was mindfully appreciative of the juxtaposition of the murals at the site:

> *"I consider myself an art lover but I'm not particularly. I mean most of the stuff I look at I don't have much knowledge about. I kind of grew up in a background where I knew about art but I think that my knowledge is fairly limited still. Still, it was interesting to observe the juxtaposition of the murals that were there and the technology that has been installed since."*

In all these descriptions there is an implied desire for learning. For Gareth there was a desire to gain knowledge about the history of the place, for Catherine to learn about the artist and for June to learn about the murals. Learning is a central component of mindfulness (Moscardo, 2009a). On many occasions, the difference between mindfulness and challenge-skills balance was very subtle, but one distinguishing characteristic of the flow dimension is the presence of a mental challenge that is being met. This challenge is typically presented by a visual stimulus that is studied in detail and then decoded or understood (Csikszentmihalyi and Robinson, 1990). The existence of a challenge was typically hidden but was implied and thus discernable from the interviews. When asked to think of another on-site experience that could match the description of flow from a Csikszentmihalyi's quote, Kirsty said:

"I guess the closest thing I can think of is seeing Picasso's Guernica. That was really one of those things that I was so in awe that I didn't feel anything for a couple of seconds. I saw it in Madrid, in a museum. Then I started analysing the shapes. I guess I am an analyst."

So, Guernica was a complex and powerful visual stimulus for Kirsty because it had many shapes (challenges) that she started to analyse (with her visual skills). Yet this experience of detailed observation was highly exhilarating because it matched the description of flow. She was therefore experiencing the challenge-skills balance.

TOTAL CONCENTRATION AND OBJECT FOCUS

Another core theme was total concentration from flow, which also normally meant focus on a particular object or aspect of the site (object focus). For the bulk of the respondents, total concentration and object focus did not occur at the sites for this study. This could possibly be due to the fact that respondents were required to engage in sightseeing for the purposes of the research. Total concentration and object focus did, however, feature in other on-site experiences of the students. Talking about a fulfilling moment from his past visit to a museum, Peter said:

"That time when I was in a museum in Madrid, I was looking at art because you kind of tend to ignore the people around you . . . Like if you are focusing on a painting or a certain work of art then it's easy to concentrate on that . . ."

Monique similarly described her total concentration and object focus at a Vietnam War museum in Ho Chi Minh City:

"I was packed in this little thing that everyone was moving through together. . . . And it kind of doesn't fit in with 'my body feels great' cause my body felt heavy (cause it was really intense) but it was the same sort of feeling I guess . . . I dunno, I agree with every other part of the quote—a complete and utter focus on what I was seeing, and what I was reading . . ."

The theme of concentration and focus was also expressed in the following way by Melissa in her account of the on-site experience at the church in Logroño:

"I wasn't paying attention to who was moving around me and stuff. And when I moved away I also didn't pay attention to what was around me."

AUTOTELIC EXPERIENCE AND PERSONAL EXPERIENCE

Autotelic or an intrinsically rewarding experience is considered a product of the other flow dimensions and is a feeling of high exhilaration and fulfillment. It is therefore not a cognitive but an affective element of immediate satisfaction. With the exception of one person, the respondents did not have autotelic experiences at the sites during the study. Autotelic descriptions of experiences by the students at other sites, however, abound.

Autotelic experiences were highly personal. Maria's comments about her cathedral visit are illustrative of how individuals in the sample described these powerful experiences:

> "It looks surreal. Inside it makes me feel at peace, content, it makes me feel like nothing else matters, it makes me feel happy, it . . . Yeah, nothing else matters . . ."

The three-times repeated phrase "makes me feel" points to this interplay between the personal and the autotelic. When asked if this was her first time at the site, Maria replied:

> "No, *this wasn't my first time, but this time the site still had the same impact on me as when I first saw it. That it's huge and it's there and it's beautiful and it's . . . I think it's amazing (repeats twice). Ummm . . . it's overwhelming . . ."*

Another example of an autotelic experience was Emily's account of her visit to Ellora caves in India. In this instance the word *amazing* is mentioned several times, which is one of the words that normally describes autotelic events (Jackson and Eklund, 2004):

> "I was in these caves—Ellora caves in India. Just lots of sets of different caves with beautiful carvings inside and it was just amazing cause they were carved in the dark. They had all these amazing techniques to do it, like water on the floor to reflect the light and then just this incredible painting with this woman with a flower in her hair and it was just amazing the way it was done! I felt completely calm inside, tranquil, really balanced, just a satisfied very calm sort of clearheaded feeling. I guess it was a content sort of happy feeling."

When asked how long she spent looking at the carvings, she said:

> "I have no idea. I didn't care how long it was. I was in a group but we were just wandering around the place, but there was no pressure . . ."

TIME TRANSFORMATION AND CALM/TRANQUILITY

Indeed, the importance of calm and tranquility to immediate satisfaction was also clearly expressed by the respondents. When asked to talk about a powerful experience from the past at a tourist site, Brenda mentioned the Alhambra fortress in Granada. To the question "Were there any specific physical attributes which grabbed your attention at the Alhambra fortress?" she replied:

> "No, it was just the overall tranquility. The architecture is such that there is not much light that can go through. So it's actually quite cool even if it's hot outside. It's calm. You can't hear noises from the city. While you are in there you can freely focus on the architecture and the designs. The ceiling in particular I found most intriguing . . ."

Alexis's visit during this study to Barcelona's Saint Paul's Hospital was also very calming:

> "I found that the hospital was beautiful. I was quite surprised how lovely actually it was. I read a few things in guide books but I didn't know it was so beautiful. The architecture is really nice. If it wasn't called a hospital and you didn't maybe pick up a few of the hospital signs you wouldn't think it's a hospital necessarily because it's sort of. . . . When you walk into the courtyard, the atmosphere is calm. The colours of the building I also found very calming—most probably used for the purpose of it being a hospital."

Time transformation (a perception that time either slows or speeds up) was commonly intertwined with the descriptions of calm and tranquility. The quote by Monique is a good illustration of the linkage between calm and tranquility and time transformation. In her description of a different powerful on-site experience, she described how she took her time to enjoy the calming atmosphere at the site:

> "When I was in Tunisia, I came across these Roman ruins in the Middle of North Africa and I found them really amazing. Maybe because I didn't have an understanding that such things existed here, but to see them! And to see the Roman ruins! There weren't so many tourists around, it was really calming and it was just nice to wander through it on your own, take your time and discover these things on your own."

Also, Brenda added shortly after her reference to tranquility that "*the time just went too quickly when I was in Alhambra*".

Monique's idea of "taking time" at the Roman ruins and Brenda's perception that time went too quickly at Alhambra show how the perception of time was distorted for the respondents during these experiences. The time transformation, together with the other flow elements of challenge-skills balance, total concentration and autotelic experiences, hence characterises immediate satisfaction of the student tourists. There was, however, one more other satisfaction theme that was uncovered.

DISCOVERY

Discovery was the last immediate satisfaction theme that featured prominently. Unlike the rest of the themes, it did not have a flow linkage in this study. The notion of active discovery has, however, been compared to the challenge-skills balance in museum visitor settings (Csikszentmihalyi and Robinson, 1990), but in this study the challenge-skills balance dimension was deemed to be more similar to the mindfulness theme.

This is how Maria expressed her discovery at the cathedral in Salamanca:

> "I was standing outside and looking at the cathedral. Every time I'm there I see things that I haven't seen before. So I can look at something and I find things. I discover things there. One of my favourite aspects today was the fact that there was someone playing the organ and they were practicing their scales on the organ. We don't have that in Sydney, they were just practicing. It was like a normal thing."

And when Jo was asked what he liked the most about Palacio Real in Madrid, he said:

> "Umm . . . When we stood up on the fence and looked inside where the plaza was. I guess it was a bit weird. We climbed on the fence and it was like we were discovering something."

Monique, who was with Jo at that time, added her commentary to the haphazard discovery:

> "Yeah, I was also interested when we looked inside the palace there from the fence. It was really cool cause one person came in and walked across the palace and I couldn't help it, but I was really curious. My imagination went wild as to what that person does . . . I thought maybe that person has actually met the king and that person was actually allowed to enter the areas for that reason . . . I dunno, because I was more relaxed my imagination started to run wild a bit . . ."

For Brenda in Granada, the discovery at the Jose Guerrero Centre (museum) was so powerful that it influenced her intention to return to the site:

> *"I was surprised to see there was an Australian painter's work. I am interested in it. I actually wanna go back to it and I am curious about it."*

So, what is interesting to note that the discoveries for the respondents never detracted from the quality of their on-site experiences. The discovery was typically viewed in a positive light, as a random, haphazard element that enriched the overall immediate conscious experience.

BACKGROUND INFORMATION

The first three interview questions were: 1) Why did you decide to do the study abroad course and come to Spain? 2) How have you found the period of time since your arrival in Spain? and 3) Which aspect of your in-country study experience do you currently find most rewarding and most satisfying and why?

The purpose was to gain an insight in the respondents' general state of mind at the time of research. Although it was initially anticipated that the students with a negative state of mind would also have negative on-site experiences, no evidence for such a claim was found. Most students were eager to fit in with the Spanish culture, improve their command of the Spanish language and overcome feelings of loneliness and homesickness. Yet these feelings did not seem to affect their satisfaction with the cultural site or their ability to talk about other fulfilling events. The case of Maria is again useful for analysis. She described one of the most fulfilling on-site experiences during this research, yet she also gave a very negative account of her initial experience of living in Salamanca and feelings of general apathy about her life in Spain at the time of the interview:

> *"Ok, when I first arrived . . . I hated it. Completely hated it. Ummmm, I was gonna go home. I was ready to go home. I hated everything. I hated the size of the city. I hated the fact that I couldn't communicate. I hated that I didn't have friends, that I was disconnected from everyone, that I was isolated, that I couldn't leave the city, ummm . . . I didn't know what there was here to do. But, as time went on, I sort of . . . I sort of learned to accept that I'm here and to make the most out of the situation. So I'm here, I'm not going anywhere, if anything I'm going to get something out of it."*

Others talk about similar issues broadly related to the culture-shock elements (Oberg, 1960), such as language issues:

> *"The language—I just assumed that after having 4 semesters of Spanish I would be speaking almost like a Spaniard. I got here and I couldn't say anything—couldn't say anything at all. My friend spoke much better than me. It was a stab in face, it was a kick when I was down. I just couldn't get by at all. And couldn't express any aspect of my personality because I had no language skills. That was the hardest thing—not being able to express myself because I just didn't have the skills. . . . Next semester we are actually in with the Spanish students. It's going to be a bit harder. But it will also be exciting because I will have more of an understanding of the language."—Lisa*

Positive contextual themes, however, also featured. The following two quotes are representative of these themes:

> *"I really wanted to do Nursing in South America so the Spanish language would really propel me there. But I didn't go to South America for International Studies because I didn't think it was very safe for me there as like, first moving out of home . . ."—Terena*

> *"I love cementing friendships over time. In my group of friends in OZ we are closed off to any new people. We've been the same group for almost 10 years. It's good not to have them as a fallback. Instead you are forced to make new friends and get to know people for the first time as opposed to knowing people already and talking crap day in and day out. It's good to have a look at someone else's life and create friends."—Peter*

At the time of the interview, therefore, the students were also concerned with satisfying their safety and comfort needs and were developing opportunities for self-growth through close friendships.

DISCUSSION

The purpose of the study was to identify immediate conscious satisfaction themes of the student group through a psychological approach. The results show that the tourist group's immediate satisfaction at a site consists of a variety of affective and cognitive elements. The tourists were immediately satisfied by feelings of calm and tranquility, time transformation and by experiences that were personal and intrinsically rewarding (autotelic) for them. For the participants, to be immediately satisfied was also about being mindful, being focused on objects and discovering new things about the sites. Total concentration on visual stimuli and a feeling of exhilaration from meeting the challenges imposed by the visual stimuli (challenge-skills balance) were also the core immediate satisfaction themes. Most of the students were experiencing culture shock at the time of the interviews. Yet, these challenges did not seem to affect their ability to have satisfying experiences at tourist sites on this occasion or to talk about other fulfilling moments from the past.

The presence of the cognitive-affective mix may sound contradictory. For example, it may be thought that experiences that are characterised by a lot of thinking, such as mindfulness and total concentration, contradict with the notions of relaxation, tranquility and time transformation. Yet the presence of both hedonic and more cognitive (thinking) themes is the essence of the flow state. Being in flow (a highly satisfactory optimal state) is as much about being engaged and attentive as it is about deriving emotional pleasure from such attentiveness and engagement (Csikszentmihalyi, 1975, 1990; Jackson and Eklund, 2004; Ryan, 1995). Aspects of this state were uncovered in the in-depth interviews. The model of flow from positive psychology has therefore embellished the conceptualisation of the immediate conscious tourist experience. Through the following flow quote, an important layer of the tourists' immediate satisfaction was brought to light.

> "*My mind isn't wandering, I am not thinking of something else. I am totally involved in what I am doing. My body feels great. I don't seem to hear anything. The world seems to be cut off from me. I am less aware of myself and my problems.*" (Csikszentmihalyi, 1982: 23)

This different layer of tourist satisfaction may not have been uncovered through more reflective Nordic methods (Crompton and Love, 1995; Hughes, 1991; Kozak, 2001; Prakash, 1984) and certainly not through expectations-based service approaches such as SERVQUAL (Parasuraman et al., 1988; Truong, 2005) or IPA (Hudson and Shephard, 1998; Martilla and James, 1977). Instead, the findings of this study complement the increasingly popular, experience-related conceptualisations of satisfaction, such as the tourist moment (Hom Cary, 2004) and existential authenticity (Steiner and Reisinger, 2006; Wang, 1999). In line with this approach, the study suggests that satisfaction is both a feeling and a cognitive evaluation and that it is at least as much about immediacy as it is about reflection. The application of the flow model and its addition to more standard tourist satisfaction concepts has therefore improved the measurement of the immediate conscious tourist satisfaction.

There are, however, limitations of the study. The fresh conceptualisation and measurement of the immediate tourist satisfaction was based on the findings obtained from a small sample of tourists who are culturally quite homogenous and who are in the similar age group (18–30 years old). Gender differences were not explored. Further, because the focus was on identifying immediate satisfaction themes, the students were also encouraged to talk about other immediately satisfying on-site experiences that may have been more powerful than their experience during the Spanish study. This procedure was risky because it could have violated the immediate conscious criterion of the study because the students were asked to also talk about satisfying experiences from the past. Despite this risk, it is believed that the criterion was not violated because the participants discussed other experiences in the context of the flow quote, which was presented in present tense and which described an immediately gratifying moment. Lastly, as with any IPA research, the interpretation of the findings should be taken with caution. The fact that the themes were cross coded and that the deductions and reasoning were thoroughly discussed has reduced the potential partiality.

Considering the limitations, this study could be conceived as an exploratory examination of immediate conscious on-site tourist satisfaction—the satisfaction type which has been overlooked in tourism studies (Hayllar and Griffin, 2004; Hom Cary 2004; Mannell and Iso-Ahola, 1987). Immediate conscious tourist experiences, such as the ones described in the exploratory study, are worthy of further research. Kubey, Larson and Csikszentmihalyi point out that researchers "must be cognizant of the milieus in which the behaviors and phenomena they wish to study actually occur in order to adopt appropriate methods" (1996: 99). They further point out that human activity takes place rapidly, in short bursts, repeatedly and over variable periods of time. Similar conclusions can be drawn about tourism, which is commonly a highly spontaneous activity. Unpredictability of events seems to lie at the heart of tourist experiences, and it is these unpredictable events which often end up being most satisfactory (Botterill, 1987; Hughes, 1991). Therefore, immediate tourist experiences need to be researched so that tourist satisfaction can be better understood and managed.

CONCLUSION

It is hoped thus that the study described in this chapter has laid a foundation for new research on conceptualisation and measurement of tourist moments, immediacy and satisfaction from the positive psychology perspective. Traditional and dominant tourist satisfaction approaches can and should be embellished by new approaches from disciplines outside tourism studies. Positive psychology ideas on immediate satisfaction are one example of this embellishment and hold much promise for better understanding tourists' satisfaction with a holiday.

A plethora of experience-based approaches is clearly replacing or complementing the more traditional, Nordic and Expectations methods of measuring tourist satisfaction. As part of these experience approaches, flow state and its methods from positive psychology could be further applied in studies of tourist satisfaction to gain more holistic conceptualisations of the complex phenomenon.

3   Time, Tourism, Host Communities and Positive Psychology

The awareness of time is of major importance in understanding our lives not only in the present but also in the contexts of the past and the future. Yet many people, particularly in the Western world, have an uneasy, even troubled, relationship with the notion of time in their daily existence. Most commonly expressed is the regret that we seldom have enough of it (Banks, 1983; Robinson and Godbey, 1997; Sullivan and Gershuny, 2001). Suggestions of a widespread time famine and of frequently experiencing time poverty are common, not only in organisational publications but also in lifestyle magazines and other popular media. This prevalent perception of time and its scarcity also seems to be in stark contrast to the findings of Robinson and Godbey, and also Sullivan and Gershuny, who generally conclude that many people in the West have in fact gained up to seven hours of additional time per week in which to relax and to pursue increased leisure and recreational activities. Robinson and Godbey further report that leisure activities now increasingly preferred have the characteristics of time deepening, a tendency to compress more activities into the time available; they find time deepening involves an accelerated rate of doing and of achieving. This, they aver, primarily focuses on those activities able to be performed quickly and likely to be accomplished more than once; activities that take longer amounts of time or that are not amenable to an immediate sense of achievement are now said to be less favoured As a consequence, these increasingly popular choices are said more likely to be accompanied by feelings of fragmentation in people's lives, and a greater awareness of time pressure and even of time dominance. There would thus appear to be a powerful association between the manner in which individuals understand and negotiate time perceptions and expressions of well-being.

Notions of time have also been found associated with changing patterns of travel. Within tourism there is now a reported trend to take more trips in each year, though of much shorter duration. Many people in the West would seem to not have the time to take the more traditional longer breaks, but rather prefer more frequent trips that are shorter and perhaps to compact more tourist experiences into these excursions.

Salt (2006) reports that social changes in countries such as Australia are influencing the patterns of tourism travel and consumption. He suggests that a range of time-related factors such as the coordination of schedules for working couples and the particular demands for meaningful travel experiences among groups such as grey nomads will alter travel frequency, activity and mode. Newbold, Scott, Spinney, Kanaroglou and Paez (2005) have found that, as the population of Canada ages, patterns of travel are changing: travel by motor vehicle for groups such as baby boomers is said to be increasing, with a lessening reliance upon other forms such as public transport. Collia, Sharp and Geisbrecht (2003) find a similar reliance upon the motor vehicle in the United States, and suggest that this increasing reliance presents looming problems in a variety of spheres for planners and government authorities. Similarly, in the United Kingdom, Dickinson, Calver, Watters, and Wilks (2004) report a growing reliance upon motor vehicle travel for shorter trips, and warn of the increasing congestion, pollution, loss of heritage values, escalating accident rate and parking problems that this will cause in host communities. Russo (2002) also warns of the destructiveness that can be caused by the swelling number of short-stay excursionist tourists, those visitors who it is said are particularly linked to the later stages of a destination's life cycle and the decline in a city's attractiveness.

Whilst there is now a growing awareness of the links between time and travel in regard to well-being, there is another area of tourism, that of host community functioning, wherein the notion of time is also closely related to personal well-being. This association between time perceptions and host community functioning would seem to be writ large in regard to relatively vulnerable groups such as senior citizens. This chapter will examine the concept of time as it relates to well-being within the positive psychology literature and will also explore the ideas of time perspective and time balance; the chapter will further present a major theoretical model, that of socioemotional selectivity theory, as it assists in the understanding of well-being among senior residents of tourism communities, exploring time perspective and well-being in a variety of tourism contexts. The chapter will conclude with a number of recommendations as to how vulnerable people such as senior host community members can receive more equitable treatment so as to maximise their well-being.

THE SELF AND TIME WITHIN POSITIVE PSYCHOLOGY

Psychologists have long been aware of the critical role played by time perception in any individual's self-perception. William James (1890/1950, 1892/1961) in the latter part of the nineteenth century observed that a period of time filled with interesting events and experiences was, on the occasion, perceived as short in duration, yet lengthy when remembered.

However, he also points out that an episode of time relatively devoid of varied and stimulating experiences seems at that time lengthy in its passage, yet on reflection at a later date, very short. The length, retrospectively regarded, would seem largely determined by the richness and meaning of the memories of the time period. It is also the case, as Levine (1997) avers, that paying attention to the passing of time changes our perceptions; time is said to pass more slowly when we become aware of it. It is also the case that when there is an absence of temporal cues so as to diminish one's awareness of time's effluxion, individuals conclude that time passes much more quickly than in fact it does (Ashoff, 1985). The experience of time, as James (1892\1961) and Harton (1939) show, can be characterised as odious, as boring, as inspired and even as exhilarating; Csikszentmihalyi (1978, 1993) has described the idea of flow as a highly stimulating and all-encompassing state wherein time appears to stand still. Positive experiences, it would seem, are generally perceived by an individual as shorter in duration, whereas negative experiences are lengthier, with time appearing to drag for that person.

Positive psychology commentators such as Seligman (2002) conclude that future selves have considerable motivational force in the lives of most individuals. Future selves contain within them expectations that involve both hopes and fears, emotional states that may lead to goal-setting and many possible life achievements; alternatively, expectations may lead to the avoidance of experiences and situations that could potentially cause distress. A fear of heights, for example, whilst visiting an unfamiliar place or city may well lead some travellers to avoid a wide variety of attractions, buildings and social contexts where elevation is a characteristic; so too many travellers may be apprehensive about the possibility of encountering incidents of crime such as mugging and therefore avoid any possible excursion, walking tour or trip that may be perceived to offer risk. In both cases these apprehensions associated with the future self, whether one regards them as major apprehensions or even mild to moderate phobias, can seriously limit the range of experiences and thus the possibility for enjoyment and learning; as a consequence, these forebodings of the future self may seriously detract from the well-being of the traveller.

Central to the entire purpose of positive psychology is the question 'what is the good life?' Such a question was posed by Aristotle, and subsequently deemed of central importance by many thinkers during periods of cultural and intellectual creativity. This question has also been uppermost in the considerations of many within the discipline of psychology in recent times (Argyle 1999, 2002; Argyle and Crossland, 1985; Diener, 1999, 2000; Diener and Seligman, 2002; Kahneman, Diener and Schwarz, 1999; Layard, 2005; Peterson and Seligman, 2004; Seligman, 2000; Seligman and Csikszentmihalyi, 2000; Seligman, Steen, Park and Peterson, 2005; and Veenhoven, 2000, 2002). Whilst a number of findings are now emanating from the ongoing research programmes of those just cited, as well as many others throughout the world, one common theme does emerge among many commentators: It is the desirability of reaching of an equilibrium in regard to the various selves that represents the past, the present and the future; it profoundly involves the achievement of an optimal balance in one's time perspective (Zimbardo, 2001, 2002; Zimbardo and Boyd, 1999; Zimbardo, Keogh and Boyd, 1997).

Zimbardo and colleagues would hold that well-being is inextricably associated with the ability to maintain a balanced time perspective. This facility involves adjustments to the temporal mode so as to accommodate the requirements of the present environmental setting or personal challenges faced by the individual. Zimbardo et al. (1997). describe this idea of the several foci upon time frames and selves at different life points as an individual's time perspective, and hold that this attachment of self to a particular time perspective is a potent determinant of everyday behaviour; it is moreover a major explanatory variable they suggest in regard to providing answers to Aristotle's question concerning the good life. Zimbardo and colleagues have asserted that the notion of time perspective has considerable value in the understanding of human behaviour, of attitudes and values in a variety of domains such as health, scholastic attainment, and vocational interest as well as choice of leisure activity. Various time perspectives are predictive of specific behavioural patterns; risk taking whilst driving, for example, has been found by Zimbardo to characterise many people possessing a present time perspective. Keogh, Zimbardo and Boyd (1999) would posit that the present time perspective is predictive of a higher propensity to engage in sexual behaviours; substance abuse involving both drugs and alcohol has also been associated with a predominant favouring of the present time perspective. Eppel, Bandura and Zimbardo (1999) suggest that unemployed people who have a future time perspective are more likely to be focused on achievement, be involved in goal-setting, and employ their time in such a manner as to maximise their chances of securing a job; in contrast, Eppel et al. find that individuals with a present time perspective are less likely to be desirous of taking concrete steps to find employment. Such individuals, they find, use more of their time for activities such as watching television.

Zimbardo et al. would argue that a predominant orientation toward one time perspective could lead to a lessening of well-being. Zimbardo (2002) cites the preoccupation of a great deal of the industrialised Western world with the future orientation; goal-setting and the achievement of increasingly higher targets within enterprises results in what Zimbardo terms a time famine. Time for enjoyment is severely truncated when the possibility of reaching a time balance is lessened; leisure time is reduced as the work role intrudes further into the home and nonwork life. In assessing the costs associated with a predominance upon one time perspective, such as that concerned with the future, Zimbardo warns that any major overemphasis does not come without cost to individual happiness. Other important aspects of life are sloughed off when a dominant future time perspective results in work largely taking over one's life; family, friends, travel, cultural and sporting pursuits as well as personal growth are likely to become casualties, according to Myers (2000). Leisure and travel activities would seem to be major casualties in this situation; taking up the role of a tourist becomes a somewhat irrelevant luxury within a future time perspective that sees work as all-important and wholly time consuming. The opportunities for nonwork travel and the enrichment that is derived from the visitation to sites and contexts of historical, cultural and natural value become severely restricted

However more leisure time alone does not necessarily guarantee higher levels of personal well-being. Argyle (1999, 2002) has made the point that many individuals report their leisure time to be relatively unsatisfying. One likely explanation of this, Zimbardo et al. suggest, is to do with the lack of balance that may be present in an individual's time perspective. They cite the example of individuals who have a predominately future time perspective that is associated with their work. Such people may struggle, often unsuccessfully, to regain a present time perspective when not in the workplace. Leisure, travel and tourist activities, often centrally located in the present, could also become relatively unsatisfying and seemingly irrelevant to those people locked into a future and an achievement-focused perspective, the expression of which is primarily within their workplace. Their answer lies in striving for a balanced time perspective, and in avoiding the enthrallment of one temporal self. Zimbardo (2002) summarises such a strategy as involving past, present and future selves that are able to blend with or forge some balance with another, so that the present situation and its needs determine the nature of the time balance required. Individuals who achieve this flexibility and suggested balance of the selves across time relate to their social and physical environments in a manner that is more effective and more likely to be appropriate to their circumstances. Thus when a person is visiting family and friends, or is visiting a cultural or historical site, they are fully immersed in the present, are with other individuals or environments in a complete sense, and so experience enjoyment and satisfaction that would not be possible for individuals whose temporal self was still locked into some future work mode. Moreover, such individuals could, whilst being entirely in the present, acknowledge a past self that was connected with family memories or with a pleasant nostalgia for past events, past travel experiences and for a continuity of self across time.

Flexibility in regard to possible selves is therefore of considerable importance in achieving well-being. Diener and Seligman (2002) suggest that aspiring to possible selves that have a balance involving past-positive and present-hedonistic maximises a person's likelihood of building personal relationships characterised as happy and rewarding. Yet these findings ought not to lead to the conclusion that a future-self time perspective is necessarily dysfunctional; Diener (2000) has found that a future time perspective is associated with a higher socio-economic status, which in turn is more likely to be associated with well-being. Overall, however, it is the balance as between these possible selves across time, and the expression of an appropriate balance for the circumstances presently facing the individual, that would seem critical in the attainment of happiness. Boniwell and Zimbardo (2004) aver it may well be this balance of selves that is ultimately related to how individuals employ their time; they consider there is a likelihood that a balanced time perspective can lead to an optimal use of the individual's time and to higher levels of contentment, culminating in a higher level of overall well-being in one's life generally. Such connections would have considerable implications for the understanding of tourism-related behaviours. Visitation to a historic site, for example, may be more satisfying and be associated with greater levels of overall well-being if the person had the opportunity to reach a balanced time perspective containing elements of both past and present selves.

WELL-BEING AMONG HOST COMMUNITY MEMBERS

The many influences, pressures and upheavals brought about by the growth of tourism within a community can have a quite noticeable influence upon the self and the time perspective of individual residents. A variety of commentators such as Allen, Long, Perdue and Kieselbach (1988), Ap and Crompton (1993), and Easterling (2005) have over the last few decades examined not only the forces for good or ill brought about by tourism development within a city or region, but also the many effects this development may have upon local people; also considered are the reactions that residents may have to those changes in their environment. It has also been noted that, whilst many community changes have been documented and residents' responses seen to be associated a variety of socio-demographic and interpersonal and economic factors, relatively little theoretical foundation has been provided in order that both changes and consequent personal reactions may be understood in a wider theoretical context (Faulkner and Tidswell, 1997; Lui and Var, 1986). One notable contribution in this area is that by Zhang, Inbakaran and Jackson (2006), who have examined resident reactions to tourism in an urban-rural border region, employing personality dimensions such as McRae and Costa's (1996) Five Factor Personality Model (FFM) as well as expectancy values theories. Research such as this holds considerable explanatory value in the area of host-guest interactions within a well-being framework.

Representations, particularly those of a social nature, have long been recognised in various areas of psychology as having a powerful influence upon behaviour. Social representations theory is now an established formulation within the area of social psychology, and has been applied to the domains of physical and mental health, and to areas such as stigma and safety campaigns. It has been suggested by Pearce, Moscardo and Ross (1996) and Ross (2007) that social representations theory can shed considerable light upon the various reactions of host communities to tourism development. Social representations afford a way for tourism researchers to reconstruct and to explicate that social reality experienced by many host community members; it moreover allows for understandings of the various forms of conflict that arise when deeply felt issues, particularly those concerned with loss of amenity, are provoked by development over which individuals perceive no control. Farr (1993, 1994) and Moscovici (1984) explain social representations as fundamentally those myths, images and ideas within thought patterns concerning objects, entities or social processes commonly experienced; reactions at the various implications of tourism development would be deemed as indicative of social representations circulating within a community. Social representations can also be understood as mechanisms, as processes community members engage so as to understand, to react to and even to initiate change so as to attain or to regain their well-being. These social representations would have the action of changing the unfamiliar into the familiar, with prior knowledge and experience being rendered into a form of understanding that facilitates new social encounters to be comprehended in a familiar context; these understandings are also likely to be perceived as being shared by other members of the host community.

Older people, it has been found, are likely to be among those who most acutely perceive the impacts of tourism on their individual selves as well as on their fellow community members (Ross, 1991, 1992, 2005a, 2008). They are likely to be among those residents more likely to employ social representations so as to comprehend the changes that are happening around them and over which they may perceive they have little or no control; social representations moreover can, given favourable circumstances, sometimes assist them to react in ways that they believe will empower them as individuals, and thus assist them to regain some measure of well-being. Certainly older residents are prominent among those who report baleful effects of tourism development in various areas of their lives, such as those involving crime and safety, environment degradation, access to community facilities and leisure opportunities. They are also prominent among those resident groups that perceive negative economic impacts, reporting that the financial benefits enjoyed by some residents and occasioned by development are perceived to pass them by and may even occasion increased financial hardship.

Older residents exhibit social representations of crime that emerge in the form of apprehensiveness and fear; whilst this fear may not necessarily provide evidence of an elevated crime rate for their age group, or indeed any age group, older community members often verbalise a heightened trepidation. This social representation may well be expressed within and regularly intensified by the repetition of media stories concerning the details of recent violent crimes as well as oft-quoted crime rates. The fear experienced by older residents is likely to occasion a further restriction of lifestyle, with older people more reluctant to leave their dwellings, to socially engage with others, and therefore likely to experience a further diminution of their subjective well-being. Some commentators have even suggested that fear of crime and apprehension about personal safety are so seriously detrimental for some older people within a community undergoing change that it could result in premature admission to residential care (Jones, 1987; Pinkerton-James, 1992). It might be concluded that issues regarding fear of crime and concern of one's personal safety are often very important yet commonly neglected issues in regard to seniors within a local community undergoing relatively rapid change as may be occasioned by development. It is also the case that the reactions to these social representations of seniors are felt at a much more visceral rather than cognitive level of functioning; it is argued that reactions are more appropriately understood within a socio-emotional model of human functioning; here, resources such as time and health, a perceived lack of personal agency and the inability to rectify and even influence negative circumstances all emerge as potent explanatory factors in understanding issues to do with the negative self among many senior residents of host communities. In short, whilst many senior host community residents understand that time and other life-span circumstances such as physical health may not be running in their favour, they also find that a more present-focussed strategy also has limitations occasioned by disrupted social networks, safety concerns and other factors such as rising living costs and the disappearance of important local cultural symbols.

Yet it must be acknowledged that not all host community members find themselves disadvantaged by tourism development and consequent changes. Conceptualisations of the self within a time perspective afford a theoretical context in which we may comprehend and systematically explore the implications of the many positive and negative representations and reactions to the growth of tourism. The perceived personal benefits received by a person has a profound effect upon the self; those residents who depend on the tourism industry, who see it as providing a secure or even a bright future for them and for their families, are likely to have a self associated with some positive expectations of the future, as well as a sense of contentment in regard to the past and the present. Lankford and Howard (1994), McGehee and Anderlick (2004), Easterling (2005) and Sirakaya, Teye and Sonmez (2002) all report high levels of affirmation for the industry as the result of this present and future source of benefit. Researchers such as Snepenger, O'Connelly and Snepenger (2001) would add, however, that many of these individuals, whilst having a positive reaction to tourism, also acknowledge that there are accompanying negative impacts that may be more keenly experienced by others. A second factor found to be influential in regard to a person's self and associated time perspective is that to do with the level of contact with tourists. Commentators such as Lankford and Howard (1994) suggest that contact with visitors, and positive experiences thereby encountered, can have an influential effect upon residents. Those residents whose interactions are satisfying in the present add to their sense of personal agency and satisfaction; within a future focus, residents may evidence expectations to the effect that contact with visitors will likely result in a sense of enjoyment and well-being. This positive present-future balance in regard to resident-visitor contact may well provide a rich source of optimism for many people.

A third area wherein the self and its time perspective may shed light upon tourism impacts on local people is that concerned with community attachment. Those residents who have lived in a community for longer periods of time, and have witnessed changes to the built, the cultural, the social and the natural environments of their community, may well evidence different responses to tourism and its continuing development when compared with those who have more recently moved to that community (Lankford and Howard, 1994; Madrigal, 1995; Ross 1991, 1992, 1998; Weaver and Lawton, 2001). It should, however, be pointed out that such an effect is not uniform; nor is it found in every tourism community undergoing change. Yet when it does appear, individuals can experience high levels of disempowerment likely to produce past, present and future time perspectives inimical to personal well-being. The following are prominent among those negative effects and associated social representations likely to have a baleful effect upon more vulnerable residents such as senior citizens.

IMPEDIMENTS TO WELL-BEING IN HOST COMMUNITIES

A number of major domains that reflect the negative impacts attributed to tourism development can be identified; each of those discussed following is likely to have a salient influence upon the self for host community members, particularly for groups such as older residents who may have spent a large portion of their lives within the community. It is suggested that social representations in regard to the degradation of historic sites, symbols and contexts, to the vitiation of cultural identity, and to the provocation of social conflict within a host community are prime among the instigators of negative time perspectives entertained by many host community residents.

1 Historic Sites, Symbols and Contexts

The historic cities and cultural centres of Asia, Europe and the Americas are now receiving more visitors each year than ever before; Venice, Florence, Hong Kong, Shanghai, New York, Paris and London are all experiencing a rising level of pollution, caused not only by greater numbers of aircraft and road traffic, but also by litter and by the utilisation of considerably more resources required to host these many extra visitors. The costs of this, together with the sheer physical presence of increasingly larger numbers of people in a community, arouse resentment among locals. Not only does it impede residents in their daily activities; for many it is also perceived to happen with no corresponding benefit to them. The arc of benefit is not seen to reach down to their daily lives. Rather, pollution and congestion appear to be the only by-products. For many older residents a time perspective reaction will involve nostalgia for a better time that has now passed, and perceived not likely to return in their lifetime. This can produce few feelings of well-being, nor does it engender good wishes towards the visitors. Moreover, it is not only the great cities of Asia, Europe or the Americas that have their historic environments impacted upon by the growth of tourist development. Many smaller aggregations of people also feel just as keenly a loss of heritage context through inappropriate or unrestrained development. In recent years, reported examples of such places include the island of Koh Samui in Thailand (Green, 2005), Urgup in Cappadocia, Turkey (Tosun, 2002), Luang Prabang in Laos (Aas, Ladkin and Fletcher, 2005), and Bath in the UK (Haley, Snaith and Miller, 2005).

Green (2005) reports local residents of Koh Samui as keenly perceiving negative changes to the historic architecture of many of their community buildings. A number of hitherto culturally important settings had been altered so as to accommodate the tourism industry, yet not the local people. Green describes a situation wherein locals, whilst acknowledging the oft-repeated truism that tourism development brings benefit, clearly feel that their historic environment has been degraded, largely for the benefit of others. Tosun (2002), in similar vein, reports that many in the city of Urgup are sceptical as to the purported benefits to their community that might eventually flow from tourism development; this development is widely perceived by the citizens of Urgup to be antithetical to their interests; they feel they have suffered the loss of, or at least the degradation of, many of their historical and cultural sites occasioned by a national government whose major concern is perceived to be macro-economic development. A picture thus emerges here of many residents who have vocalised a degree of personal powerlessness when faced with this widespread representation concerning the perceived ruin of a home that has deep symbolic meaning to them. It is likely that the time perspective of many citizens would consist of a nostalgic desire for the past, a present characterised by simmering dissatisfaction, and a future imbued with uncertainty or even dread at the quality of life that is to face them in older age as well as that to be inherited by their children.

The city of Bath in the UK is also reported to be experiencing the impacts of tourism, despite the city being an important site of visitation for many centuries. Haley, Snaith and Miller (2005) describe residents in the centre of the city as more supportive of restrictions upon visitors; they conclude that the cramped nature of many historic cities is bound to make congestion a major issue for residents. Those citizens who had lived longer in Bath were found more likely to be negative about the impacts of tourism upon the historic fabric of the city. Haley et al. further report that local people in such contexts need access to a consultation process that is both accessible and transparent; the sustainability of tourism within historic contexts such as Bath can only be assured if individuals perceive that they have some source of remedy for the perceived negative impacts upon their lives. This perception of the need for empowerment in respect of the environment surrounding them is, as Haley et al. conclude, largely absent among many of the residents of this host city. Aas, Ladkin and Fletcher (2005), commenting on Luang Prabang in Laos, discuss similar issues, though in very different circumstances. Their study found that most in the community have no effective participation in development decision making, even though 96% of respondents reported a keen desire to do so. The ability to do no more than petition was widely concluded to be insufficient. Aas et al. advance a comprehensive set of principles by which heritage management and tourism can coexist sustainably, and articulate a series of objectives by which local people can be empowered so that they might be able to preserve their heritage. These are basic mechanisms that involve the incorporation of local stakeholders in the decision making in regard to development within their community; local stakeholders, they conclude, need an inalienable right to participate in decisions that govern development, the effects of which will in all likelihood transform the local heritage and, in consequence, the way in which local citizens conceive of their community and therefore their own lives.

The picture to emerge from these various studies is one of disempowerment and frustration among host community members; many local residents, whether they be in Thailand, in Cappadocia, in Bath or in Luang Prabang, evince feelings of helplessness as they witness valued local landmarks and cultural symbols removed or degraded so as to make way for a new tourist development; they are, moreover, aware that they lack any power or right of negotiation that might mitigate changes to those symbols that so profoundly represent their personal and community values. It is likely that many residents experiencing this will evince a self that is both locked back in some nostalgic past and also constrained within a passive and despondent present self; this particular balance of selves, as Zimbardo (2002, 2004) would suggest, is inimical to adequate levels of well-being, and likely to determine a future outlook largely lacking in optimism within their civic, cultural and personal lives.

2 The Lessening of Cultural Identity

Cultural identity is, in most countries, a 'taken-for granted' part of life for the citizenry; most residents are rarely conscious of its components, its functioning or its benefits. It is only when that identity becomes challenged or diminished in some way that individuals notice change in social cohesion, in the assumed commonalities and shared values that imbue a sense of personal well-being. Fotsch (2004) has described a number of processes by which cultural identity can be changed and diminished as the result of tourism growth and development. Cannery Row in Monterey, California, is the example Fotsch provides so as to illuminate these processes of change. This community has a rich and varied history that includes the once dominant presence of a sardine-processing industry. The Row later became a revered destination for those literary travellers who sought to capture some of the spirit of Steinbeck's famous novel. Fotsch points out that in more recent times the tourism industry has striven to expand Cannery Row's appeal to many more people; changes have included alteration to the cityscape that involve the reconstruction and refurbishment of historic buildings, the purpose of which is now to provide a backdrop for the numerous gift shops, restaurants and sundry food outlets serving the visitors. He describes three processes, each of which renders this diminution of cultural identity in destinations such as Cannery Row: standardisation, commodification and historical distortion.

Standardisation is said to involve the movement toward uniformity, and embodies the deliberate tendency to reconstruct many precincts so that they resemble each other wherever they may be located in the world. This, Fotsch points out, is in no small measure due to the influence of multinational corporations operating in industries such as food, catering, retail and accommodation. A similar process, theming, is also described; here, whole areas, environments and city quarters may be fashioned so as to reflect a particular theme or currently popular style. This has the effect of standardising a great deal of the visitor's space that may have been a diverse and distinctive historical locality in earlier times. Fotsch finds evidence of this standardisation now appearing in Cannery Row: Whilst some of the façades of former canneries may have been left, many of the shops, the restaurants, the hospitality establishments and the retail stores are deliberately constructed so as to appear similar to those found in other tourism precincts across the world.

Fotsch makes the point that when historic sites and cityscapes are refashioned so as to fit a marketing perspective, the uniqueness of a place may quickly fade from consciousness. The commodification of local communities and their heritage, particularly for the purposes of furthering consumption in shopping malls and retail outlets, is said to have at least two undesirable consequences: It not only diminishes the sense of genuineness regarding the local environment for the local people, but also can result in a loss of distinctiveness, a characteristic that formerly may have persuaded many visitors to plan a visit to the destination. Whilst Fotsch finds that this process of commodification has not thus far become destructive to the individuality of Cannery Row, he warns of the possibility that it could happen if its apparent uniqueness is ever traded for the purported marketing ease of a commodified destination.

Heritage buildings and places are ever vulnerable to the loss of long-practiced traditions and truthful representations of past events and purposes of use; they can easily be turned into places where simplistic, even inaccurate, interpretations of the past are displayed. Fotsch points out that tourists are often presented with an entirely positive and thoroughly sanitised representation of the past, so as not to offend the visitor or to portray the destination in a poor light. He challenges both assumptions made here: Visitors, he avers, generally prefer the truth about a heritage site, and are much more likely to think better of a place if they leave having had an insight into both the highs and the lows of a site's history. Moreover, the distortion of history not only shortchanges the visitor; it also sends a message to the local people regarding the acceptability of their own history. Fictive accounts of their past are more likely to evoke the social representation that their past is too shameful or too irrelevant to present to a visitor. The effect on an individual's notion of self would likely be deleterious; this would most certainly be the case for the long-term older residents whose social and cultural identity is closely bound up with the history and the heritage of the place. Fotsch concludes that a process ought to exist wherein ongoing scrutiny by all stakeholders such as local people should regularly take place. The presentation of a host community's local heritage should be open for regular consideration and debate, with mechanisms available for locals to have input into how this heritage is presented

3 Social Conflict

One of the most extreme negative manifestations in the context of tourism development is that of social conflict. It can occur between host community members and visitors; it can also occur between host community members and the tourism industry, with strife occurring often as the result of disputation regarding to the usage of leisure, urban or residential spaces. This conflict is likely to have a quite detrimental effect upon the well-being of local residents, operating at both at an individual level and also at social level. Whilst open conflict is generally not common in regard to tourism, it can have quite baleful effects upon all concerned: the residents, the visitors, those involved in the tourism industry as well as those whose funds have been invested in the industry. One such example of this strife is that reported by Coomansingh (2004), who describes a situation in Trinidad and Tobago where lives have been lost in the context of tourist development. Here Coomansingh reports the development in recent times of large resorts and the appropriation of beaches; those developments have come face-to-face with the assertion of long-held locals' rights to traverse land believed to be common property and available to all residents. The deaths of local citizens are reported, together with widespread anger and grief. Such a situation, as described by Coomansingh, where disputes over contested spaces lead to the exercise of *force majeure* and even death, can very easily become the ongoing source of deeply held resentment, anger as well as despair. For many citizens in this situation, not only will there be a time perspective associated with a revered past now irretrievably lost, but also a deep pessimism associated with both the present and the future. It is also possible that, for many citizens, the high emotions engendered by such strife may well be reflected in the interactions they may have with visitors who seek to engage the local people; for both groups, it may not turn out to be a satisfying experience. Certainly for many local residents such a situation will evince a sense of self that is characterised by low levels of personal well-being.

LIFE-SPAN WELL-BEING AND SENIOR COMMUNITY MEMBERS

Happiness and its absence can have a quite major effect upon a person's life, be it in the domain of physical or mental health. Moreover, the aspiration to happiness has important resonances for all groups of people, wherever they might be in the life span. This is certainly true in regard to senior citizens within any community. There appears to be a great paradox associated with the ageing process: As people age, there is generally noted a decline in physical health and functioning. Yet contrary to what one might conclude about an accompanying decline in mental health, chronological age is not inevitably associated with a diminution in subjective well-being. Indeed, commentators in the positive psychology field such as Diener (Diener and Suh, 1997) find that well-being evidences a tendency to improve in later adulthood. This section will examine one cogent theory that has sought to explain how motivational processes among older adults account for this apparent paradox of ageing. Carstensen and associates (Carstensen, 1995, 1998; Carstensen, Isaacowitz and Charles, 1999; Carstensen, Pasupathi, Mayr and Nesselroade, 2000; Charles, 2005; Lockenhoff and Carstensen, 2004) have proposed a theoretical conceptualisation termed the Socioemotional Selectivity Theory (SST) in order to understand and further elucidate the mechanisms by which older adults maintain and in many cases improve their sense of well-being in the later periods of the developmental process. Carstensen et al. argue that, within this later phase of life, there comes a series of realisations regarding the limitations on time; a resultant reorganisation of goals and priorities very often occurs wherein goals associated with the attainment of emotional significance and meaning in the events of life are deemed paramount. Goals that relate to the longer term, to more material attainments at some unspecified future time, are regarded as being of relatively lesser value. Thus Carstensen et al. would argue that time perspectives, and not simply chronological age, motivate this shift of emphasis in later adulthood. Though age often plays a significant role in terms of assessing what time is left, they point out that it is not simply the chronological point in the life span. Carstensen and Fredrickson (1998) cite the case of young people with symptomatic HIV infections who are approaching the end of their lives; they find that a corresponding process is evoked within this group of people.

The fundamental assumptions made within the SST framework concern motivational effects of needs such as that of belonging, of novelty and of expanding horizons, be they in the fields of interpersonal affiliation, travel, financial security or intellectual achievement and knowledge acquisition. However, Carstensen et al. (Carstensen, 1995, 1998; Fung and Carstensen 2006) point out that priorities alter quite markedly at what are perceived to be later stages of the life span; they find that when an individual's future appears without apparent limit, he or she opts for goals germane to a long-term perspective, including structural personal development, the discovery of information and the acquisition of new social ties that may prove useful at some later date. When time is apparently limited, life goals alter so as to focus on the regulation of emotional functioning, the avoidance of negative emotions, the enhancement of positive experiences and the development of a personal dexterity so as to adjust emotional reactions in changing circumstances and environments. Carstensen has concluded that, whilst social network patterns can change quite markedly over the life span, and indeed undergo major processes of change in later life, there can be for, those older people fortunate enough to be embedded in a supportive social network, many benefits (Lang, Staudinger and Carstensen, 1998). A nurturing social network can serve as a hedge during times of physical or psychological stress (Cassel, 1990), and can lower the morbidity and the mortality levels in respect of many illnesses (Berkman and Syme, 1994; Cobb, 1976). Blazer (1981) has concluded that, for people in the later stages of the developmental span, the beneficial influences of supportive social networks are especially important. Carstensen would hold that, for seniors, socio-emotional selective processes in managing their social network relationships are an adaptive mechanism that provides optimal levels of well-being. When, however, supportive social networks are diminished or even lost completely, well-being decreased drastically among many senior citizens.

Senior residents, it has been suggested, are among the more vulnerable members of any host community, particularly when faced with tourism development. Yet relatively little is known about their time perspectives and the degree to which they achieve, or encounter barriers to achieving, a desired balance. In a study of senior residents of Cairns, a major tourism destination in Northern Australia, a range of tourism development impacts were examined together with temporal judgments as to tourism's impacts upon the life of the city and its senior citizens. Senior residents rated the impact of tourism development upon their community according to a range of dimensions such as recreation, entertainment, business opportunities, municipal services, safety, relationships between long-term and new residents, opportunities for social contact and privacy. Senior residents also rated the effects of tourism development upon their community as they believed it was five years ago, as they perceive it to be currently, and as they believe it will likely be in 5 years' time.

Results suggested that when senior host community residents perceive their social network relationships have been disrupted by the pressures of tourism development they are more likely to evince imbalances in time perspective, with higher levels of nostalgia for the past than satisfaction with the present; there was thus a lessened sense of equanimity about the now. They were also more likely to reveal a lack of time perspective balance as between the past and the future in the face of this social network disruption, with a higher level of nostalgia for a happier time in the past, and little expectation of a possible future characterised by optimism. It was found that the past and its recalled happiness appeared to dominate both the present and the future, and the factor associated in both circumstances involved their previously sustaining social network relationships and the injury thereto caused by tourism development within the community. The enjoyment, together with the mutual support and nurturing that senior members believed that they had derived from these networks, was in large measure vitiated. Indeed, the diminution was felt to such an extent that it had come to hold sway over the notion of self in terms of the past, the present and also the future. Such an imbalance, as Zimbardo (2001, 2002) have concluded, is likely to indicate a deep decline in personal well-being.

SENIORS, TIME AND WELL-BEING: THE WAY FORWARD

This chapter has examined well-being within a tourism context, and in particular issues concerned with time perspectives among senior members of tourism host communities. The chapter has highlighted the efficacy of a balanced time perspective in regard to higher levels of well-being, has noted the distinctive time perspectives preferred by senior citizens as well as the various changes, challenges and everyday vicissitudes encountered by senior residents of tourism communities. This chapter has also reviewed a number of studies concerned with the social, physical and cultural impacts of tourism development upon local populations, and has examined issues such as disempowerment, loss of physical and cultural heritage, disintegration of community structures and identity, as well as the manner by which social and even physical conflict can be manifested in the context of development, particularly by more vulnerable members of a host community constantly subject to change.

The chapter has also reported findings from a study of the experiences of senior residents of a host community; it has revealed that many senior residents evidence time perspectives associated with a lower level of personal well-being. The past for many seniors was much preferred to the present or to the future. Furthermore, it was the issue of social relationships that was found to predict this time imbalance; fewer opportunities for social relationships and thus less sustaining social networks were associated with this time perspective imbalance oriented toward the past. Such a life perspective is likely to evoke little life satisfaction in the present, and equally little hope for enjoyment in the future. These results would also support the predictive value of Carstensen's SST model of age-related optimal well-being, particularly the deleterious consequences for older citizens; in contexts such as host community development, socio-emotional support structures can be vitiated. A number of recommendations are offered so as to assist in the amelioration of such a situation within host communities.

First of all, future research in the area of positive psychology and host community impacts needs to move forward from that of identifying deleterious impacts upon the vulnerable. A more nuanced approach would now seem appropriate, with the focus on rectification of factors impinging upon specific groups such as the indigent, the unemployed, the dispossessed, and groups such as those who have some restrictions on their mobility or sight. Members of these groups may well be among the people who feel more keenly the impacts of large-scale tourist developments, and who experience a diminution of agency; they are likely to feel themselves among the powerless when it comes to rectifying the baleful effects in their own lives. It is also possible that these groups will suffer marked losses in the capacity to attain higher levels of well-being. Positive psychology research endeavours in this context could be directed toward the exploration of ways that these deleterious effects might be reversed, managed or at least ameliorated for them. Positive psychology interventions might then be designed and investigated for specific groups; there ought, however, be a particular emphasis upon ascertaining their perceived needs and also on attempting to meet their agency and reempowerment requirements in ways that optimise well-being in interpersonal, social and community contexts.

Host community leaders, including members of the tourism industry, ought to consider fostering regular functions that are aimed at providing contexts for seniors to renew old friendships and form new ones. This may be achieved within activities such as bowling and other sporting clubs, libraries and other learning institutions, genealogy and local history groups, as well as various hobby associations that are senior-friendly in terms of physical facilities and social attitudes. The overall aim of such functions and facilities would be to enable senior host community members to strengthen and maintain supportive social networks, and should be ongoing so that participants perceive the possibility of future support and enjoyment. It is also the case that many senior residents, for a variety of reasons, no longer have access to independent transport, particularly at a time when it is needed. It would therefore seem helpful that interests and activities such as those mentioned earlier be accessible by way of some form of suitable transport that is affordable and ideally is subsidised; minibusses such as those commonly utilised by organisations such as respite care providers in many countries would be of use here so that seniors could have regular access to those events of value to them.

The final future focus would involve the community and the tourism industry being seen to value senior citizens and to do so publicly. Whist this may appear a self-evident notion for many cultures that still esteem older people, it is by no means the case in regard to many Western contexts. It is suggested that various tourism organisations and firms regularly sponsor the publication of short biographies of senior citizens within local media outlets. The publication of a brief biographical sketch would not only celebrate the life and the contribution of that particular senior resident within the community; it would also send a message to many other seniors that their past and current life contributions are appreciated, and that their presence is unambiguously valued. This ongoing project need not cost industry a great deal; indeed, it may form a component of their social responsibility endeavours. It is likely to convey the belief that senior residents are neither useless nor unappreciated for their life's work, in whatever context that it may have been made and does presently take place. This corporate outreach, moreover, will serve to enhance the present well-being of these host community members and perhaps even afford them a future time perspective characterised by well-being. In such a manner the future will more likely represent for senior host community members a reality characterised by balance, by acknowledgment and acceptance, and by ample socio-emotional support.

4   Ethics, Tourism and Well-Being

Scandals, crises and major financial improprieties have now become quite familiar news events within the worlds of business and professional services. In the wake of this, questions have been posed as to what is the function of ethical precepts and ethical problem-solving perspectives in the provision of justice, equity and the common good, not only in regard to individual conduct but also concerning the operation of businesses and organisations, even regulatory systems. Yet such questions are not new; Aristotle in the fourth century BC posed quite similar questions albeit in different circumstances, arguing that this good, this aspiration for a life optimally characterised by happiness or eudaimonia, is achieved by way of ethics. For Aristotle, as for many philosophers and commentators since, the wisdom to understand and put into practice ethical precepts is the best guarantor of personal flourishing or completeness. Aristotle would, moreover, suggest that major ethical virtues, or values as they currently may be termed, ought apply not only in the private dealings that one person has with another, but equally ought be relevant to social, community and public domains such as those of business, of civic organisations, of family and friendship, as well as in a variety of other contexts like those of leisure, recreation and travel. Aristotle (1955) in his *The Ethics of Aristotle—the Nicomachean Ethics* paints a picture of ethics that suggests an overarching relevance when the question arises as to how best a person might attain happiness. Ethical values here are seen to form an indivisible whole that admits no selective adoption; nor do they take second place to practices such as expediency, avarice or even convenient dishonesty. The attainment of happiness, in Aristotle's view, did not come from selective virtue driven by the desire for material wealth and prestige; rather, it could only be realised by those ethical virtues such as honesty, altruism, courage and loyalty. This chapter will examine a number of perspectives wherein Aristotle's views on the good life and ethics emerge in the positive psychology movement. The chapter will elucidate a number of core dimensions associated with well-being such as wisdom, life challenges, creativity and resilience as they now emerge within and severally shed light upon tourist behaviour; tourists and volunteers within cultural heritage contexts, industry ethical challenges in the context of tourists with a disability, creative strategies in industry employment and training, work stress, mentoring and ethical climates within industry organisations will each be explored. The chapter will finally present a model adumbrating the associations that link wisdom, ethics and various tourism contexts with well-being.

POSITIVE PSYCHOLOGY: ANTECEDENTS, DIMENSIONS AND APPLICATIONS

This decade has witnessed within the discipline of psychology a widely embraced movement toward positive understandings of human behaviour; such a movement has been accompanied by the pursuit of a research program adumbrating the antecedents and dimensions of happiness, that is, 'a vision of the good life that is empirically sound' (Seligman and Csikszentmihalyi, 2000: 5). The movement is generally known as positive psychology, and aims, as did Aristotle, at the understanding and attainment of well-being. And just as Aristotle made the point that the precise nature of eudaimonia or flourishing may be endlessly debated, so too there is no universal agreement among present-day researchers who are seeking to articulate this widely desired yet still somewhat elusive and intangible notion of happiness. Lyubomirsky, Sheldon and Schkade (2005) understand happiness as frequent positive affect, high levels of life satisfaction and infrequent occurrences of negative affect. Sheldon and Lyubomirsky (2004), along with colleagues such as Diener (Diener, 1999, 2000), generally regard happiness and subjective well-being to be synonymous. Csikszentmihalyi adds a further dimension to this happiness notion, suggesting that it may also be understood in terms of the idea of flow, a state in which the person becomes so involved, so absorbed in an activity that nothing else would seem to be salient at the time (Csikszentmihalyi, 1990). Happiness for Csikszentmihalyi thus involves an altered state of consciousness that is focused on harnessing the individual's own experiences. Seligman, who is generally regarded as the researcher most responsible for the introduction of positive psychology to a wider audience in recent years, would hold that happiness is the prime goal, indeed, the raison d'être, for the positive psychology movement. He has, in various publications, sought to integrate yet also value and separately retain the various perspectives on positive psychology, such as those offered by Csikszentmihalyi, Diener, Lyubomirsky and Peterson.

Seligman et al. (Diener and Seligman, 2002; Peterson, Park and Seligman, 2006; Peterson and Seligman, 2004; Seligman, 2002; Seligman and Csikszentmihalyi, 2000; Seligman, Steen, Park and Peterson, 2005) have widely argued that the discipline of psychology has traditionally concerned itself with the negative aspects of intrapsychic life, addressing a variety of topics such as learning difficulties, addiction, schizophrenia, dementia and criminal behaviour. There is now, he suggests, a large and reliable body of knowledge in regard to topics such as these, and this knowledge traverses

domains such as physical and psychosocial abnormality, life-span development, psychophysiology, social and organisational behaviour and personality dimensions. The problem, however, is said to lie in the overwhelming
emphasis on disorder and its rectification; this negative focus has been to
the neglect of those dimensions, faculties and behaviours that are positive
and allow us to report under what circumstances life is good when we
experience it so. It is thus the case that the psychological ills and afflictions
have subsumed these states of well-being within the foci of many researchers in the psychological community.

Seligman would also seek answers to the question as to why this has
occurred. It is, he finds, because of a pervasive and powerfully held belief
that there is something fundamentally inauthentic about human happiness
and virtue; all behaviour within much of Western thinking is said to be
reducible to negative traits and states, and for this inheritance Seligman
suggests we must thank a variety of sources such as theology, political ideology and even early psychologists such as Freud. Such sources are said to
have purveyed the view that, within the practice of positive emotions such
as the display of fairness or altruism or even the aspiration to high levels
of commitment and duty, it is possible to discern some irreducible covert
negative motivation. This, Seligman forcibly rejects; he finds there can be
no evidence adduced to support such a view that suggests virtue proceeds
ultimately from baleful sources. Rather, evolution, he posits, has produced
a range of traits, positive in themselves and beneficial to the species; just
as some traits have appeared as self-seeking, such as theft or deception,
so too other more adaptive values and practices have appeared, including
altruism, cooperation and honesty. He would conclude that the 'rotten-to-
the-core' assumption regarding human functioning is but a theory, and one
that is now under increasing challenge. Positive, beneficial and life-affirm-
ing behaviours are said to be no less fundamental in the matrix of human
nature than are the negative elements.

Peterson and Seligman (2004) suggest that a core aspect of happiness
is concerned with the good life, and is, as it was for Aristotle, to do with
individuals' strengths and virtues. These are regarded as essentially activities and deliberate actions; they may involve leisure and sporting pursuits
such as hang gliding, landscape painting or the composition of music, and
can be characterised by the experience of flow when time seems suspended
and the individual becomes totally absorbed within the activity. Happiness
associated with the good life may also be concerned with the exercise of
what Aristotle described as the virtues, those moral or ethical practices
such as honesty, courage altruism and respect that, when practiced by an
individual, lead to personal flourishing. A variety of commentators, such as
Argyle (1999, 2002), Diener (1999, 2000), Layard (2005), Peterson (2000)
and Ryan and Deci (2001), have reached similar conclusions, and would
hold that a person, in exercising both these strengths and virtues, is maximally able to attain a higher level of well-being in major areas of his or her

life. A further domain that Seligman and associates would posit as being inextricably linked to positive psychology is that concerned with the meaningful life. This meaningful life is described as the combining of a person's strengths and virtues with a cause, as an ideal or quest that is much greater and more universally meaningful than that of material benefit for the individual. Positive psychology would propose that the attainment of a wider meaning for one's life is to do with the exercise of strengths and virtues that contribute to the well-being of the wider world around the person. Volunteer tourism is one such context where individuals display a level of altruism, and, as a consequence, may well experience feelings of well-being.

Whilst positive psychology often describes its debut as occurring around the turn of this century, there has been a tradition of empirical research within psychology concerned with happiness that dates back to the 1960s and 1970s. Researchers such as Argyle (1996, 1999, 2002), Argyle, Martin and Lui (1995), Diener (1995, 1999, 2000) and Veenhoven (1988, 2000, 2002) have all made theoretical and empirical contributions to the understanding of happiness. Veenhoven (2000) quotes the utilitarian philosopher Jeremy Bentham as understanding happiness to mean the sum of pleasures and pains; a more modern description he suggests would regard this state as proceeding from an overall evaluation of a person's life taken as a whole; happiness for Veenhoven may be conceived of as a life outcome (Veenhoven, 1996). He would further argue that social research can access dimensions such as degree and duration of this state which, when combined, would afford a dimension he would entitle 'happy life years'. It is also suggested by Veenhoven that, whilst some states associated with happiness such as ecstasy or great good fortune can be transient, happiness is generally not so short-lived and has about it an enduring quality; indeed, Veenhoven finds that follow-up studies conducted after a year reveal rates of stability in the vicinity of .65.

Veenhoven would also conclude that whilst there is a variable picture in regard to happiness around the world, in almost every context and for most people happiness could be enhanced. Within any society the level of happiness enjoyed by many depends largely upon access to a basic level of income, to justice and to basic freedoms. More enlightened and humanitarian social policies, reforms of the financial, educational and justice systems are likely to see a marked increase in reported levels of happiness among many citizens. Reforms at an organisational level may also enhance happiness when empowerment, autonomy and ethical aspiration become dominant characteristics of an organisation's culture. At an individual level the enhancement of happiness is said to be achieved typically by way of the development of individual skills and capacities such as social and interpersonal skills, perceptions of self-efficacy, and a sense of independence from coercion and domination of others (Veenhoven, 1991, 1994). It is, moreover, the case that an increase in happiness is said likely to be associated with an elevated awareness of and inclination toward ethical behaviour.

Happiness, Veenhoven argues, also engenders a perceived increase in social support, providing benefit to all concerned, including the individual initiating such behaviour. Associated with such benefits, he suggests, are the attainment of wisdom and creativity, as well as positive physical outcomes such as less chronic illness and even a longer life (Veenhoven, 1988),

WISDOM

The notion of wisdom is able to shed considerable light on this nexus between ethics and happiness within a tourism context. Wisdom has had a long history of inquiry among philosophers as well as scholars from many disciplines. It was Aristotle who praised wisdom as the highest of qualities that formed the basis for an ethical life among the citizenry; so too many other commentators over the last twenty-four centuries have exhorted readers to see the great value of wisdom in the attainment of moral insight and thereby well-being. Psychology too has grappled with ways of exploring the idea of wisdom within human functioning (Gluck and Baltes, 2006), with life-span psychology evidencing an ongoing interest in this concept (Clayton and Birren, 1980; Lerner, 2002; Sternberg, 1990). Two prominent scholars with a deep interest in this notion were Piaget and Eriksson. It was Piaget who explored the idea of optimal cognitive development in the context of intelligence and its functioning. Eriksson, in his efforts to understand personality and its unfolding, averred that notions such as generativity and wisdom represented hallmarks in regard to an individual's personal maturity and thus happiness as an adult.

Wisdom, for Baltes and colleagues (Baltes, Glick and Kunzman, 2002; Baltes and Staudinger, 1996, 2003), is conceived of as the exercise of expert knowledge and judgment in respect of personally significant, uncomfortable and difficult dilemmas associated with life's meaning and conduct; for Baltes and colleagues, this wisdom knowledge concerns issues and individual decisions of great personal and social salience. They would understand this concept of wisdom as embracing factual knowledge regarding life and its likely development, procedural knowledge related to optimal strategies to be employed during its unfolding, contextual knowledge concerning the everyday dynamics of living one's life, value appreciation or diversity knowledge wherein understanding and tolerance is comprehended, and finally that knowledge needed to accept and to deal with life's inherent uncertainties and ambiguities. Their research suggests that, whilst late adolescence and early adulthood tend to reflect relatively higher levels of wisdom-related knowledge, factors other than age and life-span developmental levels are likely to govern the blossoming of this wisdom. The most powerful predictors of wisdom developing in a person is related not to cognitive variables such as intelligence but instead to personality-associated attributes; they further argue that openness to experience, creativity and a reflective and careful style in the assimilation of personal and social information are fundamental in the gaining of wisdom (Baltes, Glick and Kunzman, 2002).

Kunzman and Baltes (2003) suggest that values and their emotional associations have a profound association with the attainment of wisdom; they find individuals who reveal a complex and differentiated value structure more reflective of ethical precepts such as altruism and peacemaking are likely to be higher on this wisdom knowledge. It would seem from the work of Baltes and associates that wisdom plays a vitally creative role in the self-expression of individuals who seek their well-being in helping others, in conflict resolution, in contributing to the common good of those about them, and in pursuing their own life goals in such a manner that they do not detract from the rights and resources of others. Baltes concludes that an understanding of wisdom can lead to further insights into personal well-being; the attainment of wisdom lies not in the attainment of great private wealth or personal aggrandisement but rather by way of an empathic, creative and socially aware frame of mind that in turn leads to personal and community benefits for those with whom the person lives, works and takes leisure. This particular perspective, for Baltes, essentially maximises the happiness of the individual.

One major way wherein wisdom can be seen to emerge within tourism is in the tendency for tourists to recognise their own individuality as a traveller, and not simply accept an ascribed identity as a package tour member or even be characterised as a free independent traveller; such blanket and all-encompassing ascriptions are made by the industry, by government agencies and by marketing organisations who seek to document tourism; yet they can act to deindividuate tourists. These labels often have the effect of blending people into groups, into segments and into mass movements where individuality is deemed unimportant and even best left unexpressed. However, when individuality is allowed to emerge, it can have consequences not only for the individual tourist but also for host community members in whose society they have become guests. Wickens (2002) has challenged the notion that tourists are of some unitary type, and suggests that a more insightful examination would reveal individuals as having quite distinct and even disparate interests, needs and socio-cultural awarenesses that they wish to express whilst travelling. In a study of UK holidaymakers visiting Chalkdiki in Greece, Wickens found that the host community was experienced by visitors in a varied number of ways, focussing principally though not exclusively upon holiday preference, activity preference and host community attitudes. Motivators that differentiated visitors involved perceiving value and venerability in elements of the local culture, preferences for hedonic experiences, and the security and comfort in returning to a familiar context. Wickens makes the point that tourists ought not be regarded as homogenous; rather, they are, even in the so-called mass-tourism market, diverse in their interest, basic values and personal motivations. Wickens has also identified, *inter alia*, a particular type of tourist that she refers to as the cultural heritage visitor; this type of traveller was found to seek in various ways the wisdom that may be derived from an understanding of the historical and cultural aspects of Greece and of a particular host community. An associated desire of such a visitor was the experience of traditional hospitality offered by host community members. The acceptance and warmth shown both by locals and by domestic travellers to these international travellers was not only gratefully received and regarded as enriching their holiday, but it was likely to have demonstrated to the visitors the considerable value in showing acceptance and kindness to others, in this case strangers to another country and people who were away from the comfort and security of their own homes. In short, it would seem to demonstrate the wisdom that comes from experiencing altruism, and indeed in showing it to others. There would also seem to have been revealed a wisdom that comes from experiencing the richness, complexity and sheer beauty of a venerable culture; such insights can assist a visitor to understand more deeply and to appreciate both the challenges faced and the satisfactions experienced by the people whose community they are visiting.

Uriely, Yonay and Simchai (2002), reporting on the interests and motivations of a sample of Israeli backpackers, have also found evidence to suggest that some of these younger travellers reveal quite profound ways by which they understand their own travel intentions and experiences. Uriely et al. report that experiential and existential modes of travelling were favoured by a number within this group; whilst individuals might at times opt for more hedonic and recreational experiences, they also sought more profound and individually meaningful experiences. These were often to be found within the acts of observing and of participating in the cultural and metaphysical belief systems of the host community. Such a quest for wisdom would, they suggest, seem to fall squarely within Baltes's conceptualisation of wisdom that is acquired by way of understanding, accepting and identification with those about us. Within the travel context, wisdom is accessed by way of a profound respect for the local culture by learning to listen and to observe within interactions with host community members rather than express unconsidered and insensitive statements that demonstrate little or no knowledge or understanding, and may possibly be hurtful to host community members.

Those tourists, whether a part of an organised tour or independent travellers, who do demonstrate that they are able to assume multiple roles appear more likely to enhance some measure of wisdom. This would seem particularly the case in regard to that wisdom to do with the individual negotiation of meaning and involving prized experiences and interactions. Tourists more likely to deepen wisdom knowledge were those found open to what they encountered, those being nonjudgmental in regard to differences witnessed, and those being respectful regarding the rights of others. The ideal here is thus to attain sufficient wisdom knowledge so as to enjoy the hospitality of the host community members without adopting a veneer of faux superiority. Finally, wisdom in the tourism context can be manifestly deepened by way of an unassuming attitude, being prepared to acknowledge that the visitor has still much to learn, and being prepared to accept that others, including those host community members who appear to have had very different life stories from themselves, can share cultural knowledge, insights, life skills and also modes of friendship and generosity that many visitors will have hitherto not experienced in their lives. Wisdom gained at this relational level is likely to be among the most fulfilling of all wisdom-related experiences; it will, moreover, likely to add considerably to the visitors' well-being.

Volunteering in the heritage tourism arena is another way wherein wisdom and well-being may be seen to be closely connected with ethical behaviour. Heritage contexts such as sites, displays and museums attract a wide range of volunteer workers; this is so for many tourism contexts throughout the world, and in both developing and developed countries. Volunteer workers contribute their time and talents in a variety of ways, including behind-the-scenes work such as documentation, conservation and research; they are also frequently found in roles that bring them into direct contact with tourists. Here, volunteer workers may act as room or site stewards, may have a fixed or peripatetic location about the site, may be part of the interpretation staff or may assist in areas such as a recreation centre, shop or food and drink facility. What it is that volunteer workers derive from these activities, and why it is they choose to give freely of their time and talents, have been subjects of considerable interest for a variety of researchers. It is also the case that their motives and the benefits derived from their efforts shed light upon the wisdom obtained from behaviour directed toward an ethical end as well as the subjective well-being enjoyed by the individual.

Whilst there are now various models offered so as to explain the presence and the benefits of volunteer workers in these contexts, most focus on what benefit that the heritage sector can and do derive from the volunteer workers, and also how they may better be trained and managed in the realisation of those ends (Cooper, 1996; Cunningham, 1999; Kuyper, 1993). However, a more useful way in which to understand notions such as wisdom and well-being within the tourism sphere is to focus upon possible benefits that volunteer workers gain from these experiences. Three studies of note shed some light upon the wisdom accrued from volunteer work in this sector; the results principally reveal that the volunteer workers' altruism was found to be associated with high levels of well-being among many of the individuals who participated.

The National Trust (1998) in the UK reported that 98% of volunteer workers greatly enjoyed their work, 85% revealed that they derived much benefit from meeting people and making friends through their work, 78% reported a sense of achievement, 74% declared that the work gave them an opportunity to utilise their talents, and 73% revealed that voluntary work in this sector enabled them to broaden their whole experience of life. These results, taken together, would suggest that the wisdom expressed within altruism has led to a marked increase in personal well-being. In similar vein, Goodlad and McIvor (1998) report that volunteer workers within the National Museum of Science and Industry in London found that helping others to learn and to enjoy the visitor experience gave them pleasure and increased their desire to continue their voluntary work; these same volunteer workers also reported that they too learned more and enjoyed their life experiences as the result of this volunteer work. Their helping and learning experiences engendered higher levels of well-being as the result of their altruism. The core beneficial experiences as reported by the individuals within these various studies focused on helping others whilst doing something worthwhile, and learning whilst helping. There also appeared to be a reflexive quality to wisdom here: Those whose wisdom led them to altruistic expressions in this context received much in return; their experiences of volunteering both enhanced their personal well-being and also deepened their understanding of the consequences of altruism, thus adding to their wisdom as well as having possible implications for other aspects of their life. It would thus seem, as Hitlin (2007) concludes, that ethical values such as altruism have their own rewards when practiced: there would seem to be a clear association between doing good and subsequently feeling a sense of well-being.

ETHICS, WELL-BEING AND THE CHALLENGES OF LIFE

There are perhaps few more exigent and challenging circumstance in which to understand the limits and possibilities of well-being than in contexts where individuals encounter major disabilities; there are, moreover, often circumstances wherein others, particularly those not facing similar disabilities, might regard their experiences and thus the individuals themselves as in some measure lacking the capacity to attain happiness. This, however, is said very likely to be a quite unwarranted assumption. A much different perspective involves seeking to understand, at least in some measure, how disabled people perceive their own lives, how they engage with the physical and social worlds about them, and how they conceptualise both their own capacities to attain well-being and the attitudes and behaviours of others toward them. Argyle (1996, 1999, 2002) has made the point that a person's quality of life is consequent not only upon issues such as health, but also upon that person's personality attributes; it is also closely related to that person's manner of engaging the surrounding world. Sodergren and Hyland (2000) report that illness can bring with it great pain and ongoing stress; it can also bring as a consequence the deepening of interpersonal relationships and a heightened appreciation of what great capacities and gifts the person presently possesses, and even in some cases perceptions of a better quality of life, albeit different, from the one that the person had experienced before the illness or disability. This in no way minimises the challenges faced by people with a disability; rather, it highlights the strengths of each individual and the person's determination and capacity to rise above what many others may imagine to be insuperable obstacles.

Both cultural values and economic stringencies play a very major role in the facilitation or frustration of social integration for many disabled people. Notwithstanding the many barriers and aggravations encountered by disabled individuals, great efforts are made by many within such circumstances to engage effectively with their surrounding environment. Csikszentmihalyi (2000), Csikszentmihalyi and Massimini (1985) and Massimini and Della-Fave (2000) have reported that the overwhelming majority of people, in whatever circumstances, have the strong preference to engage in and develop life activities associated with a great variety of optimal experiences (Csikszentmihalyi 2000). These optimal experiences, involving notions of environmental challenge, a proficiency in personal skills, focus, enjoyment, environmental control and competence, and intrinsic motivations such as those described by Ryan and Deci (2001), are also clearly evident among disabled people. Massimini and Della-Fave (2000) report that individuals who had encountered visual impairment, paraplegia or quadriplegia in adolescence or in adulthood recognised and reported optimal experiences in their daily lives. They find that many had encountered life-changing circumstances and now no longer have similar opportunities available for optimal experiences as they had in the past typically encountered them. Disabled people did, however, report that in their present life they were encountering optimal experiences, though of a different kind; they were now more likely to be associated with an appreciation of various media such as music, reading, Braille and TV, with work, with sport, with experiences of physical therapy and with the creative company of other paraplegic or quadriplegic people. Massimini and Della-Fave aver that there was a rediscovery of optimal experiences, an encountering of new experiences, and an adaptation of previous ones to changed capacities.

They conclude that circumstances such as physical impairments do not necessarily stop development; rather, it can be associated with the finding of different life courses that can offer optimal experiences and therefore engender transformed understandings of personal well-being. They further hold that individuals with a disability ought not be judged by others according to what is or is not optimal experiences for them, or an experience that will lead them to higher levels of well-being. Instead, an ethical stance toward other people, including those with a disability, ought to involve withholding judgment as to who might or might not attain levels of happiness similar in kind or degree to that of the person making the judgment or the assumption. Massimini and colleagues believe that disabled people ought be recognised as having the sole right to define what is likely to realise optimal experiences for themselves; they ought also, suggests Massimini, to be afforded realistic and meaningful opportunities for environmental encounters and social integration. They make the point that an ethical orientation involving the acceptance of difference and the right of others to determine what it is that represents happiness for each individual are maximally likely to foster well-being for all concerned.

Whilst the proportion of people with a disability is growing in countries such as the United States, United Kingdom, Australia, Canada and New Zealand, as is their desire to travel, insofar as tourism services are concerned the needs of these citizens are among the most ignored by industry providers (Burnett and Baker, 2001; Richter and Richter, 1999). Indeed, Ray and Ryder (2003) conclude that the travel needs of this group are largely unresearched, despite their relative importance. They argue that researchers as well as the tourism industry need a greater awareness of and concentrated focus upon the unique travel needs of people with a disability. Accessibility, they point out, varies enormously, with travel staff and tourism site personnel often deficient in both information and training so as to assist when required. Hawkins, Peng, Hsieh and Eklund (1999), Jackson and Scott (1999) and Turco, Stumbo and Garncarz (1998) have variously advocated the utility of a constraints notion regarding people with a disability that includes the intrapersonal, interpersonal and structural. Constraints to travel regarding the intrapersonal are said to involve an individual's psychological state, physical capacity or cognitive range. With this intrapersonal type of constraint, health-related issues and knowledge-base issues are said to be among the more salient concerns. These constraints may be of the antecedent kind, in that personality or socialisation may orient some individuals toward or away from particular types of activities (Henderson, Stalnaker and Taylor, 1988). Interpersonal constraints can be manifested within the context of social interactions, in friendship networks, with service providers, acquaintances and families. Indeed, an induced dependency upon others may both channel and restrain the travel experiences that people with a disability are able to enjoy (Smith, 1987). Structural barriers are those that deflect or impede an individual's preference or desire to undertake a particular travel activity. The inaccessibility of some types of transport, laws or regulations that prevent participation, and also financial limitation can all prevent people with a disability from participation in tourism.

Cavinato and Cuckovich (1992), Abeyraine (1995) and Ray and Ryder (2003) have all made the point that travellers with a disability need greater recognition in respect of the disadvantages they encounter; not only do they often experience a lessened degree of travel satisfaction, but many citizens with a disability are, by the barriers they know they will encounter, dissuaded from even considering travel as a possibility in their lives. All of the abovementioned commentators conclude that services and facilities associated with travel must go further than that minimally required by local, regional and national laws, so that this group of potential travellers can have similar opportunities for travel to those presently enjoyed and indeed taken for granted by other travellers. Ray and Ryder clearly identify these deficiencies in services, facilities, standards and staff training as involving ethical issues; they aver that neglecting to establish and to maintain standards that afford this equality of access may very well be a breach of ethical duty in areas such as health, security and accessibility. It might therefore be concluded that managers and operators in the industry need to make themselves aware of the deficiencies of opportunity for travel confronting many people with a disability; industry managers need also to apprise themselves of how these various barriers, constraints and uninformed attitudes and suboptimal skill levels only compound issues of inaccessibility. This situation of discrimination by ignorance, with its ethical issues and challenges, is said much more likely to detract from the well-being of potential travellers with a disability than the disability itself.

Darcy (2002) and Daruwalla and Darcy (2005) have also pointed out that research relating to people with a disability within a tourism context is relatively modest. They find that, within the wider research arena, there has been a significant change in perspective, with a shift in focus away from regarding disability as a personal tragedy and loss to that of disability as involving some measure of social exclusion and even oppression. In this latter perspective, a person's impairment is not diminished nor is it denied; rather, it is suggested that many of the problems and barriers encountered by the person can involve socially constructed obstacles, having the effect of segregating or excluding the person from involvement in activities taken as a right by other members of society. Within this perspective, disability is regarded as having an ethical right to equality; it does, moreover, require a moral response within social, economic and organisational spheres. This clearly includes the tourism industry and the services offered within its many manifestations. Such a perspective shifts the focus from disability as some deficiency or fault of the individual to that involving the removal of prejudices and barriers so that the person with a disability can have the opportunity to participate in experiences such as travel, and encounter similar feelings of well-being as are available to others assuming the tourist role.

While the nature and degree of impairment will in some cases govern the type of tourist experiences and activities persons may entertain, it is also the case that the social context into which the persons with a disability come will determine how welcome they feel and how equitable they perceive their treatment to be. The attitudes displayed by industry employees and managers are among the most salient of the enablers or barriers to participation. It is, moreover, the case that the code of ethics embraced by the tourist organisation, together with its interpretation, promulgation and acceptance by members of the staff, will play, in no small measure, a critical role in the degree of social exclusion experienced by people with a disability. If an organisation's code does fully embrace the principle that is the right of all individuals to attain as much participation as is possible for them, and that this is accepted and practiced within a particular tourism organisation, then people with a disability are much more likely to have access to those experiences and resultant feelings of well-being accessible by other members of the tourist community.

CREATIVITY AND THE ETHICAL LIFE

Creativity, as a component of the competent functioning of an individual, has been described as a focus-oriented capacity the exercise of which can organise the life and the well-being of a vitally engaged person (Amabile, 1983, 1996; Csikszentmihalyi, 1997; Gardner, 1993; Simonton, 1999, 2000, 2002a, 2002b). Simonton, who has made a considerable contribution to the understanding of creativity, both its antecedents and its consequences, argues that this strength essentially involves originality and adaptiveness; he holds that problem-solving solutions or strategies need, above all else, originality. Older approaches, those that are dysfunctional or ethically dubious, or that offer no acceptable outcomes, are ignored in favour of newer, more efficacious solutions. Simonton also suggests that these creative solutions must exhibit the character of adaptability, that is, they must work and do so in a manner that is morally and legally acceptable. Commentators such as Csikszentmihalyi (1997), Eysenck (1995), and Waller, Bouchard, Lykken, Tellegen and Blacker (1993) have made the point that there are considerable differences among creative individuals; this is so in regard to both environment and constitution. Genetic inheritance is one important component of creative expression; so too are the various family, societal and work environments through which a person passes during his or her life. Simonton (2000) argues that creative problem solving often doesn't simply happen; rather, it is more likely to be the fruits of a particular capacity, the learning of skills and the development of knowledge. Simonton would thus assert that the creative individual could begin with a certain level of biologically endowed potential that is then fostered and nurtured with striving, with a period of development, and also within a benign and stimulating environment. And as each biological endowment, each developmental phase and enriching environment are likely to be different, so too each creative individual will emerge in distinct form.

It is also the case, as Simonton (1999, 2000) suggests, that creative people typically exhibit similar personality dispositions. It is suggested that such individuals are more courageous than those not so creative in their style of life; creative people are also found to be more nonconforming and more independent in their styles of operating. They are said to be somewhat more passionate in their life pursuits, prefer to be better read, are often energetic and exhibit a higher preference for persistence in whatever they attempt. Indeed, such is their passion for betterment in whatever they turn to, they will assert their principles even in the face of great opposition, criticism and even personal peril. They may be characterised by others as essentially rebellious, nonconformist or uncooperative. Csikszentmihalyi (1997), however, adds a note of caution in regard to the assumption that all creative individuals will exhibit the personality characteristics described earlier; he would point out that there still remains great variability in regard to the types of individuals exhibiting creativity; some personality traits may be typical of the group as a whole, although they will not necessarily be adequate descriptors of all.

The common conclusion that emerges from the literature suggests that the exercise of creativity is characterised by a propensity for ethical decision making. Creative individuals typically devote considerable amounts of time and energy together with a passionate commitment to their chosen field of endeavour, whether that be in the arena of work, of family life, of leisure or travel. This creative disposition also appears relatively unconcerned with pleasing others, with the need for popularity among peers; rather, creative individuals tend to be independent, to hold fast to opinions and deeply held values and precepts, and not lose courage in the face of opposition or even coercion. This, it is suggested, ought not lead to the conclusion that creativity inevitably leads to antisocial behaviour, nor to the indulgence of private goals at the expense of personal or community ethical standards. Whilst highly creative people as a group are said to be diverse enough to include some who may ignore or infract the rights of others, a great many of those who are creative have sufficient intellectual and emotional skills so as to satisfy their own aspirations whilst, at the same time, striving for the betterment of others. Indeed, the consensus of commentators here is that creative people tend to be highly sensitised to the needs of others, and are likely to evidence ethical values associated with altruism, competence and courage in their efforts to assist others with whom they live.

The relationship between creativity and the expression of ethical behaviour among tourism employees can be explored usefully within the context of employee education and training. Successful participation in postsecondary school programs of study and skill acquisition is now regarded as essential in most work situations, including that of tourism and hospitality. It is also the case that learning styles and perspectives play a crucial role in educational outcomes. A more traditional approach involves remembering large portions of material, and then recalling as much as possible at crucial points in the formal educational process such as during an examination, an oral presentation or during a job selection interview. Such as style is said to represent a surface approach to learning (Entwhistle, 1981; Entwhistle and Ramsden, 1983; Marton, Hounsell and Entwhistle, 1984). Whilst this approach has often been favoured in the past for tourism industry skilling, even during some 'on-the-job' training, it is now acknowledged as not the only approach available. Others advocate a learning style wherein individuals regard themselves as creators and assimilators of knowledge; students here use their talents to make reflective judgments and to reach logical conclusions. Individuals within this frame of understanding are said to both generate new combinations of knowledge and to incorporate these insights gained within their own philosophical frame of reference. Ramsden (1984) argues that these people are more likely to look for connections of meaning and for wide linkages within their everyday life, a major element of which is their basic value system. Such persons are said to embrace learning for its own sake, and not simply as a means to an end; they interact with others and with ideas in an active and an ethical way. Entwhistle and Ramsden (1983) would sum up this style of learning as creative, reflective and analytical; it is, they assert, ultimately more successful in terms of outcomes such as comprehension, assimilation in regard to a wider worldview, utility of knowledge acquired, enjoyment of the learning process and, moreover, less exploitive of others with whom the person later comes into contact.

There is also now a growing understanding regarding the ethical values that prospective staff would bring to tourism and hospitality employment; the values of hard work, genuineness and helpfulness were found to be associated with a desire to start or to enter a tourism business. Many prospective industry entrants regarded tourism as an interesting and worthwhile career choice (Ross, 2003). It has also been found that prospective industry employees highly value trustworthiness as an attribute in managers. Indeed, trust in the personal integrity of industry management was regarded by potential industry entrants as essential for any decision to join the industry; trust for these people was perceived to be a core creative element in effective workplace problem solving (Ross, 2006). Ross has also found that individuals considering a career within the industry regard ethical values as highly important in the context of face-to-face customer service. There has, however, not always been a clear and unambiguous embracing of high ethical values within the industry itself in the eyes of some. Yeung, Wong and Chan (2002) suggest that the industry exhibits some quite distinct characteristics that make it vulnerable to ethical conflict. They conclude that ethical dilemmas tend to arise as a consequence of the varying backgrounds of both staff and visitors; this, they point out, occasions a diverse set of understandings in respect of expectations and ethical principles. Harassment, racism and even allegations of theft and confrontation may ensue, due in no small measure to the ethically ambiguous roles and expectations among both staff and visitors. They conclude, as do Vallen and Casado (2000), that a sharper and more creative pedagogical focus is required upon the examination and exploration of ethical values among those people who are to be educated and skilled for the industry.

Lashley (1997, 2000, 2002) has concluded that a radical overhaul is needed in regard to hospitality education; the industry, indeed the society in which it is embedded, is undergoing rapid social change and the pedagogical models previously undergirding this training may not now be serving the industry entrants, the industry or the wider travelling public. Lashley avers that there is now an increasing need for the educational process to produce graduates with interpersonal competencies and general management skills; equally important is the education of people that facilitates an analytical and reflective cognitive style of problem solving resonant of Simonton's notion regarding personal creativity. Lashley (2002) concludes that graduates of the educational process need not only to be practical and pragmatic; they also need to be comfortable in both an analytical and theoretical mode, demonstrating the capacity to reflect on what it is they are learning, to incorporate it into their daily operating skills, and thereby to demonstrate a more enhanced form of cognitive problem-solving style. In similar vein, Morrison and O'Mahony (2003) illustrate the clear creative value of critical analytical thinking in the problem-solving arena; this skill set, they conclude, optimally equips potential employees for the challenges of industry employment at a time of considerable social change where diverse and difficult ethical dilemmas regularly present themselves. Creativity would thus seem to be a valuable component in the training of individuals for the tourism industry. Not only does it have immediate benefits to offer the industry and also the travelling public, but it also has profound benefits regarding the well-being of the employee.

RESILIENCY AND THE CAPACITY FOR AN ETHICAL LIFE

The ideal of resiliency has been explored at a theoretical and also a practical level by Ryff and Singer (2003) and by Masten (Masten, 2001; Masten and Reed, 2002). It has been concluded that resiliency may be understood as comprising not one but rather a set of characteristics such as interpersonal assets, risks faced and also available adaptation skills that, together, comprise a pattern or grid of positive responses in the face of pressures and stresses imposed by the exigencies of ethical problem solving. Adaptation processes here include coping skills when responding to personal stress experienced, overall problem-solving styles and long-term goal setting and revising skills. It would also seem the case that resiliency is reactive in nature, the endowments of which are said to become operational when problems present themselves; in contrast, responses such as hope and optimism are much more likely to be proactive in their appearance (Masten and Reed, 2002). Coutu (2002) has made the point that an important driver of resiliency is that particular constellation of primary life values held by an individual; central among these values are the precepts to do with ethics, those beliefs and practices that make a person's life just and meaningful in their own eyes. In essence, resiliency involves those principles that are most likely to lead to the good life. Coutu (2002) warns that not all values and beliefs are necessarily ethical; it is also the case that some resilient individuals in the past have been noted for their highly unethical behaviour in the course of their acquisition of wealth and power. Notwithstanding this, Coutu asserts that a resiliency associated with ethical problem solving is likely to be of considerable value in personal functioning; those individuals more ethical are also more likely to find their resiliency to be an enduring response and also to be more to the benefit of those about them.

Resilient ethical mentors, whether they be within organisations, communities, families or travel environments, are of considerable value in the establishment and fostering of an ethical climate that is seen to be of long-term value for those about them; acting ethically in the face of opposition, adversity and even force, mentors are required to embrace a code of ethical ideals that is to do with fundamental meanings in their lives, and one that they acknowledge as being intimately connected with their own long-term happiness. Masten (2001) argues there are empirically established strategies that facilitate the development of resiliency in various contexts. These strategies involve an asset focus, a risk focus and a process focus. Strategies involve actively training mentors and significant individuals within an organisation for the benefit of more junior staff; in this training, techniques involve modelling both the benefits and the challenges that are involved in resilience for ethical problem solving. It is held that both social and resource-based supports are also necessary in this fostering process, as are the supply of information and effective communication. The fostering of trust and an acknowledgment of achievable performance levels are said to be the most effective means to avoid fear, insecurity and even failure among those being taught. Masten further advocates a process focus that emphasises strategic planning, feedback to participants, adequate rewards of various kinds, together with a high level of consistency by those undertaking the programme. Such strategies, Masten suggests, will optimally foster a resiliency among those who embrace an ethical problem-solving style. There is, however, a common condition to be found in many workplaces indicating that resiliency is starkly absent: That is the persistence of work stress and even burnout.

Jackson (2006) has pointed out that the physical well-being of individuals in the workplace is the major concern of most occupational health and safety programmes; psychological well-being is, however, not so well acknowledged, despite there being in recent years an increase in research efforts aimed at understanding the deleterious effects of work stress on organisational members at all levels. A variety of researchers, such as Gonzalez-Roma, Schaufeli, Bakkar and Lloret (2006), Grant and Langan-Fox (2006), Schabracq, Winnibust and Cooper (2003) and Warr (1987, 1999, 2007), have concluded that work stress is relatively common in many workplaces and often debilitating to the individual concerned; it typically makes substantial inroads into his or her sense of well-being and thus general resiliency in facing life's problems. Indeed, stress and burnout are now acknowledged by those actively researching this field to be among the most baleful of workplace-induced conditions, with very few people, whatever their position, tenure or skill level, being able to maintain a level of resiliency in the face of this. Schabracq et al. (2003) argue that work stress typically results in lowered creativity and an absence of personal and professional development, most often resulting in a remarkable absence of work motivation, work and life satisfaction, and overall well-being. They also note that work stress often occasions a severe reduction in the quantity and quality of social interaction, resulting in both conflict and isolation for the individual. There is a marked diminution in the person's competency, often accompanied by chronic illness and in some cases even death.

Organisations too pay a very high price when stress becomes a problem for their members. Cooper (1998), Cooper and Payne (1991), and Warr (1999, 2007) have all noted that organisations will most likely incur lower productivity levels, disruption to their production or services and even higher levels of industrial disputation. Organisations will also encounter higher levels of internal conflict, lower levels of staff cooperation, disrupted communication patterns, and generally a lower level of competent problem solving. Cooper and Warr also make the point that stress, if left unaddressed, can lead to problems with the organisation's clients, with suppliers and even with regulatory authorities. The loss of key staff, injury to the company image, together with ongoing industrial strife, escalating sick leave and an overall organisational image of a workplace generally worth avoiding only add to the problems confronting an organisation when work stress becomes entrenched. Yet many organisations either choose not to acknowledge the reality of work stress, or fail to take meaningful measures to counteract its effects. It is the case that relatively few research studies have been directed toward understanding stress within the tourism industry; there are, however, some studies involving organisational factors in the industry that reflect upon both emotional and cognitive components of organisational well-being. Factors such as morale, work satisfaction and stigma have been examined, assessing the extent to which stress and occupational well-being have been an issue among industry employees (Lam, 2003; Ross, 1995a, 1995b, 1997, 2003, 2005b; and Zohar, 1994). Studies involving industry workers have focused upon the attitudes and responses of employees and managers, organisational culture and commitment, challenge and meaningfulness, the perception of older workers, food-service workers, job satisfaction and managerial styles. Results, moreover, are generally less than encouraging of the belief that work stress is adequately addressed within the tourism/hospitality industry in many parts of the world.

Job satisfaction and work commitment are also among the most potent indicators of workplace well-being. Lam (2003) has examined these factors within the food-service context, revealing quite disturbing results. Employees, Lam reports, rarely found that typical or reasonable role expectations were encountered in the industry. Food-service jobs were often reported to lack challenge and indeed to be absent of any meaningfulness in terms of workplace accomplishment. Coworkers, moreover, were experienced as lacking in helpfulness, and even lacking in basic levels of courtesy and communication.

The study reported by Lam reveals widely held perceptions of a noticeable lack of opportunity to learn or to display competent decision-making skills, a facility vital for the successful operation of any industry organisation. Lam thus reveals an industry context wherein new employees experience chronic disappointment and boredom, in which there were found to be few if any chances for development, skill acquisition or for effective and satisfying communications with fellow workers and with management. An employee mind-set of disappointment and transience was found to characterise the food-service workplace. All of these factors, it is suggested, are powerful predictors of work stress and a diminution in the well-being of the individuals operating in such a workplace; this workplace dysfunctionality, moreover, is indicative of an ethical perspective on the part of management not only toward the employees but also, it may be argued, toward the organisation and the shareholders.

The issue of empowerment is also an important one in the context of resiliency, work stress and well-being within the tourism industry. A lack of empowerment among many employees, avers Zohar (1994) and Vallen and Casado (2000), is a prime cause of work stress and thus diminished well-being. Zohar mounts a strong argument for widespread work role design as being an important first step in tackling work stress. Disempowerment is also a theme emerging from the work of Vallen and Casado, who have examined organisational climate and burnout within hospitality employees. A strong association is reported as between work stress and those organisations that may be characterised by mistrust among members, by elevated levels of workplace control of employees, and also by an absence of teamwork and cooperation in the workplace. Researchers such as Zohar and Vallen and Casado conclude that the major sources of work stress in the industry include disempowerment, dysfunctional communication patterns and isolating work roles that include little or no opportunity for teamwork and cooperative effort. An amount of this diminished well-being may be related to the style and the interpersonal skill levels of management. Deery and Jago (2001), reporting on a study involving perceptions of hotel managers' styles, found many employees experienced managers as autocratic, as lacking in the willingness or the skill to be consultative, and as particularly deficient in communication skills in their dealings with employees. Such a situation may indicate an indifference or an incompetence on the part of management.

The various studies cited earlier evidence a common and disturbing theme in respect of well-being within the tourism industry workplace; job satisfaction, organisational commitment, work stress and burnout all point to a situation that may be understood within an ethical framework. Managerial values and interpersonal skill levels are likely to be at the centre of this malaise that is revealed in the diminution of both cognitive and emotional functioning on the part of industry employees. From an ethical standpoint, rectification lies, at least in the first instance, with management; when managers and decision makers alter their communication patterns, make changes to the design of the workplace and of roles therein, foster autonomy and more effective patterns of cooperation and communication among employees, a climate more conducive to personal resilience and well-being will emerge. However, it would appear a reasonable conclusion that an ethical understanding of how others are to be treated needs to be the prime mover of this change. It is further suggested that a mentoring model be developed in many tourism and hospitality workplaces along the lines proposed by Masten (Masten, 2001; Masten and Reed, 2002). Mentors trained in the workplace and publicly supported by management hold considerable potential in advancing the well-being of senior workers, junior food-service staff, tourism workplace teams and hospitality-staff interactions. Mentoring may also assist in fostering a workplace climate wherein ethical problem solving is seen as essential, and in so doing improve the personal well-being not only of staff but also management and the travelling public with whom they interact.

SUMMARY MODEL AND CONCLUSIONS

The model contained within Figure 4.1 proposes a causal pathway suggesting wisdom as leading to an appreciation of the relevance of ethical precepts manifested in domains such as life challenges, creativity and resilience, which, in turn, enable individuals within a range of tourism and hospitality contexts more likely to attain an enhanced measure of well-being. Wisdom, for Aristotle, and for many since, may be understood as representing an ontological frame of reference within which the entire process of ethical problem solving is understood; without an understanding of wisdom knowledge as the cornerstone and starting point for the comprehension of life values and subsequent behaviours, relatively little understanding can be gained in respect of those enduring ethical precepts that lead to greater justice and equity within the whole range of tourism contexts, and that can play a powerful role in fulfilling or denying a tourist's reasonable expectation of well-being.

Whilst there is now a growing awareness of the need for overt and transparent ethical problem-solving processes within tourism, as well as the need for industry codes of ethical practice and for workplace cultures that aspire to just and equal treatment for all, more still needs to be achieved. Three contexts have been presented in this chapter as examples of tourism situations wherein rectification is still sorely needed. Those tourists with a disability still face exclusion, and one not of their own making. This exclusion and frustration of their chances to find a measure of well-being from their travel experiences is largely so because ethical codes and organisational climates often do not yet guarantee that all tourists have equal access to experiences that match their capacity. Tourists have a right to experiences commensurate with their aspirations limited only by what is possible; to offer them less and so diminish their ability to achieve a sense of well-being would seem to be a clear abrogation of ethical duty. Tourism and hospitality industry education, if approached in a more creative and contemporary way, can equip new graduates with skills that optimise their ability to engage with ethically difficult dilemmas that increasingly confront a more diverse and swiftly changing workplace and customer base; industry employees require and are entitled to problem-solving skills that are analytic, sensitive and fair to all. That outcome is in the best interest of all, the employees, the tourists and the organisation.

Finally, the profoundly challenging issue of work stress is examined. It is suggested that an organisational climate often largely bereft of high ethical principles, and an absence of a management-supported system of problem rectification, will likely lead to much psychological suffering, staff demoralisation and staff turnover. It is argued that tourism industry management can do much to alter this, not only in the nurturing of a culture of ethical problem-solving but also in the active fostering of concrete strategies such as assisting junior staff within meaningful mentoring programs. The abovementioned various strategies suggested can assist tourists such as those with a disability, those in training for employment within the industry and those facing stress-related issues within industry employment to attain levels of well-being that are not only reasonable within the prevailing circumstances; they enable staff, particularly junior and newly appointed employees, to eschew pointless, hurtful and often frustrating obstacles that are present primarily because of unethical behaviour or an inexcusable ignorance of ethical standards. There would seem to be little doubt of Aristotle's conclusion that a life characterised by ethical principles is the primary path to well-being; this wisdom continues to have considerable resonance for the tourism context.

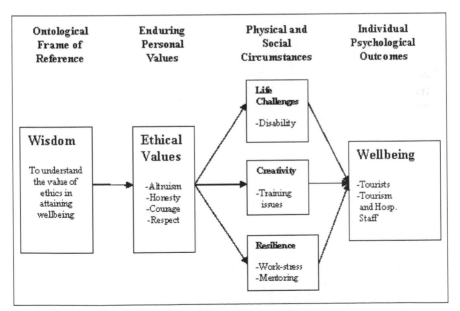

Figure 4.1 Predictive pathways among the dimensions wisdom, ethics, tourism issues and personal well-being within tourism settings.

Part II
Individuals and Tourism Contexts

The concerns of the next three chapters in this volume have some different kinds of commonality to the material presented in the preceding part. They describe separate instances of an underlying theme which sees transitions taking place in tourism contexts which fit with an expanded eudaimonic view of the good life. In the first chapter the topic of materialism is the focus of attention and its seductive powers are described as not being without problems. The treatment of materialism should not be cast as some kind of higher moral valuing of spiritual or humanitarian goals since to adopt such a stance is to foreclose on open discussion of the psychological benefits (as well as the costs) of consumption. The presence of materialist values in tourism education is however highlighted. This view of education is in line with the thinking of a suite of globally connected scholars in the TEFI organisation; some new directions are indicated (cf. Sheldon, 2008).

The next chapter offers some insights into the values of a subgroup of tourism entrepreneurs, those who conduct small lifestyle businesses. The studies of these individuals are important because a high percentage of tourism operators globally are in the small-business category, yet many of the models we have of management are formulated at the corporate level. In order to understand the qualities that are needed to run small lifestyle businesses in particular and to assess what motivates them, some of the chapter suggests that the character strengths assembled in positive psychology studies can form a rich resource. It is a key example of the way in which the field of tourism studies has considered topics of values but has only done so in an incomplete way and the opportunities to embrace a wider range of material for consideration should now be apparent.

The final chapter in this second part also reviews material from a tourism context which has a plausible a priori connection to the good life. The topic is spa and wellness tourism and the recent wave of interest in this kind of tourism is both impressive and interesting for the way in which the benefits of travel for well-being are emerging. The particular contribution of the chapter is to take the travel career pattern model of tourist motivation and assess its applicability to the motivation of groups of tourists having these kinds of spa and wellness experiences.

The selection of topics in this part is limited but hopefully indicative of the potential reach of the positive psychology as a research guiding approach to core tourism topics. The consideration of other topics with the same kinds of detailed motivational and character strength appraisals as used in this part can be envisaged for already popular areas of tourism research attention which facilitate well-being. Key examples here are volunteer tourism (Wearing and Lyons, 2008) educational travel (Ritchie, 2003) and select aspects of cultural heritage and ecotourism (Fennell, 1999; Richards, 2001). The same kinds of studies as to how travel builds knowledge, awareness and pro-social behaviour remain of interest and would seem to be easy extensions to the ambit of positive psychology application to tourism and leisure analysis. One further and not at all insignificant extension of these studies lies in a much greater attention to tourists and individuals form non-Western backgrounds. The positive psychology researchers have been diligent in ensuring the systems they have devised have broad applicability, and the challenge for tourism researchers is to test the validity of these assertions when international communities cross the globe.

5 Materialism in Tourism and Its Alleviation Through Good Values

INTRODUCTION

In their widely cited introduction to positive psychology, Seligman and Csikszentmihalyi stated:

> Entering a new millennium Americans face a historical choice. Left alone on the pinnacle of economic and political leadership, the United States can continue to increase its material wealth while ignoring the human needs of its people and those of the rest of the planet. Such a course is likely to lead to increasing selfishness, to alienation between the more and the less fortunate, and eventually to chaos and despair. (2000: 5)

Materialism, as suggested in this seminal contribution to an American journal, is of great concern to positive psychologists. Materialism thus deserves attention in this text and it can be defined in numerous ways. In social sciences, outside philosophy, materialism is defined in terms of personal values related to consumption (Polak and McCullough, 2006). The term *value* can be interpreted by economists as quantifiable monetary exchange rates (such as dollars) or as physically quantifiable environmental attributes and processes (such as trees and ecosystems), but it is in psychology known as attributes and behaviours (Dillon, 2009). There are many examples where materialism is hence defined as the personal value people attach to consumption behaviour. Some time ago, Belk (1985) defined materialism as the value a buyer places on possessions, whereas Richins and Dawson (1992) consider that the concept refers to placing of a relatively high value on the possession of wealth and material goods. More recently, Kasser, Ryan, Couchman and Sheldon (2004) employed the term *materialistic value orientation* to define the aims, beliefs, goals and behaviours of a consumption culture. A key feature of contemporary life, Kasser asserts, is that commercialisation and consumerism are embedded in modern culture: ". . . our governmental leaders continually reinforce the importance of consumerism, placing economic progress and increased consumption at the forefront of public discourse; referring to citizens more often than not as consumers, passing laws that maximise shareholder profits . . ." (2006: 200). The value people attach to money, wealth and material possessions varies but is high for materialists. Materialists define their self-concept and success in life by the quality and quantity of extrinsic possessions (Christopher, Saliba and Deadmarsh, 2009; Kashdan and Breen, 2007).

Tourism is not a frivolous leisure pursuit that operates outside the realms of this materialistic world with consumption-related values (Coleman, 2005). Tourism is often described as one of the fastest growing industries, an engine of economic growth of many countries as well as an important global social phenomenon (Jamal and Robinson, 2009). Tourists spend money in countries and societies they visit; they shop and consume the destination's resources. Newly acquired souvenirs and goods often contribute to the tourists' image and ego (MacCannell, 2002). Tourism expenditure has been increasing at an annual rate of 4% since 1995 and tourism expenditure today worldwide is in hundreds of billion of United States dollars (Fleischer and Rivlin, 2009). Some time ago, Belk (1988) controversially asserted that we are what we have and that this is arguably the most enduring fact of consumer behaviour, as also echoed by Rosenbaum (1972). Similarly, the devotion to possessions and acquisitions, as Leach (1993), Schor (1998) and Tatzel (2002) point out, is a defining characteristic of this age. Tourism can be a vehicle for fulfilling this devotion.

Considering the current trend in tourism academia to be critical of the dominance of neoliberalism and individualistic consumer values which it normally espouses (Higgins-Desbiolles, 2006; Tribe, 2008), attention to the issue of materialism, well-being and tourism is timely. Related issues, such as commodification (Wearing, McDonald and Ponting, 2005) and the spread of capitalism through global businesses (Higgins-Desbiolles, 2006), have been analysed in the tourism literature. At the time of writing this text, the world is going through a major economic crisis, with some of the most developed world economies facing a long recession (Roubini, 2009). Materialistic behaviours, business greed and self-interest have been largely labelled the key causes of such dire current economic circumstances (Folbre, 2009).

A contemporary and in-depth analysis of materialism, however, is typically beyond the scope of tourism discussions. Outside tourism studies research of materialism has flourished (Burroughs and Rindfleisch, 2002; Kilbourne et al., 2009). While some of this research shows that materialism is a symbol of a confident society and prosperity (Borgmann, 2000; Halton, 1986; Holt, 1998), there is more evidence, as suggested by Seligman and Csikszentmihalyi (2000), that materialism has negative consequences on individuals and societies (Burroughs and Rindfleisch, 2002; Christopher et al., 2009; Hirschman, 1991; Kasser, 2002; Kasser and Ryan, 1993). These negative consequences are discussed in the forthcoming section.

COSTS OF MATERIALISM IN TOURISM

Before discussing how materialism can be overcome through education, it is necessary first to consider costs of materialism in general terms. This discussion is essential because it provides a broader picture of the negative consequences of materialism on well-being of tourism stakeholders. The term *cost* here refers to disadvantages to individuals, negative impacts on groups of people and degradation of natural environments. While there are other costs of materialism, the personal, social and ecological classification is based on Kasser's (2002) thorough work. The main costs of materialism in tourism are personal costs due to overspending; social cost of diminished ethics; and environmental cost of resource degradation due to overconsumption.

PERSONAL COSTS

Perhaps the most common enduring personal cost of materialism is the diminished well-being as a result of overspending (Kasser, 2002). Materialism has been labelled as the devotion to acquisition and possessions (Tatzel, 2002), a shallow cultural value that impoverishes the human spirit and fuels narcissistic self-absorption. Materialists not only spend more than nonmaterialists, but they also spend differently (Tatzel, 2002). Luxury goods are typically acquired and consumed and their value is judged on public visibility, prestige and cost (Holt, 1998). Wealthy destinations are known for providing excellent opportunities for the purchase of quality luxury goods and services to tourists (Henderson, 2006). Tatzel (2002) explains that materialists turn their experiences such as vacations into things and obsess over acquiring possessions such as expensive souvenirs. McClure (1984) has shown that this obsession leads to diminished well-being in the sense that it causes frustration at not having reached material goals. These goals are unachievable because the appetite for spending is insatiable (Csikszentmihalyi, 1999). The whole process of obsessing over acquiring goods, spending money on luxury items and being frustrated for not having reached material goals can be termed *overspending*.

There are negative personal costs of overspending beyond mere frustration (Neuman, 2005). Richins and Dawson's research (1992) has shown that the more people agree with statements such as "Buying things gives me a lot of pleasure", and "Some of the most important achievements in life include acquiring material possessions", the lower is their reported level of life satisfaction. Other studies have confirmed that the more people endorse these materialistic goals, the less satisfied they are with life (Belk, 1985; Kasser and Ryan, 1996; Richins, 1994; Van Boven, 2005). Researchers have also shown positive correlations between materialism and depression and paranoia (Kasser and Ryan, 1993). Nickerson, Schwarz, Diener and Kahneman (2003), in their analysis of the negative psychological consequences of pursuing financial success, further noted that materialism and low subjective well-being are linked. The more research respondents supported aspirations such as "You will buy things just because you want them", the lower was their reported level of subjective well-being (Nickerson et al., 2003; Van Boven, 2005).

So clearly there are significant personal costs of overspending. Consideration of the literature on shopping in tourism is evidently relevant to this discussion. Shopping is a tourism activity of enormous contribution to the industry and with substantial contribution to the retail trade (Hu and Yu, 2007; Norman, 1998). Studies have shown that tourists spend one third of their expenditure on retail shopping, mainly apparel items and textile crafts (Grattan and Taylor, 1987; Littrell, 1996). Perhaps the most iconic manifestation of these items and crafts is a souvenir. Souvenir products are commercially produced and purchased merchandise. Hu and Yu (2007) argue that souvenir researchers have mainly focussed on understanding symbolic meanings and perceptions of souvenirs, have examined perceptions of souvenir shopping experiences, buying intentions for souvenir products, and have focused on market segmentation studies related to souvenirs and shopping. In short, academic research on the topic of souvenir and tourist shopping has grown over the years, albeit mainly in terms of understanding shopping as an integral activity of travel experience and shopping as a factor in tourist destination choice, not materialism and overspending (Hu and Yu, 2007). Yet, as materialism is directly related to acquisition of expensive tangible goods (Kasser, 2002), this lack of attention in shopping research is somewhat surprising.

The lack of attention is further surprising because shopping can be a primary tourist activity at destinations (Henderson, 2006). One of the primary and core attractions of the Singapore Tourism Board (2005), for example, is shopping. At the time of Henderson's (2006) paper, the primary shopping belt of Orchard Road in Singapore was to receive a 1.6 Singapore dollar billion makeover to attract more shopping tourists. The city of Dubai, in the United Arab Emirates, is another example of a key shopping destination: "Shopping in the souks, malls and duty free outlets is prominently advertised and regular shopping festivals are organised" (Henderson, 2006: 37).

Tourist shopping has known psychological benefits such as preservation of memories after a tourist trip through the acquired goods (Gordon, 1986) and extension of the sense of self. There are clearly, however, also detrimental effects of engaging in excessive shopping, such as lower life satisfaction, subjective well-being, frustration and depression, as shown in this analysis. An opportunity for detailed future research in this field is therefore warranted. There are, however, costs to materialism in tourism beyond overspending at shops.

SOCIAL COSTS

In terms of social costs of materialism, questions of ethics are most relevant. Hudson and Miller (2005) point out that tourism has become one of the most remarkable global social phenomena in terms of its impacts on societies and economic growth. Ethical issues are of crucial importance in the modern society due to known consequences of unethical behaviour: lost jobs, lost savings and precipitous stock declines (Giacalone, Jurkiewicz and Deckop, 2008). There is now a recognition that individual values and beliefs play a major role in ethical decision making and behaviour at work (Giacalone et al., 2008; Jurkiewicz, 2002; Lefkowitz, 2003). So the issue of ethics is an important sociological as well as psychological issue and is hence of relevance to this text on positive psychology.

Perhaps the most appropriate manifestation of unethical behaviour in tourism is the lack of corporate social responsibility (CSR). CSR is "a specific application of the notion of environmental and social auditing to business practice" and in lay terms refers to a sense of responsibility that a tourism business must have beyond making profits—to look after the people and the environment in which its operates (Hudson and Miller, 2005). Mowforth and Munt (2003) point out that the tourism industry displays astounding absence of ethical leadership and that it is behind other industries in terms of CSR.

An example of the absence of CSR in tourism is the lack of responsibility for workers in sex tourism. Beyond the health issues of unprotected sex, there is a major problem with exploitation of young women in the global sex tourism industry (Enloe, 2002; Ryan and Hall, 2001). Some time ago Truong (1990) explained that in Asia, international power relations shape sex tourism. In Asia, rich states, such as the Western, English-speaking countries and Japan, send the tourists and control the industry. Poorer states, such as Thailand and the Philippines, provide the labour and the location for exploitation of mostly young women and sometimes children (Truong, 1990). In Kenya, sex facilities, such as brothels, have flourished alongside hotels along Kenya's Indian Ocean coast. Sex tourism is one of the main activities on the coast, catering mainly to tourists from wealthy parts of Europe and the United States (Omondi, 2003; Sindiga, 1999). The Indian Ocean coast is the key tourism region of Kenya (Omondi, 2003). A recent worrying trend is a growing number of older white women from rich countries who visit Kenya for engaging in sex tourism with young African men (Clarke, 2007).

While sex tourism may be excluded from official, national tourism policies, it is apparent from the Asian and the African examples that there are businesses in tourism and government organisations that commercially benefit from selling sex to tourists with little apparent concern for the welfare of sex workers. Enloe (2002) points out that there is commonly an alliance between local governments in search of foreign currency and foreign local businesses that are willing to invest in such activities. So the issues of ethics and corporate social responsibility are crucial to the sex sector of the tourism industry. The linkage to materialism is that materialistic individuals are likely to have a lower corporate social responsibility (Kasser, 2002) and engage in unethical behaviour, such as sex worker exploitation.

In this linkage between materialism and corporate social responsibility, Inglehart's seminal (1977, 1990) distinction between materialists and post-materialists is relevant. According to Inglehart, postmaterialists value sense of community, social equity, concern over quality of life, self-expression, belongingness, love and honesty as opposed to materialists, who value prosperity, economic security and rewards over those values (Giacalone et al., 2008). Since the distinction was introduced in the 70s, a number of studies in this area have addressed the difference. Shifts in some people's values to postmaterialism have been interpreted as major components of a broader sociological, political and institutional change in the postindustrial societies (Dalton, 1996; Giacalone et al., 2008; Opp, 1990). The Inglehart (1977) dichotomy has been criticised as research has shown that a common missing element in the distinction is how the values function (Franklin, 2002). Some have suggested that the values are not mutually exclusive (Brooks and Manza, 1994), that they are too simplistic and that the values should not be conceived as polar opposites (Giacalone et al., 2008; Marks, 1997).

Nevertheless, the dichotomy continues to provide useful insights to researchers of materialism as it relates to ethics and corporate social responsibility. Many studies have shown that postmaterialists would be more ethical and would display more corporate social responsibility than materialists. For example, Finegan (1994) some time ago found that the values of love and honesty, which are associated with postmaterialism, were positively correlated with higher ethical judgment. More recently, Giacalone and Jurkiewicz (2004) assessed the relationship of materialist and postmaterialist values on sensitivity to corporate social performance (such as sensitivity to corporate philanthropy). The findings showed that "when individuals were low in materialism, increasing postmaterialism was associated with greater sensitivity to corporate social performance; when materialism was high increasing postmaterialism was not associated with greater sensitivity" (Giacalone et al., 2008: 487). So, significant interaction between materialism and postmaterialism was found; but generally it appears that materialism is associated with less rigorous standards of ethical conduct.

From this discussion it follows that the lack of CSR in tourism (Hudson and Miller, 2005) could be the result of the presence of materialist as opposed to postmaterialist values in the industry. Sex tourism is an appropriate manifestation of this lack of postmaterialist values, as the Kenyan example has shown. There are, however, ecological costs of materialism in tourism, in addition to these social and personal costs.

ECOLOGICAL COSTS

The ecological costs of materialism relate to overconsumption and depletion of natural resources at tourism destinations. As Kilbourne and Picket

(2008) point out, there are today few researchers in the environmental arena who would argue that materialistic behaviour has positive environmental consequences. Materialism in capitalist, market societies is a major cause of environmental decline as it fuels overconsumption and beliefs that are not environmentally friendly (Porritt 1984; Stiglitz 2002).

In Kilbourne and Pickett's (2008) study, the relationship between materialism and the natural environment was studied in detail. The study hypothesised a negative relationship between materialism and environmental beliefs. Through a telephone survey conducted in the United States, responses from 303 research participants were analysed. Survey construction was based on Material Values Scale and included Likert scales where respondents had to indicate their level of agreement with a statement (from 1, indicating strongly disagree, to 7, strongly agree). The rating scales included specific statements on materialism (9 items), environmental beliefs (6 items), environmental concern (6 items), and on environmental behaviour (8 items) (Kilbourne and Pickettt, 2008). The results indicated that materialism was negatively associated with environmental beliefs; a further finding was that as one's belief in the existence of environmental problems increases, their level of concern also increases (Kilbourne and Pickett, 2008).

This linkage between materialism and the negative association with environmental beliefs has significance for tourism. The linkage can be explored through the contexts of sustainability (Butler, 1999) and carrying capacity (McCool and Lime, 2001).

The term *sustainable tourism* is challenging, perhaps almost impossible to clearly define (Saarinen, 2006). The term broadly refers to "tourism which is economically viable but does not destroy the resources on which the future of tourism will depend, notably the physical environment and the social fabric of the host community" (Swarbrooke, 1999: 13). Carrying capacity can be similarly defined but does not imply global solutions and refers more to time/space–specific answers at the local level (Mathieson and Wall, 1982). Both carrying capacity and sustainability in tourism, however, refer to the scale of tourism activity that occurs in a spatial unit without major harm to the socio-cultural, economic and natural elements at a tourism destination (Saarinen, 2006). So the natural, socio-cultural and economic elements need to be integrated for successful sustainable development in tourism. The key, natural, sustainability element is at threat at some destinations due to overconsumption of natural resources by tourists.

A notable example of one such destination is the Lijiang Ancient Town in China, where tourism development has led to water pollution and water supply scarcity (Baoying and Yuanqing, 2007). Lijiang Ancient Town (LAT) is located in Lijiang City, Yunnan Province of China, and is a stunning ancient town with Naxi craftsmanship and unique architecture, built during the time of the Song Dynasty and the Yuan Dynasty. The town has numerous water canals, creating an impressive landscape with Naxi households located along the canals. Before the year 1990, the town was poor with limited tourism development, but after 1994, the town developed rapidly and tourist numbers and tourism income skyrocketed. This growth has had positive economic outcomes for the residents but adverse other outcomes. In 2007 it was reported that on average 11,000 tourists visit LAT every day, which is twice the number of local residents in LAT (Baoying and Yuanqing, 2007). The increase of tourists has led to exponential development of shops and this growth has created a significant environmental problem in addition to the commercialisation of the Naxi culture (Bao and Su, 2004); the tourists and the shop owners have put pressure on the town's water resources. The town's infrastructure for water collection and waste disposal cannot keep up with the current needs: "water waste in LAT exceeds 30,000 m3/d, whereas, the disposal capability of the sewage purification plant is only 28,000 m3/d" (Baoying and Yuanqing, 2007: 125). The unit of measurement, m3/d, stands for cubic metres per day (Ringzone, 2009).

Another example of an ecological cost due to overconsumption driven by materialism is the increased ecological footprint in the rapidly developing tourist centre of Manali, Indian Himalayas (Cole and Sinclair, 2002). Ecological footprint (EF) analysis is also called an appropriated carrying capacity analysis (Levett, 1998). It estimates the area of productive land and water ecosystems that is required to produce the resources that population consumes and to assimilate the wastes that the population makes (Rees, 1996). In Cole and Sinclair's study, changes in the size of Manali's footprint since the advent of mass tourism in the early 1980s were considered. Specifically, the direct impact that tourists had on the size of the footprint was analysed. It was concluded that between 1971 and 1995 the overall EF of Manali grew from 2,102 to 9,665 ha (hectares), which is an increase of over 450%. The results show that the town is increasingly relying on outside ecosystems for its sustenance. It is unclear whether EF in Manali in the current year of this text, 2010, has reduced since the Cole and Sinclair's (2002) study. What is more relevant to this discussion is that the reason for such a detrimental impact was due to tourists' overconsumption and materialistic behaviour. Tourists' consumption in Manali exceeded the per capita availability of local resources. Tourists in Manali were overconsuming the area's energy, housing materials, food and other resources. A tourist couple at the time of the study would commonly spend up to a double the average annual salary of a local Manali resident on a four-day trip on various consumption items (Cole and Sinclair, 2002).

So clearly there are significant ecological costs of materialism in tourism on top of the social costs of unethical behaviour and the personal, psychological costs. It is not suggested that tourism always produces these costs, but the discussion demonstrates that materialism and its negative consequences are present in tourism. Table 5.1 summarises the ecological, personal and social costs from the preceding analyses.

Table 5.1 Key Costs of Materialism in Tourism

Materialistic activity	Explanation	Examples of Costs	Types of Costs
Overspending	Obsession with shopping at tourism destinations	Frustration, lower life satisfaction, lower subjective well-being, higher depression and paranoia	Personal
Unethical behaviour	Lack of corporate social responsibility	Exploitation of workers in the industry, such as sex tourism workers	Social
Overconsumption	High ecological footprint	Resources depletion by tourists and tourism businesses	Ecological

As the discussions have shown, the costs mainly apply to tourists, tourism workers, host communities and natural environments affected by tourism. Whereas tourists and the tourism industry are responsible for alleviating the key costs presented earlier, tourism academics are responsible for teaching the right values to future generations of tourism managers and leaders so that they can prevent these costs. As tourism academia is an important target audience of this text, the remainder of this chapter focuses on exploring the issue of materialism in education.

MATERIALISM AND TOURISM EDUCATION

Materialistic values are dominant in the global tourism education. Much of tourism education is on the business of tourism (Ring, Dickinger and Wöber, 2009; Tribe, 2008). The business subjects would typically espouse values such as prosperity, individualism or economic reward (Vansteenkiste, Duriez, Simons and Soenens, 2006). Materialism is a Western concept and despite evidence that some Asian cultures are materialistic, the Western, English-speaking nations are still considered the seat of capitalism, entrepreneurship and consumer culture (Tatzel, 2002). Global tourism education is informed by this Western culture and hence by materialism (Nash, 2009). Nash (2009) refers to Böröcz (1996) to highlight how tourism has made its way gradually into Western discourse. In a recent ranking of top 100 hospitality and tourism programs by research instances (Severt, Tesone, Bottorff and Carpenter, 2009), eight out of the top ten tourism programs are from the United States and one is from the United Kingdom. Dann (2009) similarly noted that the International Academy for the Study of Tourism is in fact not international enough and is actually quite Western in its belief system and attitudes to tourism. Arramberri (2007) pointed out that the academy is predominantly a white Anglo-Saxon organisation and is essentially influenced by Western thinking. It is not suggested here that all of Western tourism education is materialistic, or that all of business education espouses wrong values, but that the Western concept of materialism has indirectly influenced the structure of tourism education courses globally.

There is further evidence for this claim. Global tourism education is based on traditional, vocational, industry needs (Inui, Wheeler and Lankford, 2006; Morgan, 2004). Perhaps the most important of these needs is to learn how to effectively maximise profits for an organisation. The traditional tourism education needs therefore resemble traditional business education needs. Traditionally, business education exacerbates socially indoctrinated materialistic aspirations (Giacalone, 2004). Three key aspirations have been traditionally indoctrinated: 1) wealth creation is the managerial *raison d'être,* 2) the pursuit of wealth is associated with positive outcomes and 3) educators should proffer the value of wealth creation over virtues such as gratitude, hope or forgiveness (Giacalone, 2004). Giacalone, however, points out that this materialistic education is not anymore in line with the business of the twenty-first century. In the business of the twenty-first century, global citizenry, self-expression, belongingness, sense of community, social equity, quality of life are valued, at least equally (and often over) material and economic rewards, economic security, control and prosperity. He adds: "The global citizenry is not becoming antimaterialist but is holding nonmaterialistic values in higher regard" (Giacalone, 2004: 417).

Yet three key concerns still pervade current business education: 1) although business of the twenty-first century has changed its value system to incorporate nonmaterialistic values, these new values are not being taught to students (Giacalone and Eylon, 2000; Inglehart, 1997; Ray and Anderson, 2001); 2) educators in business still associate the pursuit of wealth with predominantly positive outcomes, although research suggests that teaching materialistic values has negative consequences; and 3) educators fail to promote the right virtues, while teaching the wrong values (Giacalone, 2004).

Due to similar concerns, Tribe (2008) recently called for a reassessment for the way tourism education of the twenty-first century is conceived— for a shift in values. Conclusions about global tourism education, such as the one drawn by Giacalone (2004) and Tribe (2008), have also recently been drawn by other tourism and business scholars (e.g. Sheldon, 2008). There have been calls for a more balanced approach between vocational and liberal aspects in tourism curriculum development to embrace values such as ethics, sustainability, responsibility and humanism (Morrison and

O'Mahony, 2003; Ring et al., 2009). This call for the shift in values can be interpreted as part of the wider effort to make tourism education less driven by materialism. Yet little is known up to now on how such shifts can be implemented in a tourism classroom. The following sections aim to provide some insights on this issue.

BEYOND MATERIALISM

Eudaimonia

Materialism, as just implied, is associated with excess, self-gratifying, hedonic behaviours and eudaimonia is the opposite of this association. Eudaimonism, as it is known in the positive psychology literature, is an ethical theory that calls people to recognise and to live in accordance with the daimon or true self. This ethical theory has informed thinking in the education context (Michalos, 2008). Eudaimonic education is explicitly nonmaterialistic.

Waterman (1993) states that "the daimon is an ideal in the sense of being an excellence, a perfection toward which one strives and, hence, it can give meaning and direction to one's life." In lay terms, eudaimonic definition of well-being is one in which well-being is conceived in terms of higher virtues as opposed to mere pleasure. Eudaimonia is a Greek word and has its philosophical roots in Aristotle's conception of well-being (Glatzer, 2000). A eudaimonic person is good and virtuous and engages in good deeds for his/her own self and for others. Well-being in this tradition is not seen as episodic or momentary, like emotions are. Instead, eudaimonia refers to the whole life (Smith, 2005) and this is how the thinking has had an influence on education. In his discussion of eudaimonia in an educational context, Michalos states: "A good or happy life, according to Aristotle is achieved exactly insofar as one deliberately engages in the unimpeded excellent exercise of one's capacities for the sake of doing what is fine, excellent or noble . . ." (2008: 358).

Discussions of eudaimonia are very new to tourism literature but deserve further attention and future research. Aristotle's eudaimonic notions have, however, been proposed as a framework for sustainable tourism pedagogy. Tribe (2002) suggested further integration of role-plays, case studies and work experience into tourism education where phronesis (practical wisdom) can be practiced by tourism students. This practical wisdom is in line with eudaimonic thinking because it relates to having a wisdom to do the right thing and engage in good conduct. Similarly, Jamal (2004) stressed the importance of applying virtue ethics to complement current theories of obligation and rightness in tourism (Fennell and Malloy, 1999). Continuing on this eudaimonic trend, in 2006, an initiative was created by senior tourism scholars for significant changes in the content of tourism education programs; a value based education was proposed as an alternative.

Tourism Education Values

Based on an extensive literature review, Ring et al. (2009) have identified these main requirements for a future tourism education: understanding of a wider tourism world and society (namely in terms of tourism industry impacts), transferrable skills, lifelong learning, creativity, critical and flexible thinking, social skills, concern for the future of tourism, concern for sustainability, preparation for the industry and information technology needs. As the preparation for the industry still seems to be the dominant feature of tourism education (Ring et al., 2009), there is clearly room to incorporate some of the other requirements in future tourism curriculum design. In 2006, this need led to a formation of Tourism Education Futures Initiative (TEFI) (Sheldon, 2008). The vision of TEFI is to provide knowledge and framework for tourism education programs and promote global citizenship and optimism for a better world. The first TEFI meeting took place in Vienna, Austria, in which the future and current status of tourism education were discussed in detail by senior experts. Following this successful meeting, two other meetings took place and a final set of values was identified as the key to this new vision for tourism education. These values are:

1. Stewardship: sustainability, responsibility and service to the community
2. Knowledge: critical thinking, innovation, creativity, networking
3. Professionalism: leadership, practicality, services, relevance, timeliness, reflexivity, teamwork and partnerships
4. Ethics: honesty, transparency, authenticity, authentic self
5. Mutual respect: diversity, inclusion, equity, humility, collaboration

Cleary, the TEFI set addresses some of the other requirements identified by Ring et al. (2009), that is, those other than the preparation for the industry. For example, TEFI's value of stewardship and knowledge resembles the identified requirement for understanding of a wider tourism world and society; and professionalism, ethics and mutual respect broadly resemble the transferable skills and the concern for sustainability requirement.

A separate value, transcendence, however, directly addresses the issue of materialism. This value can be used in education as an addition to the TEFI set and to the proposed requirements by Ring et al. (2009).

TRANSCENDENCE

Transcendence is a way of reconsidering the materialistic foundations of business education. Giacalone mentioned empathy, generativity, mutuality, civil aspiration and intolerance of ineffective humanity to describe the transcendent business education. Empathy involves understanding the feelings of those who are underprivileged and powerless, humiliated, poor, afraid, disadvantaged. Students learn how "to feel their decisions as potential victims might, not as a shallow path to self-consternation, but to induce wisdom" (Giacalone, 2004: 418). Generativity involves making the students consider generative questions, such as: What outcomes are truly worth leaving behind for others? (McAdams and de St. Aubin, 1992). It is about caring for future generations (Giacalone et al., 2008). Mutuality is, similarly to TEFI, about understanding that success is better achieved not in personal gain but through a common victory; civil aspiration is about understanding that obedience to ethical rules and written laws can have its flaws and asks students to embrace a sense of moral consciousness, that is, to stand up when they feel something is not right. Finally, intolerance of ineffective humanity means teaching students that "decisions both impact others and define the decision maker" (Giacalone, 2004: 419). It is about understanding that singular pursuit of wealth, selfishness and disinterest define poor decision makers, and essentially poor human beings.

Transcendence, like TEFI, is in line with the eudaimonic thinking. The notion of the good and noble life which has informed much of the recent tourism education value movement (Sheldon, 2008; Tribe, 2002) is also relevant for teaching the value of transcendence. The value is blatantly nonmaterialistic, as materialism is about self-interest. Transcendence, as demonstrated, is a value that asks students to think of broad concerns. Transcendence themes hence complement but differ from the TEFI set. The themes of intolerance of ineffective humanity and civil aspiration are somewhat broader than the TEFI set of stewardship, knowledge, professionalism, ethics and mutual respect. They refer to societies as well as to individuals.

Teaching Transcendence

Transcendence might sound like an esoteric value which is challenging to teach to tourism students. Yet, standard positive psychology subjects typically cover the themes of transcendence: wisdom, as part of empathy, or hope, compassion, altruism, gratitude as part of generativity (Ben-Shahar, 2006). Positive psychology literature further covers many of the themes represented by the TEFI values (Seligman, Steeen, Park and Peterson, 2005). Seligman (2002) writes about authenticity and authentic self in the context of happiness (authenticity is part of TEFI's ethics value), and the work on flow has been linked to creativity—TEFI's knowledge value (Csikszentmihalyi, 1996). In the seminal introductory paper (Seligman and Csikszentmihalyi, 2000), the values of humility and equity are mentioned among others (TEFI's mutual respect).

It may be valuable, then, to integrate positive psychology lecture material with tourism lecture material at undergraduate and postgraduate levels. There are strong arguments in favour of this proposed integration. University courses in positive psychology are flourishing. The first master's degree on positive psychology started in September 2005 at the University of Pennsylvania (Seligman et al., 2005). Within one month of announcing the existence of the degree, over 200 applications were filled. Today this university is only one of many offering similar postgraduate courses. There is also a teaching task force at the Positive Psychology Centre (2008) working on disseminating positive psychology curricula in high schools and colleges. In the year 2006, positive psychology was the most popular course at Harvard University, widely known as one of the top three most prestigious universities in the world (Goldberg, 2006). The contents of the Harvard course may provide a way of embellishing tourism curriculum. By meshing positive psychology topics with relevant tourism material, an innovative subject or a unit within a subject can be created. In this subject, tourism students can be taught the values of nonmaterialism and the good life.

Table 5.2 presents the topics that could be covered in such lectures and the literature in positive psychology and tourism that can assist in developing the lecture material. It is beyond the scope of this analysis to suggest class assessments and/or to provide a detailed, week-by-week lecture schedule. Such an approach would be too definitive because tourism academics teach various tourism subjects in different parts of the world. The list of suggested topics is based on lecture material from positive psychology classes from Fairleigh Dickinson University (Rashid, 2002), the University of Alabama at Birmingham (Uswatte, 2003), Harvard University (Ben-Shahar, 2006) and from Central Connecticut State University (Engwall, 2009). The lecture schedules of these classes can be publically accessed online through a search engine, such as Google.

These positive psychology lectures were made for both undergraduate and postgraduate students and the topics can therefore be taught to junior as well as to more advanced tourism students. The topic suggestions in Table 5.2 and the positive psychology contributions do not represent an exhaustive list of topics and readings that are relevant to nonmaterialistic education. Instead, an effort was made to propose examples of topics and the literature that relate to the TEFI and transcendence values. Tourism contributions by the three authors are excluded, such as a paper by Pearce on humour, Filep's (2002) work on flow and Ross's papers on ethics. This omission was necessary to propose a more objective outline of tourism readings that complement the positive psychology contributions.

As can be seen in Table 5.2, the value of transcendence can be taught by drawing on the suggested literature from positive psychology and tourism studies. The list of lecture topic suggestions was based on the lecture schedule outlines from American institutions. So tourism academics outside the United States may prefer to refer to positive psychology literature with cases and examples from their countries. The table also shows areas in which tourism research has been limited. Future tourism research studies on modesty and forgiveness, love and kindness and optimism may need to be conducted to embellish the positive psychology contributions.

Table 5.2 Beyond Materialism in Tourism Education: Suggested Lecture Topics

Lecture topic suggestions	Positive psychology contributions	Tourism contributions
Positive psychology: An introduction	Seligman and Csikszent-mihalyi (2000); Seligman (2002)	Introductions of well-being in tourism (Gilbert and Abdullah, 2004), quality of life in tourism (Sirgy, 2009), tourism and welfare (Hall and Brown, 2006); and wellness tourism (Smith and Kelly, 2006)
Happiness	Ben-Shahar (2007); Diener and Biswas-Diener, (2008); Csikzentmihalyi (1999)	Nawijn (2009)
Flow	Csikzentmihalyi (1975, 1990)	Ryan (1995); Han, Um and Mills (2005)
Subjective well-being	Ryan and Deci, 2001	Michalkó, Rátz and Irimiás (2008)
Mindfulness	Brown and Ryan (2003); Kabat-Zinn (2003)	Moscardo (1996)
Optimism	Peterson (2000)	Limited or nonexistent
Humour	Martin, Puhlik-Doris, Larsen, Gray and Weir (2003)	Wall (2000)
Wisdom, judgment, fairness	Baltes, Gluck and Kunzman (2002)	Jamal (2004); Tribe (2002); Higgins-Desbiolles (2008)
Love and kindness	Hendrick and Hendrick (2002)	Limited; a discussion of tourism as a social force may be relevant: Higgins-Desbiolles (2006)
Gratitude	Emmons and McCullough (2003); Lambert, Fincham, Stillman and Lukas (2009)	Kolyesnikova and Dodd (2008)
Modesty and forgiveness	McCullough and vanOyen Witvliet (2002)	Limited or nonexistent
Altruism and empathy	Batson, Ahmad, Lishner and Tsang (2002); Cassell (2002)	Works in the area of volunteer tourism (e.g. Sin, 2009)

Positive psychology offers one way of putting the notion of transcendent education (Giacalone, 2004) into practice in a tourism classroom. It is now possible to propose a model of nonmaterialistic tourism education, based on the discussions throughout this chapter.

CONCLUSION

The model is the outcome of the discussion on defining materialism and its relationship to tourism, the costs discussion and the arguments on education made in this chapter. Figure 5.1 depicts the model.

The model proposed is exploratory in the sense that it is based solely on this conceptual discussion. The key limitation of the model therefore is that relationships suggested here have not been empirically analysed. A further limitation is that the model is based on specific literature from psychology and tourism—sociological and other contributions from social sciences may advance the figure; there is also an assumption in the model that

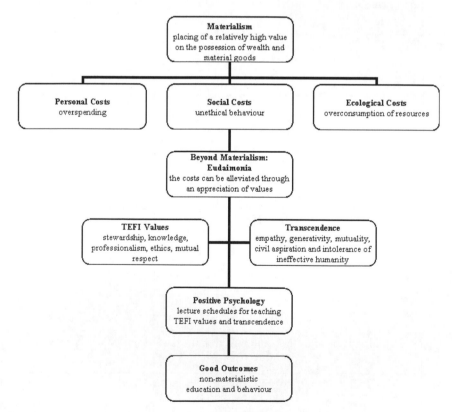

Figure 5.1   Transcending materialism in tourism through education values.

the educators of the values can provide the students with the knowledge required to change the students' thinking; finally, there might be a way of conceiving nonmaterialistic tourism education without the explicit focus on the values and this alternative path is worth exploring.

The exploratory model in its current form, however, can be applied in a university classroom of a tourism course. One way of applying the model and testing its value would be to conduct a study of subjective well-being and materialism with a cohort of tourism students before and after teaching the positive psychology concepts. Following the seminal research by Richins and Dawson (1992), the students can be asked to rate their level of agreement with these two statements from 0 (completely disagree) to 10 (completely agree): 1) "Buying things gives me a lot of pleasure"; and 2) "Some of the most important achievements in life include acquiring material possessions." The rating can be conducted before and after the positive psychology addition to the course. The two questions can be integrated with standard subjective well-being and life-satisfaction rating scales (Cummins, 2009). It would then be appropriate to observe the differences in reported levels of subjective well-being within the same group of participants before and after the positive psychology sessions. There is recent evidence that business students are more materialistic and have lower subjective well-being than students in less applied disciplines (Kasser and Ahuvia, 2002; Vansteenkiste et al., 2006); so an examination of this issue in tourism would be appropriate and timely.

Positive psychology efforts may instil in tourism students the good value of transcendence (empathy, mutuality, generativity, civil aspiration and intolerance of ineffective humanity) (Giacalone, 2004) over the bad values of selfishness, disinterest in others and greed. This dichotomy is in line with eudaimonic thinking where the good and noble is clearly distinguishable from bad and unethical. Simonton and Baumeister's words hence offer an appropriate concluding remark to this chapter (2005: 100):

"Good can triumph over bad, and often does, by force of numbers. We just need a lot more good to overcome the bad".

6 Lifestyle Businesses and Their Community Effects

In this chapter an attempt will be made to apply some of the core ideas of positive psychology to the topic of working in tourism businesses. Most attention will be given to tourism businesses and employment which are seen as generating lifestyle benefits. The chapter will also provide a smaller section considering the application of related positive psychology ideas to communities responding to these predominantly smaller kinds of tourism businesses.

There are a number of preliminary considerations which assist in clarifying the scope of these aims and their execution. It is at least necessary to provide a rudimentary identification of tourism businesses. Statistical definitions of tourism businesses tend to vary in their precision across countries (Gunn, 1994; Hall, 2005). In some locations tourism businesses are restricted to only those where the organisation's income is derived predominantly from a combination of domestic visitors and international tourists (Murphy and Murphy, 2004). Common and familiar tourism businesses identified in this way include resorts and hotels, transport and tour guiding services, attraction operators, travel agencies, bed-and-breakfast offerings and some restaurants. Typically these businesses belong to and influence tourism associations. They are studied the most by tourism researchers (Buhalis and Costa, 2006; Ritchie and Goeldner, 1994). By way of contrast the broader tourism-influenced business sector can be seen as all those organisations where at least a percentage of total revenue derives from the expenditure of travellers. Such businesses are included in the measurement of tourism satellite accounts (Smith, 2000). A diversity of businesses and organisations comprise this grouping including media and information services, cleaning services, construction companies, shopping outlets and sports events. The interest in this chapter tends to favour businesses and personnel operating in the core tourism group where most of the business income is derived from providing direct tourism services but some of the ideas discussed are applicable to the additional businesses linked to tourism.

A second consideration pertains to the scale of businesses being considered. There is abundant evidence from different parts of the globe that the tourism focussed businesses are predominantly small with less than twenty employees. Many are micro-businesses with less than ten employees

(Morrison, 2006). The generalisation seems to apply across countries and continents with locations as far apart as Scotland, Thailand, Canada, Australia and Botswana all providing consistent figures highlighting that more than 80% of businesses belong to the small- and micro-business categories (Getz and Petersen, 2005; Cottrell, Pearce, and Arntzen, 2008; Rocharungsat, 2008). The interest in this chapter will favour the study of people and businesses in this smaller enterprise category since issues of self-determination and lifestyle benefits are most relevant to this subsector.

An additional topic to be considered in this chapter is the well-being of communities strongly influenced by tourism. The focus in this discussion will be on the attitudes and representations of tourism established through the views and values of lifestyle-business operators. Throughout this chapter the approach to be taken is to consider the existing literature in the fields of interest and then focus on insights from positive psychology. In particular the application of ideas about character strengths and values, as well as concepts pertaining to the dynamic nature of attitudes and representations, will be used to reframe or augment many of the current studies.

WORKING IN TOURISM

There appears to be a clear case that working in tourism is somewhat different from working in other industry sectors. This case can be substantiated in a number of ways. In the broad surveys of lifestyle businesses, tourism is a sought-after employment area. It is an area of work people seek to join rather than a set of jobs from which people seek to escape (Marcketti, Niehm and Fuloria, 2006). This appeal seems to apply not just in one continent but is documented in work on tourism businesses in Europe, North America and Australia (Andrews Baum and Andrew, 2001; Ateljevic and Doorne, 2000; Di Dominico, 2005; Getz and Petersen, 2005; Stone and Stubbs, 2007). The defining appeal of tourism businesses seems to lie in the social nature of the jobs, the opportunity to both live and work in physically appealing and often scenic locations and the seasonal nature of such employment offering times of low stress and reduced work intensity (Andrews et al., 2001).

There are, though, some qualifications to these broad generalisations. The greatest appeal seems to exist for small owner-operated businesses where self-employment reigns. Tourism employment in large corporations may differ little from employment in other hierarchical work environments. Riley, Ladkin and Szivas (2001) report that the low rates of pay for junior employees generates employee dissatisfaction in many tourism workplaces. Further, Pizam (2000) suggests that "burnout" is also a problem with many human-service professionals. Factors affecting burnout which are applicable in the tourism world include emotional exhaustion, which is viewed as a state of depleted energy due to emotional demands on the individual

(Maslach and Jackson, 1986). This tourism-linked stress would seem to be particularly appropriate given the emotional labour and possibly the performative labour required of tourism service workers and performers (Bryman, 2004). Other contributing factors to burnout include feelings of low personal accomplishment and a phase of seeing customers as objects to be managed rather than individuals.

A slightly less obvious contributor to employee dissatisfaction among tourism employees was reported by Law, Pearce and Woods (1995), who noted that it was often the relationships with managers rather than customers which made life stressful for Australian tourist attraction employees. The staff at these attractions also reported that much of the stress was manageable if good communication was possible with other employees and where appropriate their managers. Finally, while seasonality may be appealing to some employees with rich leisure lives and the capacity to enjoy such opportunities, for others seasonality is a burden reducing their continuity of employment and lowering their income overall (Baum, 2007). As these studies observe, tourism work too can be a part of the rat race and any generalisations about the positive benefits of tourism employment need to be framed with care.

It appears that there are multiple entry paths to starting up the kinds of tourism businesses which do provide for a rewarding lifestyle. Stone and Stubbs (2007) investigated the ways in which former English residents entered tourism and tourism-linked businesses in rural areas of southern France and northern Spain. At core these individuals and couples were lifestyle migrants first and the decision about what kind of business they would take up was a delayed and secondary consideration. The motivations and values which drive such tourism workers and owners are of central interest in a positive psychology context. Stone and Stubbs report that a majority of their respondents were driven by a need for independence. At core they resorted to self-employment as an enabling mechanism for living in the new location. Typically this was not an immediate decision since the financial capital they had acquired by selling English property had given them a breathing space in which to settle into new and less expensive foreign accommodation. When the pressure to earn money to continue their new lifestyle became pressing, the interviewees reported that working for others was not a part of the new lifestyle they had envisaged. Instead, they were driven by a desire for autonomy and control. In particular, the flexibility of their working hours and the status of owning their own business were contributing factors in choosing self-employment over working for others. As these English émigrés were adapting to a new setting it is noteworthy that a subsidiary reason for the delay in their decision making was the need to develop networks for advice on fitting into the local environment. A corollary of this networking was that by establishing a business the new settlers earned a role in the community which aided their social integration. This kind of international mobility and creation of new businesses by outsiders has been noted in several contexts. Earlier, Befus et al. (1988) observed that smaller scale United States lifestyle entrepreneurs in Central America spent time settling into the new situation for a while and commenced their operations only after carefully observing local opportunities.

The studies in France and Spain reveal some specific and at times unexpected outcomes in the establishment of the lifestyle businesses (Stone and Stubbs, 2007). Many of the new business owners did in fact work quite long hours: overall 55% put in at least 40 hours per week and those in tourist and property development roles reported more than 60 hours a week. Respondents suggested there was a trade-off involved in these figures with either a short-term investment of time needed to establish the business or an ongoing rationalisation that the input of effort was acceptable when set against the overall benefits associated with the new life.

The notion that there is a short-term intensity of effort to establish the lifestyle businesses was supported by findings about future business planning and the expansion of the activities. The plans for developing the business were usually very modest—such as just to keep it ticking over—and often trying another new venture was seen as more appealing than growing the first business. Indeed, it seems that some of the lifestyle businesses, at least in this part of the world and with these kinds of restaurant, accommodation and tourism property interests, were very much about containing the growth of their operation so that the owners would not have to get trapped into bureaucratic approval processes and the management of diverse employees. Clearly they were seeking to avoid swapping a stressful past for an equally challenging present and future.

Another pathway into tourism businesses involves domestic mobility and lifestyle changes as opposed to international transfers. Popcorn and Hanft (2001), among others, have identified shifts in public values in Western countries which are potential drivers of these lifestyle changes. In particular, the processes of "cashing out" and "downsizing", which refer to transferring assets usually from one kind of urban situation to a more rural location with a less stressful employment role, appear to be common in a number of countries. In Australia and New Zealand, for example, the specific names applied to these relocating residents, many of whom move into tourism-linked businesses, are "sea changers" and "tree changers" (Murphy, 2002).

The process of jaded urban dwellers relocating to the coast and the hinterland has been going on for some time. A study by Pearce and Moscardo (1992) reviewing specialist small-scale accommodation in Australia assessed the operators' satisfaction and considered the economic performance of the sector. The occupancy rate was only 41% but more than 50% of the operators reported they were quite or very satisfied with their business. While not all of the 144 businesses surveyed and the twenty-five property owners interviewed were sea or tree changers, at least two thirds of them were people who had deliberately set about creating a lifestyle business. It is noteworthy that they reported an alignment with the interests and values of their guests. Operators noted that they enjoyed the same resources and activities as they provided to visitors such as the natural settings, local attractions and friendly Australian conversations and interaction.

A third pathway for entering lifestyle tourism businesses does not involve international or domestic relocation but instead witnesses participants deploying existing resources from their current setting. Typically this involves guest house, bed-and-breakfast accommodation or some forms of farm tourism and natural resource use. In a representative study describing this group, Di Domenico (2005) interviewed guest house owners in Scotland. Working within a symbolic interactionist framework, Di Domenico used her open-ended interviews to document how guesthouse operators in Dundee and Inverness viewed their businesses and lifestyle. The researcher was careful not to impose etic or researcher-derived meanings and perspectives on the respondents. Di Domenico concluded that the lifestyle needs were seen by her respondents to have a higher priority than business needs. This conclusion was supported by a number of specific findings. First, none of the operators desired business growth where this was identified as increasing the size of the operation, an expansion in the range of services provided to guests or the need to employ more staff. The disincentives attached to these growth activities were seen as a decrease in free time, reduced personal control and a loss of physical space in the guesthouse. The latter was of special concern because it generated the potential that the owner operators would have to reside elsewhere. Secondly, there were concerns about hiring extra staff in this Scottish study which were very similar to the reluctance to deal with staff among the Spanish and French operators. The same issues of a preference for direct control and avoiding dealing with problematic employees were common themes for these kinds of small lifestyle-driven entrepreneurs.

A further commonality with previous work was the affective link between the accommodation providers and their guests. Not only do the owners enjoy being hosts but they like to think they provide services which they would appreciate themselves. This can extend not just to the physical provision of a comfortable and pleasant place to stay but involves an enthusiastic role in guiding visitors to areas of interest and acting as a representative of the region. The importance of social capital and values such as authenticity, integrity and kindness are a key part of this kind of tourism employment and its appeal.

The relationship component of lifestyle businesses can vary in importance according to the life stage of the business owners. In studying farm tourism businesses in Ireland, Wilson (2007) observed that changes in the ages and interests of children influenced the way the businesses evolved. There were differences in the way the business was approached and managed according to the presence of young children, teenagers or university-aged young adults. These observations confirm earlier work on farm tourism in New Zealand, where some farmers used the business to educate younger children about different kinds of people and the wider world but older respondents used the contacts for their own social well-being (Pearce, 1990). Wilson observes that the dreams of the parents may die or at least not be relevant to older children and a successful transition of lifestyle businesses from generation to generation seems to be uncommon (cf. Getz, Carlsen and Morrison, 2004).

COMMONALITIES AMONG LIFESTYLE TOURISM OPERATORS

The studies already considered concerning these specialist tourism accommodation operators show some value and character strength commonalities. Autonomy, control, kindness, the importance of compatibility with the types of guests and self-limiting attitudes to business growth reoccur across the countries. These considerations can be explored more fully from some of the detailed empirical evidence provided by Getz and Petersen (2005). Their study of 184 small-tourism-business operators was undertaken as a comparative research effort in Bornholm, Denmark, and Canmore, Canada. In all such studies the context for the operators is of some importance with the island of Bornholm being described as a mature, traditional Danish destination with marked seasonality, whereas Canmore is a fast-growing resort town on the edge of the Canadian Rocky Mountains. Canmore services the adjacent ski fields and has a large number of bed-and-breakfast houses. There is a year-long demand to visit Canmore, though as a predominantly snow destination there is a clear peak winter season. The researchers generated four hypotheses from previous studies and predicted that lifestyle and autonomy goals were likely to predominate; that people with such goals are attracted to specific types of businesses; that there will be two sets of businesses, one much more profit-oriented than the other; and the profit-oriented group will select distinctive types of businesses.

All four of the hypotheses were supported by the survey results. For Bornholm, the values with the highest mean scores reported by operators were to provide me with a challenge, to live in the right environment, to permit me to become financially independent, to be my own boss and to enjoy a good lifestyle. For the Canmore sample, the highest mean scores were to enjoy a good lifestyle, to be my own boss, to live in the right environment and to be financially independent For the Canmore residents to meet interesting people was more important than to provide me with a challenge. To make lots of money was one of the least important items as perceived by both groups. Further, the issue of providing opportunities for family members or even to keep families together was also not an important motive and possibly reflects the age distribution of the respondents with over 50% of the sample being over forty-five and the cultures being studied have traditions of young adults being independent and pursuing their own careers.

A synthesis of these kinds of lifestyle and tourism studies is provided in a model constructed by Ateljevic and Doorne (2000). It forms a key link to the work on positive psychology. The model is presented in Figure 6.1 and is discussed in the following section.

Ateljevic and Doorne's model should be read as radiating from a centre point. At this core point of origin there is the strongest focus on lifestyle values and perspectives. Dedicated lifestyle businesses and their attributes are captured inside the circle. In each of the four quadrants depicted in the model there is a tension between holding to the values which promote a lifestyle orientation to business and being drawn away from those values towards more commercial and larger business concerns. For the markets quadrant, the defining lifestyle-oriented values of the small-business operator include spontaneity, a personally mediated approach to the customer and attempts to build meaningful customer experiences. The more commercial businesses tend to involve packaged and preplanned market experiences, an employee-mediated delivery and less of an emphasis on engaged and meaningful experiences. Ateljevic and Doorne use contrasting

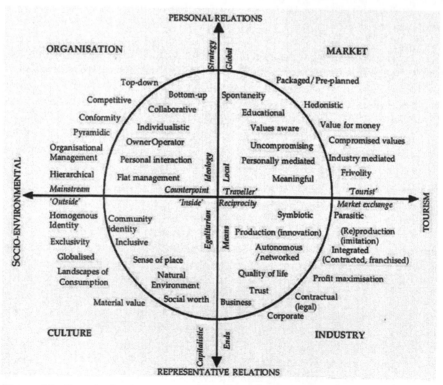

Figure 6.1   Perceived value positions for lifestyle entrepreneurs.

phrases to depict the direction of drift away from the core point for all quadrants. In the case of the markets quadrant, they emphasise that inside the circle of lifestyle businesses there is an emphasis on customers being travellers rather than tourists and there is a local as opposed to a global scale of operation.

In a second quadrant in Figure 6.1, the focus is on the administrative and organisational arrangements of the business within the tourism industry. The defining lifestyle components include a symbiotic relationship with the owners' lives and a trust-based set of administrative links. These approaches may be seen as contrasting with more contractual, legal arrangements pertaining to the corporate world where there is often a greater imitation and copying of franchised products and experience design rather than innovation. One axis used to define the contrasts in this quadrant is means and ends with the latter referring to the processes within the corporate world. The contrast here is with the lifestyle-business operators for whom engagement in the activity is more inherently satisfying. The other defining dimension is labelled reciprocity versus market exchange, which helps emphasise the contrast between the ways benefits are derived for the two classes of business.

The third quadrant explores the connection between businesses and the cultural communities in which they are embedded. The importance of this link was established in the Getz and Petersen study and its inclusion in the Ateljevic and Doorne model emphasises the contrast between those who strongly value a sense of place, context and community identity as compared to those businesses which place a material value on local resources and consume landscapes and places. Here the defining axes are egalitarianism, which establishes the connection for the lifestyle businesses to their local setting, and capitalistic, which approaches the public resources with an eye to the profit which can be realised from their use. Additionally, the axis of inside and outside is employed and can be interpreted in the dual senses of the origins of the residential and capital resources of the business.

A narrower focus on how the business is managed applies to the fourth quadrant. Here the values and mechanisms which are given priority and which define the lifestyle operators are flat management, an individualistic approach, cooperation and the generation of ideas and change through a bottom-up approach. The contrasting managerial and organisational features are a top-down decision-making system, and a more competitive and conformist work environment. The defining axes are mainstream versus counterpoint with the corporate world attracting the former label. A second defining axis is ideology, which applies to how the lifestyle value position is conceived versus strategy, which characterises the world of more formal business planning.

Ateljevic and Doorne provide their own reflections on the value and purpose of the model. They observe:

What is represented in this model should not, however, be taken as a literal structuring of concepts identified in the research. Naturally, there are many points of commonality, of contradiction and simplification, which potentially render the model artificial and contrived. However to interpret it in those terms is to disregard the objective of the process, which is simply to make abstract sense from "real world" perceptions and experiences. (2000: 388)

These slightly defensive remarks underplay the value of their organising structure. At minimum, the approach highlights the continuity of lifestyle and more fully business-oriented operations and avoids a simplistic division into neat categories. Select businesses may be moving outside the core lifestyle orientation in some quadrants while remaining committed to such values in other parts of their operation. A further source of value in the model and its explanatory text lies in connecting this area of study to related debates. As an illustration of this process, the discussion of institutionalisation in the literature about backpacking and backpacker businesses can be seen as usefully modelled by the dimensions of the approach (Cohen, 2004). The illustration of the value of the Ateljevic and Doorne model for backpacking businesses and lifestyle entrepreneurs in that sector requires a brief historical review of that phenomenon.

In Europe, Israel, India, Southeast Asia, Australia, New Zealand and South Africa, the contemporary term *backpackers* is applied to young budget travellers who have relatively flexible travel itineraries and who are involved in extended travels with a highly social component (Pearce, Murphy and Brymer, 2009). The term is thus distinct from the North American use of the term, where it tends to mean hiking and walking in remote or backcountry environments. There have been phases in this type of budget travel with early 1960s and 1970s participants attracting labels such as hippie, drifter and nomad (Cohen 2004; Riley, 1988). During the 1980s and particularly in the last two decades there has been a substantial expansion of businesses catering to the growing numbers of young budget travellers. These businesses typically provide budget hostels, adventure activities and information services. Many commentators have observed that the once very unstructured and spontaneous travel style has become a much more standardised and institutionalised phenomenon (Richards and Wilson, 2004). For the present interest it can be noted that many of the businesses catering for backpackers are managed by former backpackers who are keen to continue their links and contacts with this type of traveller and lifestyle. One case study illustrates the way lifestyle businesses can evolve. It effectively reveals the transition from inside to outside the circle depicted in Figure 6.1.

Tony and Maureen Wheeler are the founding figures behind the now well-known travel guide series *Lonely Planet*. These guides are now used by literally thousands of backpackers (Richards and Wilson, 2004). Wheeler and Wheeler (2005) provide a biographical account of their business which charts the rise of their company from opportunistic reflection on their travels to a corporate entity with a global presence. The initial ambition was well within the inner circle of Ateljevic and Doorne's model. Wheeler and Wheeler report that, as new English arrivals in Australia who had travelled overland all the way, they were frequently asked about their travels:

> Every time we went to a party or met people at a work function, questions would come up about our trip to Australia. How did we do it? How much did it cost? What's Bali like? Can you really hitch through Thailand? Are the trains in India as bad as they say? Is Afghanistan dangerous? Can we really get all the way to Europe by land? We found ourselves scribbling down notes so often that we began to draw up lists of the most frequently needed responses. We began to think about selling this information instead of giving it away. Why didn't we produce a collection of mimeographed notes on the overland trip? (2005: 39–40)

The fledging guidebook writers initially did everything themselves, including all the travel to destinations and the authentication of the recommended locations. The lifestyle and the business were initially fully integrated. The Wheelers travelled to write the first guidebooks and wrote the first guidebooks to fit into their desire to travel to new places. Significant points of departure from the lifestyle business to the corporate world were made through a series of decisions: employing others, contracting out parts of the work, sizing up the most profitable books to write and changing the management and decision-making structure. In each of the quadrants reviewed in Figure 6.1, steps were taken, sometimes slowly, sometimes together, to shift the scale and the kind of work in which the now increasingly busy owners were involved. They became much more aware of commercial markets, they adopted new management regimes for the company, they moved beyond the local cultural circle to a global connectivity and they designed systematic and contractually more sophisticated production schedules.

The documentation of their subsequent business successes reveals some of the stressors which lifestyle businesses are keen to avoid. While in general terms and in most years the *Lonely Planet* brand emerged as a strong and profitable business, along the way former friends became disenchanted with the job roles and departed, employees behaved badly and personal and family relationships were seriously strained. Dealing with investors and technical production issues moved the owners out of their areas of personal skill, creating a reliance on others for expertise and at times finance. In a number of ways these stresses indicate the challenges to growing tourism where the initial passion for a product may remain but the character strengths needed to persist and grow the business may be welcomed and successfully met by only some operators. The documentation of the *Lonely Planet* story reveals a transition in a lifestyle business and the company's history effectively illustrated the processes at work in the Ateljevic and Doorne model. The implications of these kinds of decision points are significant for the nature of tourism and the values guiding businesses in the development of regions and destinations. Key aspects of these developmental issues will be pursued in the second section of this chapter concerned with values and tourism growth in communities.

POSITIVE PSYCHOLOGY VALUES

The character strengths and values depicted in the Ateljevic and Doorne model can be mapped onto the values which have been identified in positive psychology research. In their review of the progress of positive psychology, Seligman et al. (2005) highlight the achievements of the character strengths and virtues (CSV) project. It is described as an ambitious attempt to provide a parallel to the *Diagnostic and Statistical Manual of Mental Disorders* (*DSM*), which is the leading source book for understanding the varieties of human psychological problems. Common terms which are now a part of everyday language, such as neurotic, psychotic, autistic and similar labels, are rooted in the tests and analyses provided by the *DSM*.

The broad CSV scheme is built around six superordinate virtues which the researchers have demonstrated are consistent and common across cultures (Dahlsgaard, Peterson and Seligman, 2005; Park, Peterson and Seligman, 2005). These core areas were identified as wisdom and knowledge, courage, humanity, justice, temperance and transcendence. The meaning of these terms can be better understood by identifying the specific character strengths which make up each category. The strengths which were identified under the six major virtues were selected according to twelve key criteria. These requirements were ubiquity, which required that the character strength was widely recognised across cultures. The character strength also had to be fulfilling in the sense of contributing to a broadly conceived sense of happiness as well as morally valued in its own right and not merely an instrument to achieve a further end. This kind of requirement eliminated such abilities as financial acumen and the capacity to negotiate as character strengths since they are skills, possibly learned, and a route to fulfilment rather than a moral virtue. Character strengths which were identified also had to avoid diminishing others, provoking admiration rather than more mean-spirited reactions such as jealousy. Further, the character strength should have an obvious negative counterpart. In common with the better known description of a personality trait, the character strength must differ between individuals and be able to be measured in a stable manner. All of the character strengths have to be separate from the others, and this distinctiveness should be able to be demonstrated by reference to their strong embodiment in some individuals and their precocious development in some younger people. The character strengths identified were deemed to be entirely missing in some people. The worthiness of the character strengths was validated by the final requirement, which specified that through social practices or rituals these qualities were encouraged, cultivated and honoured. The classification of the six virtues and their defining character strengths are reported in Table 6.1.

Table 6.1 The Positive Psychology View of Character Strengths Which Build Well-Being and Happiness

Virtue and strength	Definition
1. Wisdom and knowledge	Cognitive strengths that entail the acquisition and use of knowledge
Creativity	Thinking of novel and productive ways to do things
Curiosity	Taking an interest in all of ongoing experience
Open-mindedness	Thinking things through and examining them from all sides
Love of learning	Mastering new skills, topics and bodies of knowledge
Perspective	Being able to provide wise counsel to others
2. Courage	Emotional strengths that involve the exercise of will to accomplish goals in the face of opposition, external or internal
Authenticity	Speaking the truth and presenting oneself in a genuine way
Bravery	Not shrinking from threat, challenge, difficulty, or pain
Persistence	Finishing what one starts
Zest	Approaching life with excitement and energy
3. Humanity	Interpersonal strengths that involve "tending and befriending" others
Kindness	Doing favors and good deeds for others
Love	Valuing close relations with others
Social intelligence	Being aware of the motives and feelings of self and others
4. Justice	Civic strengths that underlie healthy community life
Fairness	Treating all people the same according to notions of fairness and justice
Leadership	Organising group activities and seeing that they happen
Teamwork	Working well as member of a group or team

(continued)

Table 6.1   (continued)

Virtue and strength	Definition
5. Temperance	Strengths that protect against excess
Forgiveness	Forgiving those who have done wrong
Modesty	Letting one's accomplishments speak for themselves
Prudence	Being careful about one's choices; not saying or doing things that might later be regretted
Self-regulation	Regulating what one feels and does
6. Transcendence	Strengths that forge connections to the larger universe and provide meaning
Appreciation of beauty and excellence	Noticing and appreciating beauty, excellence and/or skilled performance in all domains of life
Gratitude	Being aware of and thankful for the good things that happen
Hope	Expecting the best and working to achieve it
Humor	Liking to laugh and tease; bringing smiles to other people
Religiousness	Having coherent beliefs about the higher purpose and meaning of life

An inspection of the broad-ranging and comprehensive character strengths compiled by several cooperative teams of positive psychology researchers suggests some important parallels with the values already studied in the lifestyle business arena. Additionally, there are some values in the positive psychology inventory which warrant closer research attention and offer further research directions for tourism employment studies.

The values which can be identified as shared between the previous research, particularly as revealed in the work of Getz and Petersen, as well as that of Ateljevic and Doorne, and positive psychology include self-regulation, appreciation of beauty, leadership, authenticity, zest, open-mindedness, kindness, persistence and social intelligence. The relevant and more detailed descriptions of these character strengths indicate in more detail the alignment with the previous work. Self-regulation as a character strength is centrally about controlling what one feels and does and is revealed in the lifestyle businesses in their quest for autonomy and then the limitations they place on expanding the business to remain desirably small scale. The appreciation of beauty can be applied to situations where individuals notice the beauty, excellence and/or skilled performance in all domains of life. In the lifestyle businesses this value on recognising nonmaterial positive benefits in one's context is asserted by multiple respondents reporting the enjoyment of their surroundings and work settings.

The values of authenticity combined with zest also appear in the lifestyle choices made by such groups as tree and sea changers. Such tourism personnel seize the chance and the challenge to presenting themselves in a genuine way and redesign their lives with excitement and energy. Several of the humanity virtues characterise the lifestyle entrepreneurs in tourism. These characteristics, which broadly involve social connections with others, include kindness and social intelligence, particularly as the latter involves responding to the needs of different clients and treating them as individuals as implied by the inner circle in the Ateljevic and Doorne model. A further characteristic which may be pivotal in driving the whole process of participating in tourism employment is open-mindedness, where this is understood as thinking things through and examining them from all sides. In the case of those making the conscious decision to change employment, at least some partial open-mindedness and willingness to reconsider current situations and view future alternatives would seem to be implicit in the character-strengths analysis.

The character strength of hope is allied to a very similar term: that of optimism. In quite a large volume of work directly preceding and influencing the declaration of positive psychology as a named area of research development, the construct of optimism was shown to be insightful in explaining a variety of behaviours. Optimism, researchers have come to realise, may be defined at two levels; big optimism, which refers to large social and cultural issues, and little optimism, which is apposite to daily events and concerns (Pearce, 2009a). It is the latter which is synonymous with the individual character strength of hope and refers most directly to a positive orientation towards problem solving and approaching new ventures. This kind of optimism, assessed in various ways, has been frequently linked to good moods and morale, with connections to good health. Optimists also persevere more in problem-solving tasks (Peterson, 2000; Scheier and Carver, 1987, 1992). It is reasonable to suggest that lifestyle entrepreneurs score highly on the character strengths of optimism and hope. Evidence to support this claim derives from the choices they have made to redesign the way they live in order to achieve new goals. There is an additional link here to the character strength of persistence, which is described in Table 6.1 as finishing that which one starts. A business is an unfinished entity but the character strength of persisting and working hard to establish new enterprises has already been catalogued in the data on new lifestyle operations. Future research on lifestyle businesses could benefit from considering all of these character strengths since together they form a coherent and well-established array of attributes which could enhance and illuminate survey and interview work.

One research direction which can be highlighted in this context lies in the simple, easy-to-implement measures which can be used to assess optimism. More specifically, the approach requires that respondents provide a graded response to the state of their life or world at the present point in time and a second rating of the state of the world at a future point in time. By pairing the answers to these two questions it is possible to divide large samples of respondents into optimists and pessimists. Broadly, the optimists are those who think that in the future scenario their world will be at least as good as or better than their current state. Pessimists are those who believe their world will not be as good as the present situation. For example, if the following questions were asked about the likely performance of lifestyle business, the following items could be used and the resultant patterns described.

> Thinking about the state of your business as it is now, how would you describe its success?
>
> Very good, good, poor, very poor, don't know
>
> and
>
> Thinking about the state of your business in five years' time, would you say that it will be Better than it is now, about the same as it is now, worse than it is now, don't know.

The operational definition used to define optimists can be as follows: individuals who respond that business is very good or good and who maintained or improved those ratings can be seen as optimists. Optimists were also defined as those who thought the business was currently not doing very well but who thought it would get better. By way of contrast, pessimists would be defined as respondents who thought the business was currently very good or good but in the future thought it might be worse that it is now. The category of pessimists also included those who already thought it was poor or very poor and who considered it would either stay that way or become worse than it is now.

The concepts of open-mindedness, hope and the specific approach to optimism are also linked to another significant concept in contemporary social and cognitive psychology. Harvard psychologist Ellen Langer has developed the concept of mindfulness over a thirty-year research period (see also Chapter 1 and Chapter 7). Her work and that of her colleagues provides a sophisticated rendition of the power of positive thinking or more specifically the power of remaining open to alternate interpretations of experience (Langer, 1989, 2009). Its essence is perhaps well summarised by the story of two travellers watching the passing farm scenery from the window of their train. The first individual notes that the sheep have been recently shorn. The second murmurs agreement but adds that at least those sides of the animals facing the train have been shorn. The ability to consider new ways of looking at the world and the associated skill of avoiding being trapped by regular routines are the core of being mindful. The mindfulness concept underlines several key points. There is a powerful tendency to treat the world as if it is exactly as we see it; that is, we fail to ignore other possibilities. Further, if we make a premature mental commitment to evidence, particularly evidence others provide to us, then we will not see the other options in the setting. For entrepreneurs and business personnel this tendency to see beyond the immediate situation and to develop new products and experiences both for others and for themselves might well be the realisation of how hope and optimism influence behaviour. The open-mindedness reported in the Ateljevic and Doorne model is fully consistent with the mindfulness explanations.

It is also possible to consider the applicability of the character strengths which are not represented in the Ateljevic and Doorne model. Considering the list in Table 6.1, it can be suggested that possibly the most interesting and still relatively unexplored concept relevant to tourism and lifestyle issues is that of humour (Critchley, 2006). Bryman (2004) observes that in the broad compass of the literature on humour there has been a recent surge of studies concerning humour in the workplace. This new work is allied to long-standing interests in emotional labour and intelligence (Goleman, 1995; Hochschild, 1983). These workplace studies include not just studies involving employee responses to death, tragedy and stress but now include entertainment-related employment in a number of business and tourism settings (Lashley and Morrison, 2000). A powerful direction in this work, and one consistent with traditions shaped by the sociologist Erving Goffman, lies in emphasising the social interactional issues and cognitive demands which underpin the successful operation of humour in these work settings (Goffman, 1969, 1974; Koester, 2004; Norrick, 2006). The execution of humour and its use for customers as well as amongst staff requires good timing, a sense of what is appropriate and often the ability to laugh at oneself (Pearce, 2009b). Earlier, Stebbins (1996) made similar observations in discussing the social role of humour in defusing embarrassing or difficult situations involving people with disability. When humour works, it has multiple benefits; when it fails, it can make situations even more difficult (cf. Scott 2007).

The positive benefits of humour can be described in three key ways. Humour ensures that people are concentrating because to understand most forms of humour the participants need to be mindful. Not getting the joke shows inattention and is potentially embarrassing. Secondly, humour is mostly comforting to people because it reveals that the situation is not threatening and thus brings into play kindness and inclusiveness. The third positive function of humour is that it has the ability to connect people even across complex cultural divides. If individuals can laugh together, then their common humanity is strengthened (Evans-Pritchard, 1989; Sweet 1989). Humour thus paves the way for and reinforces the operation of other character strengths. As a recent study suggests: "The findings and applications of humour in tourism seem rather different than those being obtained about humour in other more serious, darker and challenging work environments" (Pearce 2009b: 642). For tourism operators and businesses, further studies of humour as sources of comfort, concentration and connection may be insightful as an indication of their enjoyment of the good life and the ongoing evaluation of their success.

COMMUNITY EFFECTS

Murphy and Murphy (2004) provide a comprehensive review of the extensive studies of the impacts of tourism. They consider the outcomes of tourism for a range of stakeholders including residents and community decision makers. An overview of this material suggests that while humour may be an excellent attribute for the operation of tourism and the well-being of the lifestyle tourism operators, some of tourism's negative effects are not a laughing matter. In the broad sweep of all types of tourism there are serious impacts reported ranging from disease transmission to depressing accounts of the exploitation of local resources and people (Bauer, 2008; Hunter and Shaw, 2007). Much of this work is consistent with the spirit of the cautionary platform highlighted in Chapter 1 (Jafari, 2005). It is certainly not all negative, and depending on locations, types of tourism and tourists and the focus on the type of impact at issue, considerable benefits have also been identified (Pearce, Moscardo and Ross, 1996). In particular, considerable care needs to be exercised to draw distinctions amongst the types of tourism generating the varied outcomes. The present interest is in the impacts of lifestyle tourism businesses rather than the effects of all types of tourism. This frame of interest considerably reduces the number of relevant studies of tourism's influence on the community.

In addition to focussing only on the outcomes being generated by lifestyle-related businesses, this section also searches for information pertaining to overall views of tourism's future rather than being narrowly concerned with impacts themselves. As Murphy and Murphy (2004) note, it is desirable to direct attention away from the dominant concern with tourism impacts and see how hosts and relevant stakeholders define and evaluate the future of tourism in their area. In this way tourism scholars can take an important step in the advancement of their field since clear representations of tourism and its desirable futures will provide information relevant to planning. By way of contrast, simply recording and reporting impacts can leave decision makers trapped in trying to attend to past problems.

One pathway to identify and present these views of tourism and its future lies in the application of social representation theory (cf. Beeton, 2000; Pearce et al., 1996). The term *social representation* warrants some explanation. At core, social representations are everyday theories or branches of knowledge (Moscovici, 1984). They are both held by individuals and shared by social groups. Social representations are often summarised and communicated by striking images and key phrases. An example is to see tourism as an engine of growth for a community. Less positively, tourism is seen as everyday terrorism or a vulture destroying cultures. Moscovici suggested that social representations should be applied to knowledge and belief systems that exist in ordinary communication rather than to specialist knowledge domains such as science or religion. Jaspars and Fraser (1984) observe that social representations are social in at least three senses: They originate socially, they describe or represent a coherent, easily labelled aspect of the social world and they are shared with others. A fundamental aspect of social representations for the present interest is that these dynamic systems of knowledge contain values, beliefs, stereotypes and attitudes. For the present purposes, social representations provide integrated summaries and explanations of how tourism is perceived.

It is possible to propose a new marriage of ideas in exploring and accounting for the effects of lifestyle businesses on destination communities. The social-representations approach already outlined provides the social psychological infrastructure of how people structure and communicate their understanding. It does not provide an immediate content for those descriptions. Importantly, there is an iterative procedure being suggested between impacts and representations. The representations groups hold drive their view of tourism's impacts, but the impacts themselves are stimuli which shape and reshape the representation. For example, those who hold a very positive view of tourism as an economic force may downplay the small costs of vandalism. By way of contrast, those with a lesser concern for profit and employment in the tourism sector may be deeply offended by any desecration of local heritage. Nevertheless, a very prominent vandalistic act in a community may alter the social representations of each group because such representations are dynamic cognitive summaries rather than fixed properties of individuals and groups.

The usual way to understand the impacts and views of tourism in many tourism studies lies in the application of the triple-bottom-line approach popularised by Elkington (1997). These well-known categories include a consideration of social and cultural impacts, economic impacts and the environmental impacts. An alternative to this approach lies in a broader consideration of the forms of capital which are pivotal for the development of communities. Vermuri and Costanza (2006) suggest five kinds of capital which in the present context can be seen as forming the content of social representations about development and the good life for communities. The first of these forms of capital is natural capital, which refers to the quality of the natural ecosystem which supports life and provides resources for bodies and minds. A related form of capital is physical infrastructure, which encompasses the buildings and physical infrastructure available in the community. A less obvious form of capital but one pivotal to the development and future control of community well-being is financial capital. This form of capital consists of the investments, savings and access to assets which are available to the community. Financial capital is of course also influenced by income deriving from new and changing economic activities. Social capital refers to the connections and networks a community has and includes important resources such as trust and pathways for decision making. A final form of capital lies with individuals and their health, skills and educational achievements. This is referred to as human capital. Taken together, the availability of these forms of capital provide a thorough appraisal of what constitutes the quality of life for communities (Moscardo, 2009b; Vermuri and Costanza, 2006).

There are multiple ways in which these forms of capital are influenced by lifestyle businesses. New businesses and personnel coming into a community influence the human capital, they build social capital and in time they may add to the financial and physical capital. Local community members who opt to concentrate on small tourism businesses may also be seen as contributing to the density of social networks and to the construction of human and to a lesser extent financial capital. These points are illustrated by the studies reported earlier on lifestyle operators in France and Spain (Stone and Stubbs, 2007), on rural businesses in Scotland (Di Domenico, 2005), Ireland (Wilson, 2007) and New Zealand (Ateljevic and Doorne, 2000) and on new lifestyle-related activity in Canada (Getz and Petersen, 2005).

In terms of the social representations of tourism's future, lifestyle business operators may play a pivotal role in shaping development. It has already been suggested that many lifestyle operators choose to limit the expansion of their small and micro-businesses. As Murphy (2002) notes, sea change and tree change residents, having opted for life in a new location, do not always want to see it expand to become a replica of places they have left. Similarly, Goulding, Baum and Morrison (2005) report that businesses who operate on a seasonal business in Scotland may not wish to join the tourism and economic development push for expanding business to a year-round activity. Instead, they see advantages in the recuperative value of the off-season and can be unwilling to join promotional and tourism association campaigns for expansionary growth. Taken together, these survey and study results suggest that lifestyle businesses are united in a common social representation of tourism's local future—"restrained growth preserving our quality of life".

This approach may be contrasted with another social representation which is also seen as shaping the future of rural and peripheral communities. Mitchell and colleagues present a model of creative destruction which is driven by the entrepreneurial quest for profit and the accumulation of capital (Mitchell 1998; Mitchell and Coghill, 2000; Mitchell, Atkinson and Clark, 2001). The creative destruction model is applicable to exactly the kinds of attractive landscapes, communities and areas which attract lifestyle entrepreneurs. The core of the approach is that there are five phases in the use of these resources—an early commodification phase, an advanced commodification phase, a predestruction phase, an advanced destruction phase and a final period entitled postdestruction. The model has been applied to tourist shopping villages in Canada. The core social representation underlying the activities of the organisations initiating these phases of change is that profit matters and the use of the resource is an opportunity for strategic investment.

Mitchell and colleagues provide evidence from three Canadian villages and show that the outcome of development in these communities depends on the discourses and social representations involved. Mitchell and Coghill report:

> We contend . . . that these individuals are involved in several discourses. The discourse of the profit driven entrepreneur does not dominate in Elora (unlike Niagara on the Lake and St Jacobs) but rather co-exists alongside that of other stakeholders, the preservationists and the producers . . . Elora's advancement to the next stage (of creative destruction) is highly unlikely. (2000: 100)

The work of Mitchell and colleagues, together with the notions of viewing the impacts of tourism through a consideration of the weakening or the strengthening of forms of capital, offers new pathways for studying the community effects of tourism. Such studies could address more thoroughly the way likely tourism businesses engineer changes in the communities in which they are embedded. The positive psychology contribution here could be particularly beneficial in identifying the character strengths affected or implicated in these human capital considerations.

At least from the existing studies of the lifestyle entrepreneurs in tourism businesses it can be suggested that their wider civic role is to put a brake on all-out development. This may be achieved through nonparticipation in expansionist schemes, an unwillingness to extend the opening hours or seasonality of their operation or a reluctance to hire employees. Their participation in major promotional campaigns may be limited because such efforts can contradict their character strengths and values and move them outside the inner circle of comfort and preferred operating styles indicated in the Ateljevic and Doorne model. When viewed in this way, lifestyle businesses play a role in preserving the good life not just for their operators but they help maintain existing values and attributes of the life of the broader communities in which they are embedded.

7 Spa and Wellness Tourism and Positive Psychology

In keeping with the core aim of this volume, this chapter will endeavour to apply some focussed insights from positive and contemporary psychology study to the topics of spa and wellness tourism. A particular kind of contribution is attempted. While other chapters in this volume have looked at character strengths and values as well as the concepts of ethics, time, flow and satisfaction, this chapter delineates a contribution from studies of motivation and emotion. A supplementary area of interest lies in a consideration of mind–body links and the psychological processes underlying some forms of health and well-being.

There are contested origins and definitional dilemmas in considering both the topic of spa tourism and the concept of wellness. For the term *spa,* the most common origin is traced to the widespread extension of the name of the Belgian town Spa (Smith, 2009b). This destination still provides a notable example of the use of waters and bathing for health and pleasure. It emerged as a location of significance in the fourteenth century (Altman, 2000). The Romans provided the original name for the town undoubtedly due to its abundant watery attractions since in Latin the noun *espa* means fountain and the verb *spargere* means to bubble forth. The healing qualities of water were well known to ancient civilisations, especially the Romans, so both linguistically and in terms of the way the resource was used, spas are firmly rooted in early European history (van Tubergen and van der Linden, 2002). Nevertheless, the practice of taking the waters or bathing for a combination of health and leisure purposes is undoubtedly not restricted to Europe but extends globally. Asian traditions of communal bathing in mineral springs and spas are also historic and ongoing. In China, India, Korea and Japan in particular, there is a long history of bathing for relaxation and cleanliness (Erfurt-Cooper and Cooper, 2009). Forty-nine different kinds of contemporary spa types are listed by Erfurt-Cooper (2009). A small sample of these reveals some redundancy of terms and the resourceful efforts of marketers to identify special offerings. The terms include day spas, club spas, family spas, fertility spas (possibly these precede the family spas), hot spring spas, ecospas, mineral springs spas, hotel spas, wellness spas, holistic spas and seaside spas.

The diversity of types of spas is almost matched by the array of definitions concerning wellness. Some indication of the difficulty inherent in constructing an adequate account of wellness may be obtained by considering its nearest common antonym, that of sickness. It is useful to consider the comparisons between the two states.

At this point of time and as the author writing this chapter I can clearly report that I am feeling sick with a clear case of a streaming cold and associated annoying symptoms. In addition to the personal self-pity I usually manage to generate when feeling unwell, I also recognise that I am less alert, keener to finish tasks and reluctant to socialise. Yet, I have also decided that I am not seriously sick and I am fairly confident that serious ill health would generate greater anxiety, even a fear of the future and possibly a reappraisal of what I value in my life. It would seem appropriate to suggest that wellness, like its counterpart of sickness, must at least consider the issues of self-awareness, of severity or levels of the concept and its associated emotional states.

The history of the deployment of the wellness concept in these experiential and holistic terms is somewhat contested. German researchers reject the commonly cited origins of wellness as outlined in the work of the North American research Herbert Dunn since they claim that Europeans widely used the term before its transatlantic use (Dunn, 1961; Erfurt-Cooper and Cooper, 2009). Nevertheless, some agreement about wellness does seem to exist across continents with key principles of wellness being that it is subjective and perceptual, multidimensional and underpinned by models of balance or compensation (Smith and Puczko, 2009: 54–57). The wheel of wellness which Smith and Puczko derive from their overview of other studies specifies emotional, spiritual,, intellectual, social, physical and vocational wellness components. Importantly for this chapter and volume it is suggested that studies of wellness, and that includes wellness tourism, should be oriented towards explaining the positive components of human existence rather than simply the absence of the negative. Wellness then may be explained by some of the same dimensions as applied to sickness but it is not the simple absence of the latter.

Wellness tourism must consider both experiential elements and incorporate the travel and experiential product components of a burgeoning industry sector in any full definition of the term. Bushell and Sheldon (2009) offer the following:

> Wellness tourism is a holistic mode of travel that integrates a quest for physical health, beauty or longevity, and/or a heightening of consciousness or spiritual awareness, and a connection with community, nature or the divine mystery. It encompasses a range of tourism experiences in destinations with wellness products, appropriate infrastructures, facilities, and natural and wellness resources. (2009: 11)

While this definition is long and inclusive, there are some troubling elements in this approach. As Winchester (1998) reports in discussing the history of the *Oxford English Dictionary*:

> Defining words (terms) properly is a fine and peculiar craft. There are rules—a word must first be defined according to the class of things to which it belongs and then differentiated from other members of that class. There must be no words in the definition that are more complicated or less likely to be known than the words being defined. (1998: 134)

Bushell and Sheldon's efforts do not seem to indicate a very tightly defined class of experiences and emotional states. A second troubling concern is that the definition uses other terms within the defining sentences which are themselves not clear. Three terms in particular might be singled out for attention: holistic travel, heightening of spiritual awareness and the divine mystery. Finally, their approach does not consider the issue of participant awareness; that is, do travellers have to know they are involved in something called wellness tourism which exists on several levels or is wellness tourism simply an imposed, etic label describing what tourists are already doing.

Other definitions emphasise more psychological components. Myers, Sweeney and Witmer (2005) suggest an all-embracing approach where wellness tourism is a way of life which is directed to well-being in mind, body and spirit, and its consequences assist people to live within their natural and social context. Erfurt-Cooper and Cooper cite a definition from the University of Berne which states that wellness tourism is the "sum of all the relationships and phenomena resulting from a journey and residence by people whose main motivation is to preserve or promote their health" (2009: 8).

The implication of these definitional concerns can be specified as follows. Firstly it is unfair to castigate any research team for their efforts since definitions always have to be viewed within a structure of the purpose and approach of the authors. The present interests make the authors lean towards a motivationally based definition since the expressed aim of this chapter is to consider in some detail the driving psychological forces generating wellness and spa tourism. Indeed, it can be suggested that in new areas of research, and wellness tourism is not yet full of classical studies, it is desirable that researchers spell out exactly what range of human needs, products and services they are considering. In this way a cumulative and integrative understanding of the phenomenon can be built through a combination of refining definitions and providing evidence of visitor and managerial activity.

In this chapter, two topics will be explored—motivation and the experiential components of well-being. These two concerns offer the possibility of forging new insights into spa and wellness tourism which are defined here as the broad array of services and experiences people purposefully seek while travelling to foster all forms of their health and happiness.

MOTIVATION

The topic of motivation provides a number of difficulties for tourism researchers. Firstly, motivational approaches to understanding any tourism topic need to avoid the all-too-easy solution of rephrasing participation as motivation. That is, if care is not taken, every kind of tourism is seen as directed by a suitably similar motive. For example, Chen and Prebensen (2009: 234) suggest that the motivation for wellness tourism is driven in part by the motive of health consciousness. Statistical links for sets of apparent motives described in this way and associated with the target tourist behaviour tend to reveal high correlations or factor structure linkages, and researchers would seem to be "explaining" the phenomenon. Regrettably, this approach does not provide much academic progress. If all tourist activities are treated in this way, then the canon of research effort effectively duplicates what we already know—that individuals and groups have different interests and participate in a variety of tourist activities for which we can, after the fact, frame a set of "motives". This approach would therefore tend to give us motives or a need for ecotourism, wildlife tourism needs and motives, spa tourism motives, cruise tourism motives and so on. The motives which are implicated in these sector-specific lists are in effect descriptions of the activity (e.g. the wildlife tourism motives might be the need to see animals, the desire to get close to animals, the need to learn about wildlife). The potential circularity of this effort is not helpful since research is then positioned without a more fundamental source of understanding the generic drivers of tourist behaviour.

A second and related difficulty in motivation research is to move beyond any lengthy and sometimes circular listing of motives, as described earlier, and advance a more parsimonious account of the influences on behaviour. In effect this difficulty requires that researchers grapple with motivation theories or conceptual schemes. Hsu and Huang (2008) identify three broad approaches and itemise major tourist motivation theories or schemes within each of these approaches. More specifically, they observe the importance of Maslow's needs-hierarchy approach and identify Pearce's travel career pattern proposal as an example linked to this approach (Pearce, 2005; Pearce and Lee, 2005). Hsu and Huang consider a second category to be the broad area of the push-and-pull theories and within this domain they discuss the work of Dann, Crompton, Uysal and colleagues and Klenosky (Baloglu and Uysal, 1996; Crompton, 1979; Dann, 1977; Klenosky, 2002; Turnbull and Uysal 1995; Yoon and Uysal, 2005). A further organising approach noted by Hsu and Huang is the balance between escape and seeking behaviours. Within this category they locate the work of Mannell and Iso-Ahola (1987) and add a separate heading for the allocentric-psychocentric motivation theory of Plog (1974, 2001), which has appeared in many tourism textbooks.

It is appropriate to reconsider this kind of motivation research in tourism studies from the broader framework of the history of psychology, the rise of positive psychology and the adequacy of the term *theory*. Some of these issues were introduced in Chapter 1 and all have a close bearing on how to approach tourist motivation for spa and wellness tourism.

From the historical account of psychology presented in Chapter 1 it can be appreciated that it was the work of those studying "dynamic psychology" who first popularised the study of motives and began constructing extensive lists of needs (Boring, 1950: 692). Dynamic psychology, to the extent that it continues in alternate forms and under other labels, was and is an attempt to predict people's behaviour from a core understanding of human nature. Again, as discussed in Chapter 1, dynamic psychology has antecedents in hedonism, and the work of Freud represents just one branch of its multiple approaches to capture the roots of purposeful behaviour. The contributions of Henry Murray and Kurt Lewin are of the greatest interest in assessing the continuing contribution of the early psychology researchers.

The importance of Lewin and Murray in this account of dynamic psychology lies in their focus on the socio-cultural needs of individuals. While motivation has been recognised for some time as the sum of biological and cultural forces which drive behaviour (cf. Boring, 1950), the task of inventing a language and definitions of socio-cultural needs has been the hardest part of the formulation. Compared to the basic biological drivers of food, drink, sex, physical shelter and safety, socio-cultural needs must admit international variability and interpretation.

In motivational theories, biological needs are sometimes also referred to as instincts since very specific physical reactions and localised parts of the old brain are implicated in the operation of these forces (Greenfield, 2000). While McDougall and others happily used the term *instincts* to try to describe the nonbiological forces shaping behaviour, it became apparent that this concept was too mechanistic to allow for the subtlety of social and cultural forces. In Murray's system, the term *need* was employed and in Lewin's work the term *tension* was used. The concept of need is the one which has survived best. A need, Murray suggested, is characterised by its effect, not by the particular movements which may accompany it. Needs are directional because they aim at effects or outcomes. The achievement of the effect abates or diminishes the power of the need, at least temporarily. As an example, the need to affiliate with others is directional because it pushes individuals to seek the company of others and socialise. The need, then, is not to go to a party or have a drink or meals with others but it is the goal (effect or outcome) which, in this instance, is being with others which dispels the urgency of the need. Expressed in this way, needs should be reserved for the smaller class of driving socio-cultural forces which can be realised in multiple ways.

Murray in particular was content to describe many socio-cultural needs but other psychologists tried to be more succinct. It is important to reflect that much of this psychological inquiry was directed at understanding the way personality was shaped and those analysts and clinically minded researchers were often intent on describing unusual features of individual functioning. It is, though, worth recording some of these itemised needs since it is against this background of a smorgasbord of socio-cultural drivers that the work of Maslow and later humanistic psychologists foreshadowing positive psychology interests can be understood. Table 7.1 provides some of these identified needs.

Many tourist motivation studies borrow and reuse one of the major unidimensional needs such as anxiety or arousal. As demonstrated in Table 7.1, there are plenty of seemingly interesting needs to consider. Given the lengthy compilations of needs illustrated, it is perhaps easier to appreciate

Table 7.1 A Sample of Needs Identified in Psychology Writing and Research

Theoretical approach	Theorist/ researcher	Motives or needs emphasised
Psychoanalytic theory	Sigmund Freud	sex; aggression; emphasis on unconscious needs
Psychoanalytic approach	Carl Jung	arousal; creativity and self-actualisation (development and growth)
Modified psychoanalytic	Alfred Adler	competence; mastery to overcome incompetence
Modified psychoanalytic	Harry Stack Sullivan	acceptance, love
Modified psychoanalytic	Karen Horney	control anxiety; acceptance, love and security
Learning theory	Clark Hull	tension reduction and management
Trait theory	Gordon Allport	repeating intrinsically satisfying behaviours
Social learning theory	Albert Bandura	self-efficacy or personal mastery
Social approaches	David McClelland, John Atkinson	achievement
Humanistic	Carl Rogers	self-development
Humanistic	Abraham Maslow	hierarchy of needs, from physiological needs to safety needs to love and relationship needs to self-esteem to self-actualisation
Cognitive approaches	David Berlyne	curiosity; mental stimulation
Ethogenic (social and philosophical)	Rom Harré	respect and avoid contempt of others
Sociological theory	Stanley Cohen, Laurie Taylor	escape; excitement and meaning
Personal construct theory	George Kelly	predict and explain the world; control
Humanistic approach	Mikhail Csikszentmihayli	peak experiences

why Maslow constructed a hierarchy of needs as he examined the lives and personalities of successful people (Maslow, 1954). The questions Maslow faced in dealing with human motivation were more acute than many of his predecessors who were seeking to trace the origins of particular kinds of dysfunctional human frailties. Maslow was interested in the development trajectories of successful citizens and required an integrative approach to organise the needs he detected in his interviews and assessments. It was from this basis that he developed a fluid hierarchy of needs. It was not a fixed step-ladder of accumulating and achieving goals as some have imagined (Rowan, 1998) but an attempt at the layering of key needs as patterns of development in successful lives. Most importantly, the lower level needs do not disappear from the individual's frame of motivational influences as some bowdlerised textbook versions seem to suggest, but instead remain a continuing force on which other patterns of needs are built and constructed.

In making the transfer between motivations as studied in psychology and motivation as applied to tourist behaviour, there are some issues for scholars to consider. Initially it is important to remember that the institution of tourism, like leisure, is one of those mixed public–private sector social constructions which permits individuals some freedom to choose how to spend their time and money. It thus becomes a likely venue for the expression of well-being and an embodied performative opportunity to enhance one's sense of life satisfaction. Participating in tourism can be started at almost any age and, equally, discontinued at any point in the life cycle. The experience of being a tourist tends for most people to be discontinuous with intervening periods of work, study or other leisure pursuits. Additionally, in most instances the experiences from one holiday period to the next tend to vary, particularly if there is a change of venue, companions and style of travel. The influence of close relationships in particular can be a powerful moderator of individual motivation in tourism experiences.

A further defining characteristic of tourist motivation is that it needs to be cast within a framework of considering preferred future states for individuals. More specifically, many tourists aim to extend and embellish their worlds through the tourism experience rather than simply return their existence to a previous steady state. The implications of these characteristics of tourism are important for the study of tourist motivation. The episodic, dynamic, relationship-dependent, future-oriented and varied experiences imply that there is likely to be a complex pattern of learning about being a tourist and what satisfies the individual. Tourism experiences and the motivations which drive them are perhaps more like a series of separate affairs rather than a stable and continuous relationship. Further, the career trajectories in tourism may be more complicated than those in leisure where the concepts of specialisation and consumer involvement have been useful explanatory devices. Whereas tourists may become specialised in their travel interests and preferences, there is also the obvious perspective that different locations provide an array of new experiences and prompt a multilateral expansion of interests and needs.

Loyalty or intention to revisit a style of tourism may be transferred to similar but novel opportunities rather than closely linked to exactly the same provider or destination.

A consideration of these distinctive tourism features requires the articulation of a special set of conceptual requirements for the development of a motivational approach to tourism. In Chapter 1 the issue of the appropriateness of the term *theory* to tourism studies was considered. It was suggested that the term is overused and a more appropriate label is conceptual scheme or framework since many of the formal requirements of the larger term theory are not met by the present state of tourism work. Nevertheless, the term *theory* has become such a convenient shorthand for describing organising systems of knowledge in social science that the expression is sometimes used (albeit mindfully) in the following section so as not to be overly pedantic. Seven key requirements for a good conceptual scheme or theory of tourist motivation have been outlined in previous work (Pearce, 1993). These requirements integrate the discussion about the distinctive characteristics of tourism and the legacy of psychology inquiry concerning motivation and its role in shaping personality. The seven requirements are presented in Table 7.2. They are supplemented by an eighth requirement drawn from a consideration of the role of positive psychology.

Assessments of the existing tourist motivation conceptual schemes indicate that the approaches differ in terms of satisfying the criteria set out in Table 7.2 (Hsu and Huang, 2008; Pearce, 1993). The principal schemes to be considered include the psycho-centric–allocentric dimensional approach of Plog, the travel career pattern work of Pearce and colleagues, the arousal-based approaches identified with the work of Iso-Ahola and Mannell, contemporary versions of the push–pull approach typified by the studies of Uysal and colleagues, and the expectancy value approaches which has been claimed recently as an additional way to view tourist motivation (Correia and Moital, 2009). Each approach has certain strengths but arguably all require fine tuning and further development to meet all the criteria identified. In a previous detailed assessment of these schemes according to seven of the eight criteria outlined in Table 7.1, it was noted that the travel career ladder approach had some advantages in terms of fulfilling more of the criteria specified than other approaches (Goeldner and Ritchie, 2002; Pearce, 1993). In particular, it offered promise as better meeting the dynamic, multi-motive and intrinsic components of a good tourist-motivation theory.

Since that assessment, the travel career pattern approach has been formulated as an improved version of the travel career ladder approach (Pearce, Morrison and Rutledge 1998). This extension prompted by the limitations noted by Ryan (1998) and others has seen the earlier simple ladder approach rejected in favour of an emphasis on patterning (Filep and Greenacre, 2007; Bowen and Clarke, 2009). Importantly the new eighth criteria identified in Table 7.1 for a good tourist motivation theory is that of having a clearer future oriented approach and suggests motivation schemes

Table 7.2   Requirements for a Conceptual Scheme to Understand Tourist Motivation

Requirement	Explanation
It functions as a true theory	The motivation theory must integrate existing tourist needs that have been described in previous studies. It should organise the known needs and provide a new orientation for future research.
It appeals to different users	The motivation theory must appeal to several different groups, including specialist researchers investigating tourist behaviour and market researchers designing survey questions.
It is easy to communicate	In order to appeal to researchers, market survey workers and even tourists, the motivation theory should be easy to explain. A perspective which is limited to one country or one class of customers is likely to be of little international appeal.
It suggests ways to measure motivation	Some theories in social science, while they make sense and can be communicated readily, fail to influence other researchers because they offer no guidelines or suggestions as to how they can be measured or tested with data. The motivation theory must be amenable to practical study, and its ideas capable of being translated into questions and responses for assessment purposes.
It allows for many motives	The motivation theory must accommodate the view that travellers seek to satisfy several needs at once, rather than having just one goal, such as "to escape". It is likely that one or two motives may be dominant in an individual's desire to visit a specific location, but ideally the theory should be a multi-motive one, providing a pattern or tapestry of motives rather than focus on one need.
It is dynamic	Both individuals and societies change over time, and the motivation theory must have enough subtlety to monitor changes in groups and individuals. As with the issue of multiple motives, the need is for a theoretical formulation which accommodates an overall pattern of motives, rather than a single-issue approach.
It accounts for intrinsic and extrinsic motivation	The motivation theory should be able to detect that travellers are sometimes motivated by intrinsic, self-directed, self-satisfying needs, while at other times they respond to the opinions of friends, relatives and work colleagues.
It permits a future-oriented view of human striving	The motivation theory should incorporate items permitting the assessment of expanding or enhanced human potential and character strengths.

should incorporate a breadth of items sensitive to the strivings of people for a better life. This criterion is consistent with a positive psychology emphasis and the travel career pattern model fits this requirement. The basis for this assertion lies in the view that by emphasising a very wide range of motives drawn from an emic and then a structured etic approach to drawing together all the relevant motivational needs, the travel career pattern material effectively encompasses the kinds of humanistic and positive psychology striving towards both eudaimonic and hedonic well-being. This coverage of the range of social and cultural motives thus permits researchers using the full fourteen motives of the travel career pattern approach (and the underlying items which constitute these factors) to explore the important issues of change, development and human growth over time.

The development and consideration of the travel career concept is chosen in this chapter to further the understanding of motivation in relation to spa and wellness tourism. There are several reasons for this choice. The approach does receive an adequate rating according to the key criteria for a tourist-motivation theory even though commentators have tended to suggest it is promising rather than complete (Filep and Greenacre, 2007; Hsu and Huang, 2008; Ryan, 1998). Additionally, it is the approach among those discussed which is most influenced by and matches the positive psychology emphases.

SPA AND WELLNESS TOURISM MOTIVATION

Several kinds of evidence are permissible in determining the patterns of spa and wellness tourism motivations. Some of this material is collected without any explicit recognition that the assembled data can contribute to a patterned interpretation. Additionally, this section will report some data collected specifically with the purpose of showing how the reasons for attending spas and participating in wellness tourism might be blended into a full consideration of travellers' careers and motives.

Since there is an explicit decision in this section to attempt to use the travel career patterns approach in framing the motivation for spa and wellness tourism, it is necessary to outline the core methods and patterns which have been employed and established in this framework. A very long list of motives and needs was considered in the construction of the travel career patterns. Some of these needs were derived from intensive qualitative research with a small number of travellers varying in travel experience while many needs were extracted from previous studies and the psychology literature on motivation. Setting aside synonyms and idiosyncratic responses, seventy-four motives were then subjected to principal component analysis after appropriate checks on the adequacy of the sample size. Fourteen factors were identified in a survey of over 900 Western (mostly Australian and United Kingdom) travellers. A repeat of the quantitative component of the work was undertaken with over 700 Asian travellers (Korean respondents) and the details of these studies reported in Pearce (2005) as well as in Pearce and Lee (2005). The fourteen resultant motives which were corroborated across the two samples were, in order of importance, novelty, escape/relax, relationship strengthening, autonomy, seeking nature, self-development through involvement with hosts or the site, stimulation, self-development of a personal kind, relationship security (enjoying being with similar others), self-actualisation (getting a new life perspective), isolation, nostalgia, romance and recognition (prestige of travelling). The key feature of the travel career pattern approach was then to use the levels of travel experience reported by the respondents to formulate a three-part model which described the relationships between these fourteen motives and the amount of travelling which the respondents had undertaken.

The varied importance of the motives suggested that a pattern could be imposed on the data such that for all travellers there was a core layer of motives which were very important. These motives were to escape and relax, to experience novelty and to build relationships. These motives were relatively unaffected by how much travelling the participants had experienced. There were also motives which could be distributed into a middle and outer layer of importance. For those who had travelled the most, the middle layer of motives was more important than the outer layer, whereas for those who had travelled little, all the remaining motives tended to be seen as important. There was also a link between the travel motives and the stage of the travellers' life cycle but here there were some Asian and Western cultural differences. For Western travellers, later stages of the life cycle also tended to be linked to more travel experience but this was not a consistent finding for the predominantly Korean travellers in the Asian sample. Younger Koreans had often travelled more than older Koreans, so the links between travel experience and later stages of the life cycle were not strong. This discrepancy is readily explained since the availability of travel as a discretionary leisure pursuit is a more recent phenomenon in Korean society (Kim et al., 1996). Indeed, most of the variability in the Korean data was better explained simply by the amount of travelling rather than by the age and life-cycle stage of the respondents. Overall, the motive structures were broadly consistent both for Asian and the Western travellers. The two large-scale studies confirmed the notion that individuals tend to have a travel career with their holiday experience together with the stage people are at in their life cycle building a different pattern of importance for their travel motives. A succinct representation of these ideas is presented in Figure 7.1.

The highest loading item(s) for the factors are in brackets and the direction of the arrows indicates changing emphases with increasing traveller experience. The critical questions for the present analysis is Where do the motives for wellness and spa tourism fit into this pattern? Three kinds of

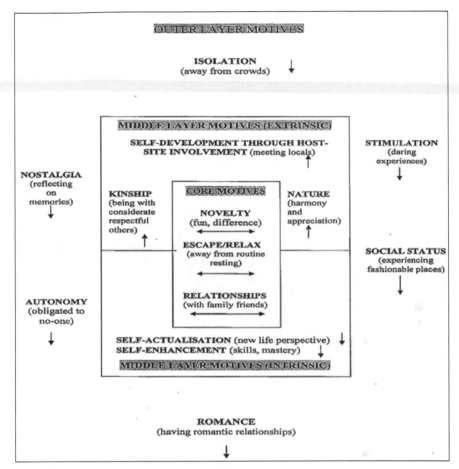

Figure 7.1   The core structure of the travel career patterns (TCP) approach.

information can help address this issue. The first material to be considered derives from a set of studies seeking to identify special defining characteristics of different types of tourism. Next, a detailed analysis will be provided of a recent research effort to explore the motivations of spa goers from Hong Kong. This work will be supplemented by preliminary results exploring motivations and directly applying the travel career pattern material from respondents in India, Thailand and the Philippines.

In seeking insights into travel motivation, several kinds of data and information sources can be used. Some material can be sought in an indirect fashion and the motivation of travellers inferred from their reported post-travel experiences and activities. A more direct approach is to ask tourists either prior to visiting a destination or at the destination why they have travelled to that location and more specifically what they are seeking out of their holiday experiences. There are good reasons for linking these two sources of information into a tapestry of motivational appraisal. The direct-questioning approach may be thorough but it does inherently set up a social situation with demand characteristics and social desirability values. A well-designed questionnaire and assurances of respondent anonymity may limit these effects but potentially they still exist. The value of appraising motives with another pathway is a potentially useful check on these limitations. It is important, though, not to overstate the limitations of questionnaire and survey material since to do so can trap researchers into assumptions that there is a "false consciousness" in their respondents' views. That is, it is dangerous for authors to suggest that while the data they have collected show a certain pattern of results, it really means something else because the tourists surveyed were unwilling to express their honest views. This kind of thinking undercuts the value of research efforts since it is based very heavily on untestable researcher assumptions. A better pathway for the checking of motivational perspectives is to use alternate qualitative and interpretive materials rather than rely on researcher reinterpretations.

Morrison et al. (1996) and Moscardo et al. (1996) provide some detailed empirical work on travellers' activities implicitly linked to motivations for different types of holidays. Both studies re-analysed large-scale secondary data with over 12,000 cases drawn from the Pleasure Travel Market survey studies conducted by the Longwoods organisation for Tourism Canada. The appeal of selecting these studies for the present interest lies in identifying the comparative experiential views of different types of tourism. Both studies compared tourists' responses to different types of holidays and noted how activity participation varied according to the type of trip. In the Morrison et al. study, the trip types were cruises, beach resorts, casino resorts, ski resorts and summer country resorts, whereas the research conducted by Moscardo et al. considered the additional choices of theme-park holidays, urban city resorts, touring holidays and outdoor vacations. The Moscardo et al. study used a multidimensional scaling approach to provide figures illustrating the patterns of perceived similarity of the experiences. In both studies, cruise, summer and beach tourism were seen as the most relaxing while cruise tourism also scored highly on being romantic, fun, adventurous and exciting. Casino-based resort holidays were seen as less relaxing and adventurous than other types of holidays but were related highly for excitement. Ski holidays were seen as exciting and adventurous and, possibly surprisingly, educational. Theme-park holidays were among the most exciting but also expensive, less romantic and less relaxing than their counterparts.

In addition to providing these descriptions of the holiday types, both studies also considered the frequency of a set of activities which broadly fall in to the spa and wellness considerations. Items for closer inspection under this rubric include the travellers' responses to the use of saunas, hot tubs, fitness clubs and gyms as well as participation in aerobics, walking and swimming. For both studies there were variations in the participation rates for these activities in the different types of resorts. The use of hot tubs and saunas, for example, was greatest in the ski resorts whereas fitness centres were used more on cruises. Aerobics participation was also highest in the cruise context but was an infrequent activity in other settings. Summer and outdoor resorts had the highest level of swimming in freshwater and ocean settings but casinos had high levels of use of gyms as did beach resorts (Morrison et al., 1996: 22; Moscardo et al., 1996: 61).

Two key points can be outlined in relation to this kind of data. By working "backwards" from activities to the needs driving those activities, much in the manner suggested by Murray in defining a need, it can be suggested that there are coherent patterns of needs for different types of holidays. Further, many of the descriptions provided of the holiday types reinforce the patterns of needs such as escape, relaxation, novelty, stimulation and excitement which have been previously described in the motivational research. This, in itself, is an indirect confirmation of the travel career pattern approach which emphasises tourist motivation as a multi-motive tapestry of combined driving forces. A second point to link these studies with the central interest here in motivation is that motivational studies of spa and wellness tourism can clearly be developed at different scales. The data reported in the Moscardo et al. and the Morrison et al. studies are North American and are very broad. Additionally, they only consider a limited set of health and wellness activities. As suggested earlier, research efforts need to be pursued in different contexts and with clearly specified types of spa and wellness products to build an understanding of motivation. The following studies explicitly direct attention to Asian research focussed specifically on actual spas and wellness tourism facilities.

One direct consideration of the motivational underpinnings of spa and wellness tourism lies in the work of Mak, Wong and Chang (2009). The researchers studied over 300 residents of Hong Kong and asked them to respond to twenty-one items describing their motives for visiting spas. Mak and colleagues argued that spa and wellness properties have become an important part of Asian tourism and they cite the expansion of such facilities in Thailand, China, Japan and Korea as being of particular interest and appeal to the travellers from Hong Kong. A dominant context for the study was the hotel spa experience (cf. Erfurt-Cooper and Cooper, 2009) since over 50% of the convenience sample studied had experienced this kind of spa operation. It is perhaps noteworthy in interpreting the findings that hotel spas are generally luxurious and a part of the high-quality services offered to guests rather than being facilities which are distinctive attractions in themselves. In some senses hotel spas are akin to day spas, which had been visited by 37% of the sample, since day spas too are often a convenient part of a broader travel schedule. By way of contrast, mineral springs spas, which had been visited by 35% of the sample, can be seen more as a focussed choice of a holiday experience. Overall, 34% of the total sample had visited spas once, 53% had visited spas between two and five times and only 12% had more than five spa experiences. From these figures it would be appropriate to suggest that the sample had a relatively low level of previous visit experience. Over three quarters of the sample studied by Mak and colleagues were women, and while this is not atypical of the distribution of hotel and day-spa goers in general, and might be assumed to reflect distinctive gender needs, the researchers found limited differences between males and females in the motives for visiting.

The core findings of the study were presented in three ways. The means of the individual motives were provided and a factor analysis was conducted of all twenty-one items resulting in five factors. It is important to stress that this study was not designed according to the travel career patterns (TCP) approach but it will be argued that the results are highly congruent with the model. Mak and colleagues report that the two most important factors are relaxation and relief and escape. These two factors have the highest grand means—for relaxation the grand mean is 3.67 and for escape it is 3.45 on the 5-point scale where 5 is the highest value. The next motive identified from the twenty-one items is self-reward and indulgence with a grand mean of 3.32. There is some interesting variability of item means for this factor which warrants further attention.

The key items, the loading on the factor and their mean for importance are as follows: Indulgence in luxurious experience (0.77), mean 3.22; desire to be seen as fashionable (0.68), mean 2.47; pamper oneself (0.66), mean 3.82; reward oneself for working hard (0.55), mean 3.78. It is noteworthy here that the status issue, expressed in this item as the desire to be fashionable, has the lowest mean score for the respondents. Correia and Moital (2009) argue that prestige motivation is a neglected and pivotal topic in tourist motivation studies, and Mak et al. themselves cite Schutte and Ciarlante's (1998) reworked model of Maslow's hierarchy to claim that status and admiration are the pinnacle motives in Asian consumer experience. The evidence collected in this study is directly contradictory to these assertions. The respondents have recorded the importance of the desire to be fashionable as the lowest for this factor and indeed it has the lowest mean score for all twenty-one items. These data are a precise illustration of the point made earlier in this section about researchers having to deal with discrepant data and the caution that a false consciousness should not be invoked lightly. That is, it might be suggested that respondents are concealing their true status-oriented needs and in public not admitting to their desire for recognition and respect. More simply, it may be the case that some tourist activities because they are now common and widely available have little status value. Interestingly, both for the Western tourist sample and the Korean sample in the travel career pattern work, recognition and status are rated as the least important of the fourteen motives (Pearce, 2005: 61, 72). A distinct possibility exists that researchers have assumed that status issues operating within a culture are necessarily applied to tourism experiences which may be much more intrinsically motivated than is often appreciated. This interpretation of the intrinsic value of health and wellness experiences as an intrinsic motivational need linked to the travel career pattern approach may apply to both Asian and Western travellers.

The remaining factors identified by Mak et al. are health and beauty needs and relationship needs as expressed in a friendship and kinship factor. Both have grand means substantially below the relaxation and escape motives with the health and beauty motive grouping (3.15) being somewhat more important than the friendship factor (2.86). Neither is as important as the self-reward and indulgence set of items (3.32). If these motives were to be classified according to the structure of the TCP approach as portrayed in Figure 7.1, then escape and relax would be core items, and both the self-reward and indulgence factor and the health and beauty factor would fit into a mid-layer set of motives. The friendship factor for the spa experience would lie in an outer layer set of motives. The Mak et al. study did not sort the motive structures according to previous experience, but an implication for the data can be drawn by its restructuring into the TCP model. Such an activity permits further testable hypotheses for spa motivation research. According to the TCP approach, with mounting experience the emphasis on the mid-layer motives should increase with both the self-reward and indulgence factor and the healthy and beauty factor gaining in importance with more spa experiences. The reward and indulgence factor should gain the most because it is more of an intrinsic motive as opposed to the somewhat more externally oriented beauty factor. By way of contrast, the friendship factor will decline in importance whereas there is a predicted stability in the importance of the escape and relaxation items. It is perhaps possible for future researchers to grapple with these possibilities. An important recommendation here would be that researchers should be encouraged to use the full range of motivational factors in the travel career patterns approach rather than a limited or restricted range of motives.

A second application of the TCP approach to studies in wellness tourism lies in considering the findings concerning motivation in the recently completed doctoral level work of Voigt (2010). Using both an intensive qualitative phase of research and then a larger sample of respondents in a quantitative phase, Voigt explored the benefits expressed by three kinds of wellness tourists. The groups studied were beauty wellness tourists, resort lifestyle visitors and spiritual wellness seekers. Based on the qualitative findings, a generic underlying theme of transforming the self was identified. This result emphasising the self distinguished Voigt's interviews from the more outward looking and socially conscious wellness tourists idealised in the work of Hall and Brown (2006).

The quantitative results from Voigt's work were built on forty-six items organised around six benefit factors of transcendence, physical health and appearance, escape and relaxation, important others and novelty, re-establish self-esteem and indulgence. The larger sample in the quantitative study did not respond in quite the same way as the more intensively inter-viewed respondents. The results indicated a key role for the escape and relaxation set of benefits. The grouping of outcomes represented by the term *transcendence* (to contemplate what is important to me and to gain a sense of renewal) had the second highest grand mean of all the benefit factors. Voigt reports some close links to the findings of Pearce and Lee (2005) and the TCP, especially in terms of the primary role of escape and the lower importance levels of the other benefits, but points out that the intrinsic and extrinsic levels appear to be working a little differently in her study. She highlights the perspective that transcendence, an intrinsic benefit analogous to the middle-level-order self-development label used in the TCP factors, appears to be distinctive and especially important part of the pattern in wellness holidays. It can be suggested that for wellness holidays transcendence is equivalent to the defining benefits for casinos (excitement) and cruise ship holidays (romance) reported by Moscardo et al. and Morrison et al.

A recently completed study by Panchal and Pearce (forthcoming) pur-sued the application of the travel career pattern approach to spa and wellness tourism motivation for respondents in India, Thailand and the Philippines. Nearly 300 domestic and international tourists were surveyed with approximately even numbers of visitors in each country contributing to the findings. Filipino (80%) and Indian (68%) residents made up a larger part of the sample in their respective countries, but in Thailand 90% of the sample were international visitors. The dominant treatments experienced were body massage either taken solely or combined with facial scrubs, body wraps, body scrubs and local traditional health treatments and therapies. The genders were balanced in the sample and there was some variability in age (with most being under 50 years old). The professional status of the respondents varied widely.

The core approach used in the Panchal and Pearce study was to obtain information on a structured questionnaire on seventy-one motive items including all items from the previous travel career pattern studies and two additional items directly assessing "maintaining my current health condi-tion and improving my current health condition". The means for impor-tance of these items for all the respondents were obtained and the results were again assessed using principal component analysis. The crucial ques-tion under examination in this study was: Where do the motive items for health fit within the travel career pattern model? The answer to this ques-tion is that not only are both the health items rated in highly similar ways but also the level of importance assigned to the health items locates them in the moderately important motives framework when travellers have little or only modest travel experience and in the outer layer of motives when travellers are more frequent holiday takers. This result conforms to pre-vious travel career pattern research and again witnesses the tendency for less experienced travellers. Additionally and importantly, the way in which

Indian, Filipino and Thai respondents rated travel motivation items was markedly similar to the Western and Korean patterns already described.

These recent studies in travel motivation conducted with relevance to or specially focussed on spa and wellness tourism form a beginning for studies in this area. The travel career pattern approach was demonstrated to have value both as an organiser for existing work and as planning tool for the design of studies. In this sense it can be seen as functioning as a 'true theory' of motivation as required in Table 7.2. It can also be suggested that the future use of the conceptual scheme can be justified since it can generate predictions for travellers with different levels of travel experience. It will necessarily be the case that studies in other Asian settings as well as Europe, North America and beyond will deal with different contexts and types of spa and wellness tourism and this core product style consideration will need to be addressed sensitively when comparisons with existing studies are made. Nevertheless the approach adopted in this chapter which is consistent with the purposive striving of individuals towards positive goals opens the way to deal systematically with the statement by Bushell for spa and wellness tourism "Questions of tourist motivation need more research" (Bushell, 2009: 36).

MIND–BODY LINKS AND SPA/WELLNESS TOURISM

Until quite recently two separate lines of inquiry have considered the effects of spa and wellness tourism. Some components of the first kind of work have already been reported in this chapter. These contributions consist of the efforts of social science researchers in tourism and the studies have tended to describe the products, locations and growth of the spa and wellness sector. The work of these scholars has been informed largely by their backgrounds in geography, sociology, economics, marketing and business studies. There is, though, the possibility of providing further insights into this field from a somewhat separate approach. The additional line of inquiry is medical science, sometimes with a strong physiological emphasis and at other times linked to more clinical forms of positive psychological inquiry. There are well-established publication outlets reporting the work of medical scientists and related researchers, particularly in terms of stress reduction and better health deriving from travel experiences (Sonmez and Apostolopoulos, 2009). A succinct review of this work and a suggested positive psychology interpretation of some of the underlying mind–body links may usefully point the way to new research studies in tourism and wellness research.

Anecdotes and striking examples of the positive effects of travel on health and well-being have been noted for some time. In Victorian England, the almost blind traveller James Holman became the world's most celebrated holiday taker. Holman is now an obscure figure in the history of travel but in his age he became a unique celebrity and his accounts of his journeys strongly influenced Charles Darwin, Joseph Conrad and Charles Dickens. For the present purposes, the remarkable feature of Holman's life was that he was persistently strong and healthy when travelling, even in extreme conditions, but repeatedly became unwell, emaciated and melancholic when sedentary and at home. The queen's physician, England's most important medical figure, was moved to write a clear prescription for Holman's health: "a continual change of scene and climate, together with unrestrained exercise of his mental and physical powers prolonged for a period of at least three years" (Roberts, 2006: 307).

The connection between holiday taking and human well-being now extends beyond the notable stories about individuals and several pockets of research have developed. Some of the findings in these studies can be viewed as surprising since together they offer a rather more positive view of the physiological and psychological benefits of travel than might be expected from everyday cynical observers. The suspicion that travel and holiday taking might be only marginally beneficial to its participants perhaps derives from the view that any benefits of holiday taking have a rapid "fade-out" effect. In short, this view suggests that despite the joys of the holiday, after a few days back at work the benefits are swamped by the mountains of work now to be completed combined with the stress of everyday life. Westman and Eden (1997), Westman and Etzion (2001) and Etzion (2003), all of whom studied the relationship between job burnout and the value of holidays, did find that there was a fade-out effect but positive perceptions of work and reduced stress levels lasted for at least three weeks.

The benefits in tourism and holiday taking are arguably somewhat more powerful and durable than these specific studies suggest. It is important to remember that holiday experiences have both an anticipatory and a reflective phase. That is, holidays may have a positive function in that people reduce stress by looking forward to them as well as reflecting on them. Some solid evidence that a consistent pattern of holiday taking confers or is at least associated with physiological benefits comes from a number of longitudinal or panel data studies reported in the medical literature. In the data tracking the social habits and behaviours of over 5,000 United States citizens collected in the Framingham Heart Study, it was demonstrated over a twenty-year period that women who took two or more vacations a year suffered significantly less from forms of cardiovascular disease (specifically, myocardial infarctions) than those taking few and infrequent vacations (Eaker, Pinsker and Castelli, 1992). In a similar kind of study over a nine-year period, more than 12,000 middle-aged men were assessed on a battery of physical, psychological and behavioural measures. Gump and Matthews (2000) report that compared with those who did not take vacations, the regular holiday takers were 31% less likely die of cardiovascular disease. As all researchers and analysts will be quick to realise, these kinds of cohort studies show relationships and links and do not necessarily indicate a causal pathway. For those who are taking regular holidays there may be other powerful determining variables linking the health–holiday relationships. For example, it may be that those who take holidays have better quality relationships which in themselves are well known as major stress reducers (Argyle 1999), and on holidays they have time to enjoy those good relationships. More simply it might be that the ability to save the kind of money required to purchase holidays is a healthy joint cooperative family exercise which itself frees the participants from stress.

Another set of studies closely tied to the present interests in spa and wellness tourism and conducted in Austria helps build the case that is the vacation experience which plays a key role. In these studies pre- and post-holiday physiological and psychological measures of health and well-being were assessed. In studies typical of this genre, Strauss-Blasche, Ekmekcio-glu and Marktl (2002, 2003), and Strauss-Blasche et al. (2004) assessed participants who enjoyed a three-week spa therapy holiday at an Austrian resort. The holiday included specialised spa treatments, mud baths, and simply time to relax. Various measures of serum cholesterol were taken and strong benefits were found for the reduction of these unwanted high levels, particularly for the men, who reported high demands at work. In the 2004 study, mood and quality sleep were reported as improved for up to four weeks after the spa experiences. The researchers suggested from their data that the health benefits of holidays, both psychological and physiological, were greater when holiday takers were getting good sleep, socializing in a warm climate and having enough time to attend to their needs and focus on their well-being (Strauss-Blasche et al., 2005).

These studies, while not definitive, tend to suggest that there are substantial health benefits of certain types of holidays. Additionally, the spa and health resort holidays studied in this research provide some of the clearest evidence for this relationship. A closer examination of what is actually happening to people in their spa and health resort experiences leads to some interesting explanations connecting fundamental mind–body issues in psychological and philosophical inquiry.

Dann and Nordstrand (2009) provide a compelling account that a multisensory approach to tourism promotion should enhance the appeal of a variety of destinations including spa and wellness tourism destinations. Within this sensory framework, one modality can be highlighted in spa and wellness tourism—the sense of touch. The importance of touch, sometimes combined with a the sense of smell, is an important component in health tourism settings. It is relevant to all those practices involving massage (person-to-person touch) as well as bathing and water treatments (substance-to-person touch). Nevertheless, interpreting the meaning of touch is not a straightforward process.

As Argyle (1975) and Argyle and Henderson (1985) have noted, touch is a significant communication tool in relationships with strongly prescribed social and cultural rules as to who can touch whom. In many countries and cultures it is only medical personnel and nursing professionals who are permitted to touch strangers and then only in certain ways and within set frames (cf. Goffman, 1974). Massage therapies often involve prolonged touching of others and exist within these kinds of defined frames, but the lexicon of interpreting touch allows for some diverse interpretations. Touch, for example, can be unpredictable, ticklish, cold, warm, soothing, relaxing, sensual and even erotic, but above all it has to be interpreted as appropriate and comfortable by the holidaymaker.

A small sample of studies from the varied research fields which have considered the therapeutic and psychological value of touch suggest it has a special power in affecting well-being. Murray (1908) drew links among the sensations of being tickled, responding to an itch, feeling pressure and experiencing pain. The sensations arising from being tickled are usually responses to a light form of touch, but social context and the sense of unexpected may modify the sensation. In behavioural terms, the response is a rapid and active attempt to avoid the behaviour while psychologically it is often linked to fun and laughter and may derive from an evolutionary need to respond to dangerous tactical stimulation in the form of insect threats or preconscious awareness of danger. Pressure, by way of contrast, and particularly as found in massage treatments, has established medical and psychological benefits particularly in terms of blood circulation, lymph gland functioning and efficient muscular function (Bright, 2002: 162–163; Clark, 1986: 209). Pressure-based touch is also viewed as having social benefits, particularly in connecting the sense of dependency and intimacy between participants in both commercial and caring settings (Clark, 1986; Verghese, 2009)

As Gergen (1997) and Verghese (2009) have argued, in exploring intimacy there is a strong learning and interpretive component here and arguably touch produces mindfulness, since to be touched by others is not a routine process. The experience of bathing in waters of different temperatures and chemical compositions is also an inherently novel activity, and whether or not it is pleasant involves combinations of cognitive and affective interpretations of bodily sensations. A common element in the psychology of spa and wellness tourism, then, is that actions or activities are effectively performed on the human body and the participant has to assess the meaning and value of these contacts. The recourse to the concept of mindfulness provides an important clue to the explanations of the positive effects of spa and wellness tourism.

A brief diversion to report one of the key studies which resulted in the formulation of the mindfulness concept is relevant to the explanations of how bodily sensations and cognitive appraisals are linked. Langer (2009) reports that she and colleagues conducted a study where they immersed a group of older men in a staged environment which was set up to simulate a period in their lives twenty years ago. The props were impressive. The respondents in the experimental condition lived for a week in the time period of two decades earlier and all conversations were held in the present tense. The programs on television, including the news, the comedies and even the baseball games, were replicated. The retrofit of an old monastery complete with appropriate furniture and food choices enabled the researchers to have complete control of the cues in the setting. A control group of men matched in age and health status with those in the experimental condition were also a part of the study, but this group reminisced about the past rather than lived it as if it were the present. Langer's results indicated that the fully immersed group living in the present tense showed some marked physical changes. These included improvements in height, weight, posture, manual dexterity, and grip strength. Observers who did not know which men were in which condition assessed the experimental group as looking younger and fitter. Additionally, the men showed levels of independence in looking after themselves that surprised their relatives and caretakers. Langer and colleagues concluded that if you truly pay attention to the possibilities in the situation including focussing on your potential improvements in health, then there is a mental influence on bodily well-being. Mind and body meet here through the active mental process of considering and thinking directly about the embodied experiences.

Clearly, there is a close parallel between Langer's experiment and its explanation through the cognitive process of mindfulness/possibility and the spa and wellness experiences. Langer writes:

> Pursuing possibility regarding our health may result in the desired end, but in addition pursuing the psychology of possibility is itself empowering. It feels good to have a personal mission, it contributes more to a positive outlook in general and it works against the idea that the rest of us (our bodies) are soon to . . . fall apart. (2009: 16–17)

It seems appropriate to follow Langer's advice not just at a personal level but at a scientific level as well and explore more fully the possibilities of using mindfulness as a key explanation of the health benefits of spa and wellness tourism. It is suggested here that it is how people think about and react to the somewhat novel sensory (especially tactile) spa and treatment experiences and the way they view these procedures which provide the possibilities for a healthier life. Studies measuring mindfulness and listening to the verbal explanations tourists provide about their spa/health treatments experiences as well as eliciting travellers' views of their own health would all seem to be important further factors to explore in this sector of tourism.

8 Summary, Synthesis and Future Directions

The final chapter summarises and synthesises the beginning of a relationship between the fields of tourism and positive psychology. Like most incipient liaisons, the future of tourism and positive psychology is unknown. Yet at this early stage it looks bright and promising. While sceptics might predict its quick demise as many new initial pairings fail, it is evident from the preceding chapters that there are many adhesive synchronicities between the two fields of study. The concept of well-being, whether interpreted hedonically, eudaimonically, in a momentary or a reflective manner, is central to both fields. Beginning with the introductory discussion on the history of psychology and tourism scholarship, and then through the sections on satisfaction, time and ethics, the analyses of consumption and materialism as forces underlying tourism and the physical and human capital which serves tourism, it was shown that the positive psychology-tourism symbiosis provides fresh perspectives on well-being.

There are also broader conclusions which reach beyond the provision of additional perspectives on well-being. There is a clear ideological underpinning to this volume. Aristotelian notions of the righteous, noble and good life are the foundations of positive psychology reasoning. It is this reasoning which was applied to tourists, tourism workers, students, educators and other relevant stakeholders throughout the volume. Additionally, the authors remain sensitive to the expression of hedonic pleasure and recognise that a high-minded elitism towards the execution of fun times can lead to ignoring elements which are widespread in contemporary tourism.

This awareness, coupled with the ideological values of positive psychology, constitutes a stance which is similar to contemporary ideological positions in tourism on ethics (Jamal, 2004), education (Sheldon, 2008) and relevant and recent analyses of the good life and good actions in tourism (Jamal and Menzel, 2009). Our perspective is reinforced through the discussion of tourism education values in this concluding chapter. The contributions in this book also presented an array of specific methodological and conceptual tools from positive psychology. These tools are outlined in this final chapter. Two specific directions for future research, among many possibilities, have been identified. They are the analyses of relationships among positive psychology, tourism and health; and explorations of different cultural perspectives in the context of positive psychology and tourism. Brief reviews of the preceding chapters, syntheses of the contributions and an exploration of the future directions follow.

SUMMARY

Scholarship in Psychology and Tourism

The introduction to this text provided an overview of the history of psychology to flesh out the building blocks of positive psychology scholarship on well-being. Historical psychological analyses are typically beyond the scope of tourism discussions. Psychology is often linked to consumer behaviour research in tourism. Many consumer behaviour discussions do not provide an in-depth overview of core psychological theories and schemes of relevance to tourism. On the contrary, detailed analyses of sociological and anthropological foundations in the tourism field are much more common (see, for example, the latest handbook of tourism edited by Robinson and Jamal, 2009). Core psychological topics were therefore analysed in detail in this chapter: empiricism and positivism in the discipline, hedonism, dynamic motivation, attitudes, values, phenomenology, the experimental method and the application of evolutionary theory. The topics were traced through a historical frame, highlighting the key phases in the development of psychology and then positive psychology. The chapter also included discussions of social, environmental and cross-cultural psychology; it was shown that these discussions provide a strong foundation for exploring the application of positive psychology to tourism. Ten key areas of application were identified: 1) anticipating experiences, 2) on-site experiences, 3) reflections on pleasure, 4) building personal qualities, 5) power of emotions, 6) relationships in context, 7) patterns of motivation, 8) positive individual interventions, 9) positive institutions and 10) ethical tourism development.

Following this introductory chapter, many of these issues were developed and illustrated in more detail. In the first part, which consisted of three chapters, the emphasis was oriented more towards the effects and outcomes of the tourism context for the individuals themselves. The focus in this first part was therefore not exclusively on tourist behaviour and experiences—actions and impacts of individuals in the tourism system were also considered. The first chapter of the part dealt with the tourist experiences quite directly through a qualitative study of on-site satisfaction. Other chapters in this part included perspectives on time as a potential harmonising force for establishing well-being and analyses of character strengths and virtues, such as wisdom in the contexts of tourism.

Flow and Tourist Satisfaction

This chapter addressed the second of the applications of positive psychology to tourism: on-site experiences. Little is known about the nature of the real-time on-site tourist experience and immediate satisfaction at tourist sites. Yet unpredictable and haphazard moments of tourists make up any tourist experience, and it is these tourist moments that often end up being most satisfying in tourists' minds. The chapter showed how positive psychology can improve our understanding of immediate satisfaction. Various ways tourist satisfaction has been understood and appraised in the tourism literature were first considered: the dominant, expectations approaches; the qualitative, Nordic approaches; and those that can collectively be labelled experience approaches. An approach from positive psychology, called the flow-state approach, was then discussed as part of the experience approaches. Flow state, as an enjoyable state of immediacy and involvement, has previously been discussed in the tourism literature (Ryan, 1995). In-depth analyses of flow-state methods and assessment approaches were, however, beyond the scope of these previous analyses. To employ the positive psychology model and demonstrate its value, a study was described which aimed to ascertain immediate satisfaction of a group of tourists at cultural heritage sites. It was shown that the tourists' near immediate conscious satisfaction was characterised by flow themes of challenge-skill balance, total concentration, autotelic (intrinsically rewarding) events, time transformation and other satisfaction themes of mindfulness, object focus, personal experience, calm/tranquillity and discovery. A different layer of tourist satisfaction was brought to light. It was shown that satisfaction is at least as much about momentary reactions as it is about reflection. Positive psychology aids in conceptualisation and appraisal of tourist moments and immediacy and it improves our understanding of tourists' on-site experiences and satisfaction. The new layer of satisfaction would have been challenging to uncover through standard, reflective satisfaction methods (Crompton and Love, 1995; Hughes, 1991; Kozak, 2001; Prakash, 1984) or dominant, service quality approaches (Parasuraman, Zeithaml and Berry, 1988; Truong, 2005).

Time, Tourism, Host Communities and Positive Psychology

The second chapter of this part addressed the third key area of application of positive psychology: reflections on pleasures. It dealt with reflections and time issues in some depth, focussing again at the individual level and using senior members of host communities as a convenient group to illustrate temporal concerns. The notion of time as it applies to senior host community residents was examined in this contribution. Recent conceptual and empirical developments in positive psychology now hold the ability to shed light upon the functioning of tourism host communities, including vulnerable groups of people within those destinations. Issues of time perspective and time balance were specifically covered and related to this host community group. It was suggested that time could be perceived as boring and odious, but also as inspiring and exhilarating and can hence affect well-being adversely as well as in a positive way. Time perspective refers to several foci upon time frames and selves at different life points; a balanced time perspective is more conducive to well-being—the perspective which involves adjustments to the temporal mode so as to accommodate the requirements of the present environmental setting and challenges that the individual faces. The chapter then progressed to describe a theoretical model of socio-emotional selectivity theory with an aim of assisting the understanding of well-being among senior residents of tourism communities. Impediments to well-being in host communities, such as the degradation of historic sites, symbols and contexts, the lessening of cultural identity and the provocation of social conflict within a host community, were analysed. The contribution concluded with a number of recommendations as to how vulnerable people such as senior host community members can receive more equitable treatment so as to maximise their well-being. These included a range of positive psychology interventions. The interventions comprise the eighth application of positive psychology to tourism. The positive interventions included: organisation of regular functions that would aim at providing context for seniors to renew old friendships and form new ones; and publicity and corporate outreach by the tourism industry that would value vulnerable host communities, such as the senior citizens.

Ethics, Tourism and Well-being

The third and final contribution in the tourist section addressed the fourth application of positive psychology: building personal qualities. This chapter first reviewed Aristotle's views on the good life and ethics and related these commentaries to contemporary research in positive psychology. Wisdom—the nexus between happiness and ethics—was then discussed in detail; it was argued that wisdom, in line with the Aristotelian thinking, represents an ontological frame of reference within which the whole process of ethical problem solving can be placed. Physical and social circumstances, such as life challenges, creativity and resilience, are circumstances or domains in which ethical issues arise and in which wisdom is required. Each of the three domains was discussed in detail and tourist examples were used whenever possible. Volunteer work by tourists was referred to in the general discussion and life challenges were discussed in the context of tourists with a disability. Creativity and resilience were related to tourism worker and training issues, work stress and mentoring in the industry. The chapter ended with a model that presented the associations that link wisdom, ethics and various tourism contexts to well-being. The model suggested that when individuals have wisdom they display ethical values (such as altruism, honesty, courage and respect), and these values can be employed to deal with life challenges through resilience and creativity. The outcome of these actions is an improvement in the psychological well-being of tourists and other stakeholders.

The next three chapters in this volume dealt more specifically with tourism, as opposed to individuals. Materialism and its impacts on well-being were evaluated, followed by analyses of lifestyle businesses in the tourism sector and the rise of spa and wellness tourism. Positive psychology perspectives informed each of these topics.

Materialism in Tourism and Its Alleviation Through Good Values

The materialism chapter tackled the tenth area of application of positive psychology to tourism raised in Chapter 1—ethical tourism development. It devoted considerable attention to discussions of costs of materialism in tourism, such as the lack of corporate social responsibility. Materialism or the placing of a high value on possessions and wealth is a topic of growing interest to positive psychologists but it is also an important part of tourism. Materialism is often associated with negative consequences (for example, greed and selfishness) and it normally has a detrimental effect on people's well-being. Personal costs (such as frustration and depression) and ecological costs (such as natural resource depletion due to overconsumption) were addressed alongside the social problem of the lack of corporate social responsibility. The second half of the chapter examined the issue of materialism in the context of tourism education. It was shown that materialism themes, such as wealth creation, economic rewards, security and property, are still fostered by tourism educators over nonmaterialistic topics such as global citizenry, quality of life or sense of community. It was argued that tourism education needs to continue to shift towards a value-based education model—to incorporate the values of transcendent business education (empathy, generativity, mutuality, civil aspiration and intolerance of ineffective humanity) with the TEFI tourism values (stewardship, knowledge, professionalism, ethics, mutual respect). The chapter suggested a list of lecture topics from positive psychology which are in line with this value-based orientation and which could be integrated into tourism units. The outcome of the chapter is an exploratory model of transcendent, nonmaterialistic tourism education incorporating the preceding analyses.

Lifestyle Businesses and Their Community Effects

The second chapter of the tourism part focused on the topic of working in a tourism business; a minor section of this chapter explored the implications of lifestyle businesses for the community responses to tourism. The scope, size and definitions of tourism businesses were first considered. Much of the discussion then explored the lifestyle of working in and managing relatively small tourism enterprises, commonly family owned. Pathways for entering these tourism businesses, such as deployment of existing resources from current settings, international relocation and domestic relocation (typically from urban to rural zones), were discussed. Commonalities among tourism operators who make these lifestyle changes were highlighted with examples from Canada, Europe, New Zealand, Australia and other world regions. It was suggested that operators of lifestyle businesses seek greater autonomy and control in their lives and compatibility with the types of guests that they would be serving. An additional common theme identified was the reoccurring tension between establishing and persisting with the modest business lifestyle and running a more serious business venture. The Lonely Planet business by Tony and Maureen Wheeler was used as an illustration, in addition to other examples of this tension. The remainder of the chapter dealt with positive values and community effects. It was suggested the positive psychology values complement the previously identified values of operators who seek a lifestyle orientation in their business as opposed to a profit-focused orientation (Ateljevic and Doorne, 2000). This values discussion was hence aligned to the fourth application of positive psychology to tourism: building personal qualities. The values which were identified as shared between the previous tourism work and positive psychology research were: self-regulation, appreciation of beauty, leadership, authenticity, zest, open-mindedness, kindness, persistence and social intelligence. These values could be investigated more closely in future studies, and positive psychology research of optimism, mindfulness and humour may further enhance understandings of the good life of lifestyle business operators. Lastly, it was argued that lifestyle businesses could play a role in not only preserving the good life of their operators but of the communities in which they are embedded. Issues of sustainability, restrained growth and social representation were debated in this final section. Through this shorter community effects discussion, the chapter also addressed the relationships in context application of positive psychology to tourism.

Spa and Wellness Tourism and Positive Psychology

The tourism section concluded with a discussion of contemporary perspectives from positive psychology to spa and wellness tourism. Following an analysis of origins and definitions of spa and wellness tourism, an in-depth discussion of motivation was provided. While the preceding chapters addressed applications such as personal qualities, ethical tourism development, on-site experiences and reflections on pleasure, this contribution addressed the first and seventh area of application of positive psychology to tourism: anticipating experiences and patterns of motivation. The motivation discussion covered the need raised by Bushell (2009) to deal more closely with the questions of motivation in the context of wellness. The recent adaptation of the travel career ladder (Pearce and Caltabriano, 1983) approach, the travel career patterns (TCP) model, was analysed in detail as a model of tourist motivation useful in understanding spa and wellness motives. The model proposes that tourist motivation occurs in a patterned and layered fashion and that it is dependent on previous travel experience. Misunderstandings of the model were clarified and its criticism was addressed. The core tourist motives according to the TCP theory are: escape and relaxation, relationship strengthening and novelty. The model has roots in humanistic psychology, notably the works of Maslow (1954) and his hierarchy of needs. This work is essentially related to positive psychology, for it was Maslow's work that has later influenced the foundations of the positive psychology movement. Examples of motivation studies in spa and wellness tourism with North American and Asian samples were provided. The findings of the studies were related back to the TCP model, confirming the argument that TCP is useful for studying motivation patterns of spa and wellness tourists. The remaining section of the chapter (the mind/body links in the context of spa and wellness tourism) dealt with the physical and mental health benefits of spa and wellness activities. These health benefits remain to be further explored and will be highlighted later in this chapter. A synthesis of the preceding contributions follows.

SYNTHESIS

The summary section has identified a set of contributions that this introductory volume has made. These contributions are presented in Table 8.1 and relate to the ten applications of positive psychology to tourism. The applications and the contributions can further be tied to core research themes from a major handbook of positive psychology by Snyder and Lopez (2002). The main contribution of the first chapter (a historical review of psychology, positive psychology and the intersections with or applications to tourism) is omitted from the table. This is because the applications were identified in this chapter.

The associations from Table 8.1 should be interpreted in a more fluid manner than the table implies. The materialism chapter, for instance, also relates to building personal qualities as it contains a section on education values. Some repetition is also acknowledged (note that the building personal qualities application is linked to both Chapters 4 and 6). Further, the handbook themes were not explicitly examined in the chapters. In essence, the table shows broad commonalties between the

Table 8.1   Positive Psychology and Tourism: Synthesis of the Core Contributions

Contribution	Key application	Positive psychology handbook themes
flow and tourist satisfaction (Chapter 2)	On-site experiences; power of emotions	flow
time and host communities (Chapter 3)	reflections on pleasure; positive individual interventions	compassion, humility
ethics, wisdom, well-being (Chapter 4)	building personal qualities	wisdom, creativity, resilience, positive ethics
materialism and values (Chapter 5)	ethical tourism development; positive institutions	moral motivation
lifestyle businesses (Chapter 6)	building personal qualities; relationships in context	optimism, mindfulness, humour
spa and wellness tourism (Chapter 7)	anticipating experiences; patterns of motivation	goal setting

chapters on one hand and the applications and the handbook themes on the other. A tight interrelationship exists between the two research fields and this is what the synthesis table suggests.

Nevertheless, only select topics from the comprehensive list of positive psychology themes were addressed in our chapters (for a full list of handbook themes, refer to Snyder and Lopez, 2002). Important handbook themes that remain to be explored in future tourism texts are: authenticity from a positive psychology perspective, spirituality, self-esteem, emotional intelligence, self-efficacy and forgiveness (Snyder and Lopez, 2002). A more detailed look at positive emotions (joy, interest, contentment and love), as identified by Fredrickson (2001) and applied in her broaden and build theory, will also be required to better understand the underexplored area of emotions in tourism contexts (Fennell, 2009). A special mention must be made here of the power of mindfulness (Langer, 2009) for providing a key understanding of how individuals can realise more possibilities in their worlds and expand their lives with positive implications for well-being.

Two broad contributions, however, have emerged from this introductory volume and can be drawn from Table 8.1. The first is the positive psychology contribution to understanding values in tourism; the second is a fresh set of conceptual and methodological tools for evaluating the tourist experience and the good life. These synthesised contributions are not meant to represent the totality of the potential value of positive psychology to tourism or the totality of the symbiosis between the two fields but, instead, they represent the two most dominant themes of this text.

Good Values, Education and Positive Psychology

A significant section of this volume was devoted to discussions of values and character strengths that positive psychology has identified. The chapters explained how these values can contribute to education (Chapter 5) and how they are relevant in understanding the value sets of tourism entrepreneurs and host communities (Chapters 3, 4 and 6). The values discussion is most closely linked to the core ideological position taken in this book—tourists, tourism and well-being as seen through Aristotelian versions of the good and noble life—the perspective that has shaped positive psychology theories and models. Similar perspectives are shaping current philosophical thinking in tourism studies. Themes such as rightness, goodness and practical wisdom (phronesis) were recently promoted by Jamal and Menzel (2009) in their discussion of good actions in tourism. Jamal and Menzel outlined three ethical paradigms that are relevant to understanding the notion of good in tourism: the utilitarian ethic of the greatest good, a Kantian ethic of respect for persons and an Aristotelian virtue ethics. In the Aristotelian philosophical discussion, they discussed eudaimonia and virtuous character and it is particularly this ethical paradigm to which this volume on positive psychology has contributed. Table 8.2 presents the values discussed in the chapters in the context of tourism education.

Although Table 8.2 synthesises the values in the context of tourism education, it is of course apparent that positive psychology values do not apply only to this context. Our discussion here deals with education, primarily due to our likely academic and educator audiences seeking to apply and add personal meaning to the topics reviewed. It is argued in the following section that the identified positive psychology character strengths and the transcendent business education values have the potential to complement and further advance the TEFI value set.

Table 8.2   Proposed Values for Tourism Education

Positive psychology character strengths	Transcendent business education values	TEFI values
temperance	empathy	ethics
wisdom and knowledge	generativity	knowledge
humanity	intolerance of ineffective humanity	stewardship
transcendence	civil aspiration	professionalism
justice	mutuality	mutual respect
courage	-	-

In terms of complementing TEFI, some connections are clear; examples include the humanity strength, intolerance of ineffective humanity transcendence value and the TEFI's stewardship value. Intolerance of ineffective humanity is about understanding that singular pursuit of wealth, selfishness and disinterest define poor decision makers (Giacalone, 2004); humanity is similarly defined as a character strength that incorporates love, kindness and social intelligence (being aware of the motives and feelings of self and others) (Peterson and Seligman, 2004). The similar notion of being aware of the needs of others and displaying a humane service to the community is an important aspect of the TEFI's stewardship value (Sheldon, 2008).

Positive psychology also offers the potential to advance the TEFI set. For example, it is worth examining the character strength of courage more closely. Courage (defined as emotional strengths that involve the exercise of will to accomplish goals in the face of opposition) incorporates the qualities of authenticity, bravery, persistence and zest (Peterson and Seligman, 2004). The question can be asked: How often do tourism educators provide a context in which students are encouraged to present openly and critically what they and their subculture value without any implicit limiting evaluations, threats and fear of failure? Courage advances our understanding of the TEFI's knowledge, professionalism and ethics values. Knowledge and professionalism are about critical thinking, innovation and leadership and the TEFI's ethics value is partially about building authenticity and the authentic self. These are qualities that a person with courage would possess. Further, the exercise of the TEFI's stewardship value by students and how they respond to the challenges of humanity as expressed, for example, in the Millennium Development Goals arguably require the character strength of courage. Whereas some students may naturally possess more courage than others, the character strength could be further developed through role plays, interactive activities in tourism classes and by encouraging students to engage in public debates. It is timely then to ponder over some of these linkages even if the connections here have not been empirically tested or if they are not immediately obvious. Such contemplation is necessary for a critical appraisal of the widely promoted TEFI value set and for its potential enrichment. The positive psychology values could also be placed within broader contexts to highlight their contribution to the student education and to the society. An example of the broader context is a set of principles in the higher education management field—the principles of responsible management education (Principles of Responsible Management Education, 2010). Within this broad context, values are incorporated under a set of six principles: principle 1—purpose; principle 2—values; principle 3—method; principle 4—research; principle 5—partnership; and principle 6—dialogue. The discussion of the six principles is beyond the scope of this synthesis, as they are not specifically addressed by the book chapters. Future research could, however, examine the suggested linkages between the TEFI values set on one hand and the positive psychology contribution to the values on the other, as well as their context within some of these broader sets of principles.

Tourist Experiences, the Good Life and Positive Psychology

In addition to the implications of appraising character strengths and values, conceptual and methodological tools have emerged from this volume. These tools assist in understanding the good life in the context of the key tourist experience phases: the motivation/expectations phase, the on-site experience phase and the reflections/memory phase (Larsen, 2007). Table 8.3 presents these conceptual and methodological tools. It is acknowledged that there are some tools that were mentioned in the chapters but are not included in the table because they could not directly be linked to the three phases. A notable omission is the measurement and application of optimism, which was discussed in the context of lifestyle businesses. Optimism is addressed in the forthcoming health section.

In the expectations phase, the TCP motivation model emerging from Maslow's work and positive psychology has been shown to be a useful model for understanding motivation in the context of spa and wellness tourism. This usefulness was demonstrated by comparing the findings of several international studies to the patterns of motivation proposed by the model. Congruence between the findings and the model was highlighted. Notably, the recent thorough study of motivations and characteristics of spa goers (Mak, Wong and Chang, 2009) was compared in detail to the model; although Mak et al. (2009) did not employ TCP methodology, the spa motivation results were framed effectively by the travel career patterns motives.

Table 8.3   Positive Psychology Contributions in the Tourist Experience Phases

Expectations phase	On-site phase	Reflections phase
Travel career patterns (TCP) motivation model for spa and wellness tourism	Flow-state measures and satisfaction	Time
	Creativity, resilience, dealing with challenges	Wisdom
	The ethics of on-site behaviour and tourist consumption	Health benefits

The contribution of the TCP model can be further strengthened by the fact that recent qualitative analyses of perfect days (a common positive psychology motivation assessment approach) have been shown to produce similar results to those proposed by the TCP (Filep and Greenacre, 2007). In the perfect-day analysis, tourists were asked to describe their perfect day at a destination in narrative essays. Through the descriptions of perfect days by a group of tourists, Filep and Greenacre found that the identified perfect-day themes of relationship/belonging, curiosity/mental stimulation, safety/comfort and self-development resembled the core motives suggested by the TCP model: relationship strengthening, novelty, escape/relaxation and the noncore motive of self-actualisation. The TCP's contribution in the context of understanding tourist motivation for well-being is hence meaningful and ongoing.

Positive psychology tools in the second tourist experience phase can also be identified. Flow-state methods (flow interviews, flow-state scales and experience sampling) were discussed as alternative methods for analysing engagement, satisfaction and immediacy at tourist sites. Through a qualitative study in which the positive psychology flow model was employed, immediate satisfaction themes were identified that could not have been uncovered through standard satisfaction measures. There were also further conceptual contributions in this on-site phase study. Certain tourist groups, such as tourists with a disability, face multiple challenges at destinations, and the positive psychology tools on building resilience, creativity and wisdom are appropriate for understanding how the challenges can be overcome. Some fresh perspectives on ethics were also provided and these are relevant to the on-site phase, as shown in Table 8.3. Personal, social and ecological costs of materialistic behaviours of tourists at destinations were highlighted. But the destructive costs can be reduced through a higher awareness of positive psychology values, positive individual interventions with the host communities and through wisdom. Important problems, such as degradation of historic sites, symbols and contexts, the lessening of cultural identity and the provocation of social conflict within a host community, could therefore be tackled through positive psychology.

In the reflections phase, positive psychology conceptual tools (time, wisdom and perspectives on health) assist in understanding the third component of the good life—meaning (Seligman, 2002). Memories that tourists acquire create powerful meanings to them over time (Larsen, 2007). The positive psychology contributions on time perspectives can assist in understanding these memories and meanings better. The time contribution sheds light on the desirability of reaching an equilibrium in regard to the various selves that represent the past, the present and the future (Zimbardo, 2001). Additionally, the contribution on wisdom could assist in further understanding the outcome of engaging in or working in tourism. It was shown, for example, that wisdom, well-being and ethical outcomes are highly interrelated. It was further demonstrated that positive psychology contributes to an understanding of the physical and mental health benefits of holidays, such as spa and wellness tourism holidays (a discussion of health is forthcoming).

So positive psychology presents insightful conceptual and methodological tools for understanding tourists, tourism and the good life in the three experience phases and adds to our appreciation of values. There are at least two promising directions that the future research related to the values and the tourist experience can take. The first is a health direction; the second is a cross-cultural research direction. The rationale for identifying these two directions is that senior scholars in both fields currently see a need to explore these issues not as tangential areas of interest but as major future research agendas.

FUTURE DIRECTION 1: HEALTH RESEARCH

One could argue that time is right for both tourism and positive psychology to deal in detail with the topic of human health. The co-founder of positive psychology, Martin Seligman, has recently mapped out a new field—positive health—which he sees as one that builds on the positive psychology research. He does not predict the end of positive psychology but rather an opportunity for integrating the field within positive health. We are reminded by Seligman (2008: 4) that the World Health Organisation defines health as "a state of complete positive physical, mental and social well-being and not merely the absence of disease or infirmity". Seligman, however, notes that thus far health has been seen as a lack of disease. Hence, he argues, there is a need for positive health—a state beyond the absence of illness. Such a field can be operationalised and each of its components can be measured.

In his conceptual framework, Seligman identifies three kinds of independent variables as parts of positive health: subjective, biological and functional. Subjective variables refer to a person feeling excellent and includes standard positive psychology qualities (examples are optimism and life satisfaction and their measures); biological variables include more traditional and standard health indicators, such as blood pressure analysis, temperature and pulse rate, full blood count, urine analysis, liver function tests and similar health indicators. The last of the variables (the functional variables) includes an array of data relating to human movement (Seligman, 2008): laboratory test data (such as laboratory measures of positive physical capacity in terms of flexibility, walk time, balance, etc.) and the data on an individual's personal ecology (the optimal state of adaptation between bodily functions and physical requirements of one's lifetimes: work, love and play).

In the tourism field, major research interest in the topic of health is also evident. There has been a phenomenal academic and industry rise of research on wellness (Bushell and Sheldon, 2009; Smith and Kelly, 2006), well-being (Gilbert and Abdullah, 2004), welfare (Hall and Brown, 2006), quality of life through tourism (Neal, Uysal and Sirgy, 2007; Sirgy, 2009) and medical tourism (Medical Tourism Association, 2010). All of these are terms and concepts that, at least partially, relate to the subjective and the aforementioned functional variables. The recent book contribution by Smith and Puczkó (2008) on health and wellness tourism and the specific mention in their volume of some health studies in the spa and wellness area are a further testament to the contemporary interest in health.

A series of positive psychology and tourism health studies could be conceived. One idea is to further the understanding of the value of optimism as it applies to lifestyle businesses. In the chapter examining the values of lifestyle business entrepreneurs, a discussion on optimism was provided. It was argued that optimism can be assessed quite efficiently by asking tourism entrepreneurs about the state of their business as it is now and about how its future success is perceived. It was suggested that those individuals who would rate the business as doing very well or well and those who thought the business was currently not doing very well but who thought it would get better can be defined as optimists. The rating questions can be combined with other optimism measures in positive psychology such as the Attribution Style Questionnaire proposed by Seligman (2008) or the Optimism–Pessimism scale used in a study by Kubzansky, Sparrow, Vokonas and Kawachi (2001).

The relationship between optimism and improved health is solid (Seligman, 2008). In Kubzansky's et al.'s (2001) research, a robust positive correlation was found between increasingly high levels of optimism and increased protection against cardiovascular health problems. In an earlier study, dispositional optimism was associated with faster rates of recovery from hospitalisation and a speedy return to normal living (Scheier et al., 1989). More recently, Kubzansky and Thurston (2007) found a solid positive relationship between emotional vitality and the lack of cardiovascular disease.

It may well be argued, then, that by understanding the levels of optimism of tourism entrepreneurs through subjective evaluations (positive psychology measures of optimism) we could better understand the entrepreneurs' biological health. While such studies may appeal to health and medical researchers, they may also be of interest to tourism researchers and practitioners concerned with the issue of work–life balance. For example, the optimism findings might have implications for human resource decision making at larger tourism organisations, such as decisions on staff satisfaction and work stress issues. Optimism therefore is a novel theme for examining the relationship between health and tourism and it can be assessed through different methods. It is appropriate for tourism and positive psychology to advance the topic of human health through detailed studies of optimism.

FUTURE DIRECTION 2: CROSS-CULTURAL RESEARCH

A notable feature of optimism measures, however, as with most positive psychology measures, is that they are necessarily focused on the individual. Within positive psychology, though, as well as within tourism, there is a new trend to take into account collectivist, qualitative and cross-cultural insights and perspectives (Christopher, Richardson and Slife, 2008; Tribe, 2009). Much of the discussion in both fields centres on the idea that Western and largely positivist interpretations of reality are inappropriately dominant in research and are biasing conceptions of happiness, well-being, the good life, tourists, tourism and subsequently good tourists or good tourism (Christopher et al., 2008; Wheeller, 2003).

Within positive psychology, the need for cross-cultural research is reinforced by the argument that non-Western perspectives embellish the field in three main ways. The fresh perspectives provide the conceptual tools to: 1) critique the assumptions and values that shape psychological theory and research; 2) move beyond the dichotomies that underlie Western thought and the individualistic perspectives that arise from those dichotomies; and 3) allow for new ways of thinking about cultural meanings and their manifestations (Christopher and Campbell, 2008; Christopher and Hickinbottom, 2008; Richardson and Guignon, 2008; Slife and Richardson, 2008).

In tourism studies, parallel criticisms exist. In a recent critique of academic tribes, territories and networks in the academy, Tribe (2010) argued that the cultural studies literature provided a useful frame for studying important topics in tourism such as values, race and gender. Similar to the positive psychology critiques, the issue of contextualising knowledge was referred to: "Knowledge rather emanates from somewhere, from someone, from embodied researchers who carry with them acquired cultural blueprints for action" (2010: 15). Tribe then refers to Haraway's (1991) critique of the assumed objectivity of Western conceptions of reality—the "gaze from nowhere", as Haraway puts it. An important message can be drawn from Tribe's paper: ethnocentrism is present in tourism research and, at the very least, researchers should recognise the limitations of their work and their reasoning.

Although the cross-cultural research in psychology was briefly discussed in Chapter 1, the revisiting here is crucial. Future research into non-Western philosophies of the good life in the context of tourists and tourism would be valuable and may fulfil the above demands in both tourism and positive psychology. Seligman's (2002, 2008) conception of the good life has been promoted and defended in this text. As a reminder to the reader, this conception is made up of the pleasant life (positive emotions that explain immediate pleasure), the engaged life (exercise of talent and virtues or 'signature strengths' and can be characterised by the flow state) and the meaningful life (a purpose or a dedication to something larger than oneself). Such a conception of the good life has recently been criticised because it is essentially in line with conceptualising the good life in terms of individual satisfaction: "the notion of a fixed, essential self that is separate from others and the world it inhabits" (Christopher and Hickinbottom, 2008: 566). In our defence, Seligman's (2002) conception of the meaningful life does in fact mention spirituality and the connection towards something greater than oneself—the overarching purpose or the belief in God(s). Further, the three-lives distinction is based on an extensive review of not only previous research in psychology. The conception was based on reviews of research and literature on happiness and well-being from other social sciences, as well as basic interpretations of Eastern philosophies, such as Buddhism (Duckworth, Steen and Seligman, 2005).

Nevertheless, there is room for advancing and understanding the authentic happiness theory (Seligman, 2002) in a more contextualised manner. There is a multitude of non-Western philosophical ideas which could be used to understand the notion of good life. It is impossible to consider all these in a summary chapter. Three broad new themes of future cross-cultural research into good life can, however, be formed. They are presented following and are based on Christopher and Hickinbottom's (2008) critique. These themes can serve as starting points for organising future studies into the cross-cultural applicability of the good life theory in tourism and positive psychology:

1. interconnectedness between the nature and the self;
2. authenticity research, particularly understandings of existential authenticity;
3. realms of meanings investigations.

Future studies could, for example, compare what the meaningful life means to a host community in Bali, Indonesia, as opposed to a Caucasian, and predominantly Anglo-Saxon, host tourism community in Australia. For many Balinese there are two realms of reality (Christopher and Christopher, 2008): *sekala*, the ordinary realm of daily life (one that is visible to most tourists) and *niskala,* the spiritual world and a deeper level of reality that is invisible to the untrained but which influences what happens in *sekala*: "It is not possible for the Balinese to talk or think about the self, emotions, illness, well-being or the good life without reference to Hinduism and a shared understanding of *niskala*" (Christopher and Hickinbottom, 2008: 571). Such comparisons and investigations might reveal different layers of the meaningful life. The depth and complexity of the topics such as spirituality and meaning also open the door to new methodological approaches beyond the traditional, commonly used quantitative, positive psychology assessments. Action research, cognitive mapping and observational techniques could successfully complement or replace the traditional, quantitative research instruments. Ryan, Gu and Wei (2009) reiterate these themes in the context of tourism research in China. They observe:

China . . . potentially offers many gifts for western researches through forcing a re-evaluation and questioning of taken for granted assumptions about the research paradigms used and the cultural milieu in which they are formed. (2009: 336)

Addressing ethnocentrism as it applies to tourism and positive psychology is an evolving process, and sharing the richness of positive psychology with international tourism researchers can be a part of this mutual development effectively enhancing approaches and tools to study what different cultures view as the good life.

CONCLUDING REMARKS

The future research directions, the syntheses and the contributions of the volume have now been outlined. In these concluding remarks it may be worthwhile addressing key criticisms of various forms of good or alternative tourism (Butcher, 2003; Wheeller, 2003). Despite expressing our awareness of the limitations of the good life theory proposed, this book might fall into one of Jim Butcher's or Brian Wheeller's categories of the "preachy, good, tourism books". Key criticisms of these books are that the previous contributions to good tourism (such as the one by Wood and House, 1991) have been divorced from the harsh realities of tourism, that they are stating nothing new and that they are idealistic. Butcher and Wheeller both skilfully paint a fairly depressing picture of the world of tourists and tourism, implying that some of these research endeavours are futile. So let us imagine an alternative world of tourism research for a moment. The world of tourism research in which no new books on welfare, well-being, happiness, quality of life through tourism, good and alternative tourism are produced and in which no new academic ideas on sustainability are created and shared with others. In this world there would be no point in producing these academic contributions because there would be a prevailing belief that their contents are too idealistic and divorced from reality. There would be no need to try. Our point here is simple—while constructive criticism of any new field and research direction should be encouraged, some new concepts and ideas should be given a chance to develop so that we avoid a significant destructive outcome: little or no new academic knowledge on tourism and the good life to share with others. Optimism, we have said, is an important positive psychology construct and we need to share this value, embody it and express it in the work we conduct.

The positive psychology movement is now global; the researchers in this field display a strong commitment towards advancing their knowledge of positive dimensions of human existence because people desire well-being in its own right, above and beyond the relief of suffering (Seligman, 2008). As many new research areas in tourism, the positive psychology field may need to first develop in the realms of academic discussions and later in more practical and applied realms; the name itself might change to positive health (Seligman, 2008) or another variant, but its foundations are solid. The field displays evidence that it is not divorced from the reality of implementation as critics might suggest. For example, the integration of the positive psychology materials into tourism lecture units could commence in a class almost immediately, following a critical appraisal of such materials by tourism educators. This integration would be in line with the value-based orientation that is currently being promoted by senior and well-established tourism scholars globally.

Suffering is an important topic, but one that has been extensively addressed in psychology. In the tourism field, suffering and the problems of tourism are also sometimes relevant topics for discussions. We do believe, however, that suffering and problems are against the basic tenets of tourism. In the phenomenon we study, the production of fun, satisfaction and well-being are central concerns. Disneyland, for example, likes to remind us that it is the happiest place on earth. More broadly, tourism is a global mechanism for the production of the good life (positive emotions, engagement and meaning), and positive psychology is an appropriate lens through which this global phenomenon can be studied, understood and enhanced.

Bibliography

Aas, C., Ladkin, A., and Fletcher, J. (2005). Stakeholder collaboration and heritage management. *Annals of Tourism Research, 32*, 28–48.

Abeyraine, R. I. R. (1995). Proposal and guidelines for carriage of elderly and disabled persons by air. *Journal of Tourism Research, 33*, 52–59.

Allen, L. R., Long, P. T., Perdue, R. R., and Kieselbach, S. (1988). The impact of tourism development on residents' perceptions of community life. *Journal of Travel Research, 27*, 16–21.

Altman, N. (2000). *Healing springs—the ultimate guide to taking the waters—from Hidden Springs to the world's greatest spas*. Rochester, VT: Healing Arts Press.

Amiable, T. M. (1983). *The social psychology of creativity*. New York: Springer-Verlag.

Amiable, T. M. (1996). *Creativity in contexts*. Boulder, CO: Westview.

Andrews, R., Baum, T., and Andrew, M. A. (2001). The lifestyle economics of small tourism businesses. *Journal of Travel and Tourism Research, 1*, 16–25.

Ap, J., and Crompton, J. L. (1993). Residents' strategies for responding to tourism impacts. *Journal of Travel Research, 32*, 47–50.

Applegate, J. F., and Clarke, K. E. (1987). Satisfaction levels of birdwatchers: An observation on the consumptive-nonconsumptive continuum. *Leisure Sciences, 21*, 81–102.

Aramberri, J. (2001). The host should get lost. Paradigms in the tourism theory. *Annals of Tourism Research, 28*(3): 738–761.

Aramberri, J. (2007). Unpublished letter to the president of the International Academy for the Study of Tourism of 8 May that was subsequently circulated to the membership on 9 May.

Argyle, M. (1975). *Bodily communication*. London: Methuen.

Argyle, M. (1996). *The social psychology of leisure*. London: Penguin.

Argyle, M. (1999). Causes and correlates of happiness. In D. Kahneman, E. Diener and N. Schwartz (eds.), *Well-being: The foundations of hedonic psychology* (pp. 3553–373). New York: Russell Sage Foundation.

Argyle, M. (2002). *The psychology of happiness* (3rd. ed.). London: Methuen.

Argyle, M., and Crossland, J. (1985). The dimensions of positive emotions. *British Journal of Social Psychology, 26*, 127–137.

Argyle, M., and Henderson, M. (1985). *The anatomy of relationships*. Harmondsworth, UK: Penguin.

Argyle, M., Martin, M., and Lui, L. (1995). Testing for stress and happiness: The role of social and cognitive factors. In C. D. Spielberger and I. G. Sarason (eds.), *Stress and emotion* (pp. 173–187). Washington, DC: Taylor & Francis.

Aristotle. (1955). *The ethics of Aristotle—the Nicomachean ethics*. Trans. J. A. K. Thomson. London: Penguin.

Ashoff, J. (1985). On the perception of time during prolonged temporal isolation. *Human Neurobiology, 4,* 41–52.

Ateljevic, I. (2009). Transmodernity: Remaking our (tourism) world. In J. Tribe (ed.), *Philosophical issues in tourism* (pp. 278–300). Bristol, UK: Channel View.

Ateljevic, I., and Doorne, S. (2000). 'Staying within the fence': Lifestyle entrepreneurship in tourism. *Journal of Sustainable Tourism, 8*(5): 378–392.

Ateljevic, I., Pritchard, A., and Morgan, N. (eds.). (2007) *The critical turn in tourism studies—innovative research methodologies.* Amsterdam: Elsevier.

Babakus, E., and Boller, G. W. (1992). An empirical assessment of SERVQUAL. *Journal of Business Research, 24,* 253–268.

Baloglu, S., and Uysal, M. (1996). Market segments of push and pull motivations: A canonical correlation approach. *International Journal of Contemporary Hospitality Management, 8*(3): 32–38.

Baltes, P., Gluck, J., and Kunzmann, U. (2002). Wisdom. In C. R. Snyder and S. J. Lopez (eds.), *Handbook of positive psychology* (pp. 327–347). Oxford, UK: Oxford University Press.

Baltes, P. B., Glick, J., and Kunzmann, U. (2002). Wisdom: Its structure and function in successful life-span development. In C. R. Snyder and S. J. Lopez (eds.), *Handbook of positive psychology* (pp. 327–350). New York: CUP.

Baltes, P. B., and Staudinger, U. M. (eds.). (1996). *Interactive minds: Life-span perspectives on the social foundations of cognition.* New York: CUP.

Baltes, P. B., and Staudinger, U. M. (2003). Wisdom: A metaheuristic (pragmatic) to orchestrate mind and virtue toward excellence. *American Psychologist, 55,* 122–136.

Banks, R. (1983). *The tyranny of time.* Downers Grove, IL: InterVarsity Press.

Bao, J. G., and Su, X. B. (2004). Studies on tourism commercialization in historic towns. *Acta Geographica Sinica, 59*(3): 427–436 (in Chinese).

Baoying, N., and Yuanqing, H. (2007). Tourism development and water pollution: Case study in Lijiang Ancient Town. *China Population, Resources and Environment, 17*(5): 123–127.

Barsky, J., and Nash, L. (2002). Evoking emotion: Affective keys to hotel loyalty. *Cornell Hotel and Restaurant Administration Quarterly, 1,* 39–46.

Batson, C. D., Ahmad, N., Lishner, D. A., and Tsang, J. A. (2002). Empathy and altruism. In C. R. Snyder and S. J. Lopez (eds.), *Handbook of positive psychology* (pp. 485–498). London: Oxford University Press.

Bauer, I. (2008). The health impact of tourism on local and indigenous populations in resource-poor countries. *Travel Medicine and Infectious Disease, 6,* 276–291.

Bauer, T., and McKercher, R. (eds.). (2003). *Sex and tourism: Journeys of romance, love and lust.* Binghamton, NY: Haworth.

Baum, T. (2007). Human resources in tourism: Still waiting for change. *Tourism and Management, 28*(6):1383–1399.

Baumgarten, A. (1936; first published 1735). Reflections on poetry. In B. Croce (ed.), Aesthetica. Rome: Bari.

Beardsley, M. C. (1982). Some persistent issues in aesthetics. In M. J. Wreen and D. M. Callen (eds.), *The aesthetic point of view.* Ithaca, NY: Cornell University Press.

Becher, A., and Trowler, J. (2003). *Academic tribes and territories.* Milton, UK: Open University Press.

Beeton, S. (2000). 'It's a wrap'. But what happens after the film crew leaves? An examination of community responses to film induced tourism in Lights, Camera, Action: Spotlight on tourism in the new millennium (pp127–136). *31st Annual Proceedings of the Travel and Tourism Research Association,* San Fernando Valley, California.

Befus, D., Mescon, T., Vozikis, G., and Mescon, D. (1988). The characteristics of expatriate entrepreneurs. *International Small Business Journal, 6*, 33–44.

Belk, R. W. (1985). Materialism: Trait aspects of living in the material world. The Journal of Consumer Research, *12*(3): 265–280.

Belk, R. W. (1988). Possessions and the extended self. *Journal of Consumer Research, 15*(2): 139–168.

Benckendorff, P., Moscardo, G., and Murphy, L. (2006). Visitor perceptions of technology use in tourist attraction experiences. In G. Papageorgiou (ed.), *Proceedings of cutting edge research in tourism: New directions, challenges and applications*, 6–9 June 2006. Surrey, UK: The School of Management, University of Surrey.

Ben-Shahar, T. (2006). *Psychology 1504—Positive psychology: Lecture schedule outline.* Harvard University. Available: http://isites.harvard.edu/fs/docs/icb.topic134044.files/1504-Syllabus-2006.htm.

Ben-Shahar, T. (2007). *Happier.* Maidenhead, UK: McGraw-Hill.

Berkman, L. F., and Syme, S. L. (1994). Social networks, host resistance, and mortality: A nine year follow-up study of Alameda County residents. In A. Steptoe and J. Wardle (eds.), *Psychosocial processes and health: A reader* (pp. 43–67). New York: CUP.

Black, N., and Rutledge, J. (1996). *Outback tourism.* Townsville, QLD: JCU Tourism.

Blalock, H. (1967). *Theory construction: From verbal to mathematical formulations.* Englewood Cliffs, NJ: Prentice Hall.

Blazer, D. G. (1981). Social support and mortality in an elderly community population. *Dissertations Abstracts International 42* (2-B): 579.

Boniwell, I., and Zimbardo, P. G. (2004). Balancing TP in pursuit of optimal functioning. In D. A. Linley, S. Joseph and I. Boniwell (eds.), *Putting positive psychology in practice.* Hoboken, NJ: Wiley.

Borgmann, A. (2000). The moral complexion of consumption. *Journal of Consumer Research, 26*(2): 418–422.

Boring, E. G. (1950). *A history of experimental psychology* (2nd ed.). New York: Appleton-Century-Crofts.

Böröcz, J. (1996). *Leisure migration: A sociological study on tourism.* New York: Pergamon Press.

Botterill, D. (1987). Dissatisfaction with a construction of satisfaction. *Annals of Tourism Research, 14*(1): 139–141.

Botterill, D. (2007). A realist critique of the situated voice in tourism studies. In I. Ateljevic, A. Pritchard and N. Morgan (eds.), *The critical turn in tourism studies—innovative research methodologies* (pp. 119–129). Amsterdam: Elsevier.

Bowen, D., and Clarke, J. (2009). *Contemporary tourist behaviour.* Wallingford, Oxon, UK: CABI.

Branson, R. (2009). *Business stripped bare.* London: Virgin Books.

Bratec, M. (2008). *Sustaining through gastronomy: The case of slow food movement in Slovenia, its impacts on socio-cultural environments and tourism development.* Paper presented to BEST EN Think Tank VIII—Sustaining Quality of Life through Tourism conference, 24–27 June, Izmir, Turkey: Izmir University of Economics.

Bright, M. A. (2002). *Holistic health and healing.* Philadelphia: F. A. Davis Company.

Brooks, C., and Manza, J. (1994). Do changing values explain the new politics? A critical assessment of the postmaterialist thesis. *Sociological Quarterly, 35*(4): 541–570.

Brown, K. W., and Ryan, R. M. (2003). The benefits of being present: Mindfulness and its role in psychological well-being. Journal of Personality and Social Psychology, *84*(4): 822–848.

Brown, T. J., Churchill, G. A., and Peter, J. P. (1993). Improving the measurement of service quality. *Journal of Retailing, 69*(1): 127–139.

Bryman, A. (2004). *The Disneyization of society.* London: Sage.

Buhalis, D., and Costa, C. (eds.). (2006). *Tourism business frontiers: Consumers, products and industry.* Amsterdam: Elsevier.

Burnett, J. J., and Baker, H. B. (2001). Assessing the travel-related needs of the mobility-disabled consumer. *Journal of Travel Research, 40*, 4–11.

Burroughs, J. E., and Rindfleisch, A.(2002). Materialism and well-being: A conflicting values perspective. *Journal of Consumer Research, 29*(3): 348–370.

Bushell, R. (2009). Quality of life, tourism and wellness. In R. Bushell and P. Sheldon (eds.), *Wellness and tourism: Mind, body, spirit, place* (pp. 19–36). New York: Cognizant Communication Corporation.

Bushell, R., and Sheldon, P. (eds.), (2009). *Wellness and tourism: Mind, body, spirit, place.* New York: Cognizant Communication Corporation.

Butcher, J. (2003). *The moralisation of tourism—sun, sand . . . and saving the world?* New York: Routledge.

Butcher, J. (2009). Against ethical tourism. In J. Tribe (ed.), *Philosophical issues in tourism* (pp. 244–260). Bristol, UK: Channel View.

Butler, R. (1999). Sustainable tourism: A state-of-the-art review. *Tourism Geographies, 1*(1): 7–25.

Butler, R. (ed.). (2006). *The tourism area life cycle, Vol. 2: Conceptual and theoretical issues.* Clevedon, UK: Channel View.

Carson, S. H., and Langer, E. J. (2006). *Mindfulness and self-acceptance. Journal of Rational-Emotive and Cognitive-Behavior Therapy, 24*(1): 29–43.

Carstensen, L. L. (1995). Evidence for a life-span theory of socioemotional selectivity. *Current Directions in Psychological Science, 4*, 151–156.

Carstensen, L. L. (1998). A life-span approach to social motivation. In J. Heckhausen and C. S. Dwerk (eds.), *Motivation and self-regulation across the life-span.* New York: CUP.

Carstensen, L. L., and Fredrickson, B. L. (1998). Influence of HIV status and age on cognitive representation of others. *Health Psychology, 17*, 494–503.

Carstensen, L. L., Isaacowitz, D. M., and Charles, S. T. (1999). Taking time seriously: A theory of socioemotional selectivity. *American Psychologist, 54*, 165–181.

Carstensen, L. L., Pasupathi, M., Mayr, U., and Nesselroade, J. R. (2000). Emotional experience in everyday life across the adult life-span. *Journal of Personality and Social Psychology, 79*, 644–655.

Cassel, J. (1990). The contribution of the social environment to host resistance. In R. E. Ornstein and C. Swencionis (eds.), *The healing brain: A scientific reader* (pp. 31–42). New York: Guilford Press.

Cassell, E. J. (2002). Compassion. In C. R. Snyder and S. J. Lopez (eds.), *Handbook of positive psychology* (pp. 434–445). London: Oxford University Press.

Cavinato, J., and Cuckovich, M. (1992). Transportation and tourism for the disabled: An assessment. *Transport Journal, 31*, 46–53.

Charles, S. T. (2005). Viewing injustice: Greater emotion heterogeneity with age. *Psychology and Aging, 20*, 159–164.

Chen, J. S., and Prebensen, N. (2009). Wellness as tourist motivation: Case of Taiwan. In R. Bushell and P. Sheldon (eds.), *Wellness and tourism: Mind, body, spirit, place* (pp. 231–238). New York: Cognizant Communication Corporation.

Childress, R. D., and Crompton, J. L. (1997). A comparison of alternative direct and discrepancy approaches to measuring quality of performance at a festival. *Journal of Tourism Research, 36*(2): 43–57.

Christopher, A. N., Saliba, L., and Deadmarsh, E. J. (2009). Materialism and well-being: The mediating effect of locus of control. *Personality and Individual Differences, 46*(7): 682–686.

Christopher, J. C., and Campbell, R. L. (2008). An interactivist-hermeneutic metatheory for positive psychology. *Theory and Psychology, 18*(5): 675–697.

Christopher, J. C., and Christopher, S. (2008). *Moral visions of well-being and health among traditional healers and their patients in Bali and Thailand.* Manuscript in preparation.

Christopher, J. C., and Hickinbottom, S. (2008). Positive psychology, ethnocentrism, and the disguised ideology of individualism. *Theory and Psychology, 18*(5): 563–589.

Christopher, J. C., Richardson, F. C., and Slife, B. D. (2008). Thinking through positive psychology. *Theory and Psychology, 18*(5): 555–561.

Clark, C. C. (1986). *Wellness nursing: Concepts, theory, research and practice.* New York: Springer Publishing Company.

Clarke, J. (2007). *Older white women join Kenya's sex tourists.* Reuters. Available: http://www.reuters.com/article/idUSN2638979720071126?sp=true.

Clawson, M., and Knetsch, J. L. (1966). *Economics of outdoor recreation.* Baltimore: Johns Hopkins Press.

Clayton, V. P., and Birren, J. E. (1980). The development of wisdom across the lifespan: A re-examination of an ancient topic. In P. B. Baltes and O. G. Brim, Jr. (eds.), *Lifespan development and behavior* (Vol. 3; pp. 103–135). New York: Academic Press.

Cobb, S. (1976). Social support as a moderator of life stress. *Psychosomatic Medicine, 38,* 300–314.

Cohen, E. (1988). Authenticity and commoditization in tourism. *Annals of Tourism Research, 15,* 371–386.

Cohen, E. (2004). Backpacking: Diversity and change. *Tourism and Cultural Change, 1, 2,* 95–110.

Cohen, E. (2004). *Contemporary tourism: diversity and change.* Amsterdam: Elsevier.

Cohen, E. (forthcoming). Tourism, leisure and authenticity. *Annals of Tourism Research.*

Cole, V., and Sinclair, A. J. (2002). Measuring the ecological footprint of a Himalayan tourist center. *Mountain Research and Development, 22*(2): 132–141.

Coleman, R. (2005). *UNT professor gives advice for holiday overspending recovery.* Available: http://www.unt.edu/inhouse/january282005/christmas-debt.htm.

Collia, D. V., Sharp, J., and Giesbrecht, L. (2003). The 2001 national household travel survey: A look into the travel patterns of older Americans. *Journal of Safety Research, 34,* 461–470.

Coomansingh, J. (2004). The nasty side of tourism development: An example from Trinidad and Tobago. *eReview of Tourism Research, 2,* 1–7.

Cooper, C. L. (1998). *Theories of organizational stress.* New York: OUP.

Cooper, C. L., and Payne, R. (eds.). (1991). *Personality and stress: Individual differences in the stress process.* Chichester, UK: Wiley.

Cooper, V. (1996). *Laying the foundation: Policies and procedures for volunteer programs.* Calgary: Glenbow Museum, Art gallery, Library and Archives.

Correia, A., and Moital, M. (2009). Antecedents and consequences of prestige motivation in tourism: An expectancy-value motivation. In M. Kozak and A. DeCrop (eds.), *Handbook of tourist behaviour theory and practice* (pp. 16–32). New York: Routledge.

Costanza, R., Fisher, B., Ali, S., Beer, C., Bond, L., Boumans, R., et al. (2007). Quality of life: An approach integrating opportunities, human needs, and subjective well-being. *Ecological Economics, 61,* 267–276.

Cottrell, S., Pearce, P. L., and Arntzen, J. (2008). Tourism as an income earner. *Botswana Notes and Records, 39,* 13–22.

Coutu, D. L. (2002). How resilience works. *Harvard Business Review, 80,* 46–55.

Coyle, A., and Olsen, C. (2005). Research in therapeutic practice settings: Ethical considerations. In R. Tribe and J. Morrissey (eds.), *Handbook of professional and ethical practice for psychologists, counsellors and psychotherapists* (pp. 249–262). Hove, UK: Brunner-Routledge.

Coyle, A., and Rafalin, D. (2000). Jewish gay men's accounts of negotiating cultural, religious and sexual identity: A qualitative study. *Journal of Psychology and Human Sexuality, 12*(4): 21–48.

Critchley, S. (2006). *On humour.* London: Routledge.

Crompton, J. (1979). Motivations for pleasure vacation. *Annals of Tourism Research, 6*(1): 408–424.

Crompton, J., and Love, L. L. (1995). The predictive validity of alternate approaches to evaluating quality of a festival. *Journal of Travel Research, 34,* 11–25.

Cronin, J. J., and Taylor, S. A. (1994). SERVPERF versus SERVQUAL: Reconciling performance-based and perception-minus-expectations measurement of service quality. *Journal of Marketing, 58,* 125–131.

Crossley, J., and Xu, Z. (1996). Three satisfaction models compared in surveys of Taiwanese tourists. *Visions of Leisure and Business, 15*(2): 4–14.

Csikszentmihalyi, M. (1975). *Beyond boredom and anxiety.* San Francisco: Jossey-Bass.

Csikszentmihalyi, M. (1982). *Beyond boredom and anxiety* (2nd ed.). San Francisco: Jossey Bass.

Csikszentmihalyi, M. (1990). *Flow: The psychology of optimal experience.* New York: HarperCollins.

Csikszentmihalyi, M. (1997). *Creativity: Flow and the psychology of discovery and invention.* New York: HarperCollins.

Csikszentmihalyi, M. (1999). If we are so rich, why aren't we happy? *American Psychologist, 54*(10): 821–827.

Csikszentmihalyi, M. (2000). *Beyond boredom and anxiety.* San Francisco: Jossey-Bass.

Csikszentmihalyi, M., and Csikszentmihalyi, I. (eds.), (2006). *A life worth living: Contributions to positive psychology* (pp. 200–214). Oxford, UK: Oxford University Press.

Csikszentmihalyi, M., and Larson, R. (1987). Validity and reliability of the experience-sampling method. *Journal of Nervous and Mental Diseases, 175,* 526–536.

Csikszentmihalyi, M., and LeFevre, J. (1989). Optimal experience in work and leisure. *Journal of Personality and Social Psychology, 56*(5): 815–822

Csikszentmihalyi, M., and Massimini, F. (1985). On the psychological selection of bio-cultural perspective. *American Psychologist, 55,* 115–138.

Csikszentmihalyi, M., and Rathunde, K. (1993). The measurement of flow in everyday life: Toward a theory of emergent motivation. In J. E. Jacobs (ed.), *Nebraska Symposium on Motivation, 1992: Developmental perspectives on motivation* (pp. 57–97). Lincoln: University of Nebraska Press.

Csikszentmihalyi, M., and Robinson, R. E. (1990). *The art of seeing—an interpretation of the aesthetic encounter.* Los Angeles: The J. Paul Getty Museum.

Csikszentmihalyi, M., and Rochberg-Halton, E. (1981). *The meaning of things: Domestic symbols and the self.* Cambridge, UK: Cambridge University Press.

Cummins, R. (2009). *The influence of tourism on the subjective well-being of host communities*. Exploring Well-Being Seminar, Melbourne, Australia: Victoria University.

Cunningham, I. (1999). Human resource management in the volunteer sector: Challenges and opportunities. *Public Money and Management* (April–June): 19–25.

Dahlsgaard, K., Petersen, C., and Seligman, M. (2005). Shared virtue: The convergence of valued human strengths across culture and history. *Review of General Psychology, 9*(3): 203–213.

Dalton, R. J. (1996). *Citizen politics: Public opinion and political parties in advanced industrial democracies*. Chatham, NJ: Chatham House.

Daniel, Y. (1996). Tourism dance performances: Authenticity and creativity. *Annals of Tourism Research, 23*, 780–797.

Dann, G. (1996). The people of tourist brochures. In T. Selwyn (ed.), *The tourist image: Myths and myth making in tourism* (pp. 61–82). West Sussex, UK: Wiley.

Dann, G. (2009). How international is the International Academy for the Study of Tourism? *Tourism Analysis, 14*(1): 3–13.

Dann, G. M. S. (1977). Anomie, ego-enhancement and tourism. *Annals of Tourism Research, 4*(4): 184–194.

Dann, G., Nash, D., and Pearce, P. (1988). Methodology in tourism research. *Annals of Tourism Research, 15*(1): 1–28.

Dann, G. M. S., and Nordstrand, K. B. (2009). Promoting tourism via multi-sensory tourism. In R. Bushell and P. Sheldon (eds.), *Wellness and tourism: Mind, body, spirit, place* (pp. 125–137). New York: Cognizant Communication Corporation.

Dann, G., and Phillips, J (2001). Qualitative tourism research in the late twentieth century and beyond. In B. Faulkner, G. Moscardo and E. Laws (eds.), *Tourism in the 21st century*. London: Continuum.

Darcy, S. (2002). Marginalised participation: Physical disability, high support needs and tourism. *Journal of Hospitality and Tourism Management, 9*, 61–72.

Daruwalla, P., and Darcy, S. (2005). Personal and societal attitudes to disability. *Annals of Tourism Research, 32*, 549–570.

Darwin, C. (1872). *The expression of emotions in man and animals*. Chicago: University of Chicago Press.

Dawkins, R. (2009). *The greatest show on earth: The evidence for evolution*. London: Bantam Press.

De Botton, A. (2002). *The art of travel*. London: Penguin.

De Botton, A. (2009). *A week at the airport: A Heathrow diary*. London: Profile Books.

Deery, M., and Jago, L. K. (2001). Hotel management style: A study of employee perceptions and preferences. *Hospitality Management, 20*, 325–338.

Dickinson, J. E., Calver, S., Watters, K., and Wilkes, K. (2004). Journeys to heritage attractions in the UK: A case study of national tourist property visitors in the south west. *Journal of Transport Geography, 12*, 103–113.

Dickinson, J. E. (2007). 'Travelling slowly': Slow forms of travel as holiday experiences. In Extraordinary Experiences Conference: Managing the consumer experience in hospitality, leisure, sport, tourism, retail and events, 3–4 September 2007, Bournemouth University, England.

Di Domenico, M. (2005). Producing hospitality, consuming lifestyles: Lifestyle entrepreneurship in urban Scotland. In E. Jones and C. Haven-Tang (eds.), *Tourism SMEs, Service Quality and Destination Competitiveness* (pp. 109–122). Oxford, UK: CABI.

Diener, C., and Suh, E. (1997). Subjective well-being and age: An intergenerational analysis. In K. W. Schaie and M. P. Lawnton (eds.), *Annual Review of Gerontology and Geriatrics, 8*, 304–324.

Diener, E. (1995). Methodological pitfalls and solutions in satisfaction research. In M. J. Sirgy and A. C. Samli (eds.), *New dimensions in marketing and quality of life research* (pp. 27–46). Westford, CT: Quorum Books.

Diener, E. (1999). Subjective well-being: Three decades of progress. *Psychological Bulletin, 125*, 276–301.

Diener, E. (2000). Subjective well-being: The science of happiness and a proposal for a national index. *American Psychologist, 55*, 56–67.

Diener, E., and Biswas-Diener, R. (2008). *Happiness: Unlocking the mysteries of psychological wealth*. Hoboken, NJ: Wiley.

Diener, E., and Seligman, M. E. P. (2002). Very happy people. *Psychological Science, 13*, 81–84.

Dillon, D. (2009). *Values: Dollars, trees or feelings?* BEST EN Think Tank IX Conference: The Importance of Values in Sustainable Tourism, June 15–18. Singapore: James Cook University.

Djikic, M., and Langer, E. J. (2007). Toward mindful social comparisons: When subjective and objective selves are mutually exclusive. New Ideas in Psychology, 25, 221–232.

Downward, P., and Mearman, A. (2004). On tourism and hospitality management research: A critical realist proposal. *Tourism and Hospitality Planning and Development, 1*(2): 107–122.

Drake, D., Pratt, J. B., Rogers, A. K., Santayana, G., Sellars, R. W., Strong, C. A., et al. (1920). *Essays in critical realism*. New York: Macmillan.

Duckworth, L. A., Steen, T. A., and Seligman, M. E. P. (2005). Positive psychology in clinical practice. *Annual Review of Clinical Psychology, 1*, 629–651.

Dunn, H. L. (1961). *High-level wellness*. Arlington, VA: Beatty Press.

Eaker, E., Pinsker, J., and Castelli, W. (1992). Myocardial infarction and coronary death among women: Psychosocial predictors from a 20 year follow-up of women in the Framingham Study. *American Journal of Epidemiology, 135*(8): 854–864.

Easterling, D. (2005). Residents and tourism: What is really at stake? *Journal of Travel and Tourism Marketing, 18*, 63–78.

Ekman, P., and Davidson, R. J. (eds.). (1994). *The nature of emotion: Fundamental questions*. New York: Oxford University Press.

Elkington, J. (1997). *Cannibals with forks: The triple bottom line of 21st century business*. Oxford, UK: Capstone.

Elliot, R., Fischer, C. T., and Rennie, D. L. (1999). Evolving guidelines for publication of qualitative research studies in psychology and related fields. *British Journal of Clinical Psychology, 38*, 215–229.

Emmons, R. A., and McCullough, M. E. (2003). Counting blessings versus burdens: An experimental investigation of gratitude and subjective well-being in daily life. *Journal of Personality and Social Psychology, 84*(2): 377–389.

Engwall, D. (2009). *PSY 444: Positive psychology: Lecture schedule outline*. Central Connecticut State University. Available: www.psychology.ccsu.edu/engwall/P444Spr09.doc.

Enloe, C. (2002). The prostitute, the colonel and the nationalist. In C. Enloe, *Maneuvers: The international politics of militarising women's lives* (pp. 19–41). Los Angeles: University of California Press.

Entwhistle, N. J. (1981). *Styles of learning and teaching*. Chichester, UK: Wiley.

Entwhistle, N., and Ramsden, P. (1983). *Understanding student learning*. London: Croom-Helm.

Eppel, D., Bandura, A., and Zimbardo, P. G. (1999). Escaping homelessness: The influence of self-efficacy and time perspectives on coping with homelessness. *Journal of Applied Psychology, 29,* 575–596.

Erfurt-Cooper, P. (2009). Use of natural hot and mineral springs throughout history. In P. Erfurt-Cooper and M. Cooper, *Health and wellness tourism* (pp. 49–109). Bristol, UK: Channel View.

Erfurt-Cooper, P., and Cooper, M. (2009). *Health and wellness tourism.* Bristol, UK: Channel View.

Etzion, D. (2003). Annual vacation: Duration of relief from job stressors and burnout. *Anxiety, Stress and Coping, 16*(2): 213–226.

Evans-Pritchard, D. (1989). How "they" see "us": Native American images of tourists. *Annals of Tourism Research, 16,* 89–105.

Eysenck, H. J. (1995). *Genius: The natural history of genius.* Cambridge: CUP.

Farr. R. M. (1993). Theory and method in the study of social representations. In G. M. Breakwell and D. V. Canter (eds.), *Empirical approaches to social representations.* Oxford: Clarendon Press.

Farr, R. M. (1994). *The roots of modern social psychology.* Oxford: Blackwell.

Faulkner, B., and Tidswell, C. (1997). A framework for monitoring the community impacts of tourism. *Journal of Sustainable Tourism, 5,* 2–28.

Fennell, D. A. (1999). *Ecotourism: An introduction.* London: Routledge.

Fennell, D. (2009). Ethics and tourism. In J. Tribe (ed.), *Philosophical issues in tourism* (pp. 211–226). Bristol, UK: Channel View.

Fennell, D. A. (2009). The nature of pleasure in pleasure travel. *Tourism Recreation Research, 34*(2): 123–134.

Fennell, D. A., and Malloy, D. C. (1999). Measuring the ethical nature of tourism operators. *Annals of Tourism Research, 26*(4): 928–943.

Filep, S. (2007). 'Flow', sightseeing, satisfaction and personal development: Exploring relationships via positive psychology. In *Proceedings of 2007 Council for Australian University Tourism and Hospitality Education (CAUTHE): Tourism—past achievements, future challenges,* 11–14 February. Sydney, NSW: University of Technology, Sydney and the University of New South Wales.

Filep, S., and Greenacre, L. (2007). Evaluating and extending the travel career patterns model. *TOURISM: An International Interdisciplinary Journal, 55*(1): 23–38.

Finegan, J. (1994). The impact of personal values on judgments of ethical behavior in the workplace . *Journal of Business Ethics, 13*(9): 747–755

Flax, J. (1992). The end of innocence. In J. Butler and J. W. Scott (eds.), *Feminists theorize the political* (pp. 445–463). London: Routledge.

Fleischer, A., and Rivlin, J. (2009). More or better? Quantity and quality issues in tourism consumption. *Journal of Travel Research, 47*(3): 285–294.

Folbre, N. (2009). *Sin cycle: When greed isn't good.* Available: http://economix. blogs.nytimes.com/2009/03/05/sin-cycle-when-greed-isnt-good/.

Fotsch, P. (2004). Tourism's uneven impact—the history of Cannery Row. *Annals of Tourism Research, 31,* 779–800.

Franklin, A. (2002). *Nature and social theory.* London: Sage.

Franklin, A., and Crang, M. (2001). The trouble with tourism and travel theory. *Tourist Studies, 1*(1): 5–22.

Fredrickson, B. L. (1998).What good are positive emotions? *Review of General Psychology, 2,* 300–319.

Fredrickson, B. L. (2001). The role of positive emotions in positive psychology—the broaden-and-build theory of positive emotions. *American Psychologist, 56*(3): 218–226.

Fredrickson, B. L., and Losada, M. F. (2005). Positive affect and the complex dynamics of human flourishing. *American Psychologist, 60*(7): 678–686.

Fung, H. H., and Carstensen, L. L, (2006). Goals change when life's fragility is primed: Lessons learned from older adults, the September 11th attacks and SARS. *Social Cognition and Aging, 24,* 248–278.

Furnham, A. (2009). *50 psychology ideas you really need to know.* London: Quercus.

Gable, S. L., and Haidt, J. (2005). What (and why) is positive psychology? *Review of General Psychology, 9*(2): 103–110.

Gardner, H. (1993). *Creating minds: An anatomy of creativity seen through the lives of Freud, Einstein, Picasso, Stravinsky, Eliot, Graham and Ghandi.* New York: Basic Books.

Gergen, K. (1983). *Toward transformation in social psychology.* New York: Springer-Verlag.

Gergen, K. J. (1997). The place of the psyche in a constructed world. *Theory and Psychology, 7*(6): 723–746.

Getz, D., Carlsen, J., and Morrison, A. (2004). *The family business in tourism and hospitality.* Wallingford, Oxon, UK: CABI.

Getz, D., and Petersen, T. (2005). Growth and profit-oriented entrepreneurship among family business owners in the tourism and hospitality industry. *Hospitality Management, 24,* 219–242.

Giacalone, R. A. (2004). A transcendent business education for the 21st century. *Academy of Management Learning and Education, 3*(4): 415–420.

Giacalone, R. A., and Eylon, D. (2000). The development of new paradigm values, thinkers, and business: Initial frameworks for a changing business worldview. *American Behavioral Scientist, 43*(8): 1217–1230.

Giacalone, R. A., and Jurkiewicz, C. L. (2004). The interaction of materialist and postmaterialist values in predicting dimensions of personal and social identity. *Human Relations, 57*(11): 1379–1405.

Giacalone, R. A., Jurkiewicz, C. L., and Deckop, J. R. (2008). On ethics and social responsibility: The impact of materialism, postmaterialism, and hope. *Human Relations, 61*(4): 483–514.

Gilbert, D., and Abdullah, J. (2004). Holidaytaking and the sense of well-being. *Annals of Tourism Research, 31*(1): 103–121.

Gill, A. M. (2000). From growth machine to growth management: The dynamics of resort development in Whistler, British Columbia. *Environment and Planning A, 32,* 1083–1103.

Gill, A.M. (2004). Tourism communities and growth management. In A. A. Lew, C. M. Hall and A. M. Williams (eds.), *A companion to tourism* (pp. 569–583). Oxford, UK: Blackwell.

Gill, A. M., and Reed, M. (1997). Tourism, recreational and amenity values in land allocation: An analysis of institutional arrangements in the postproductivist era. *Environment and Planning A, 29,* 2019–2040.

Glatzer, W. (2000). Happiness: Classic theory in the light of current research. *Journal of Happiness Studies, 1*(4): 501–511.

Gluck, J., and Baltes, P. B. (2006). Using the concept of wisdom to enhance the expression of wisdom knowledge. *Psychology and Aging, 21,* 679–690.

Goeldner, C. R., and Ritchie, J. R. B. (2002). *Tourism: Principles, practices, philosophies* (9th ed.). New York: Wiley.

Goffman, E. (1959). The *presentation of self in everyday life.* New York: Doubleday.

Goffman, E. (1974). *Frame analysis.* Cambridge, MA: Harvard University Press.

Goldberg, C. (2006). *Harvard's crowded course to happiness: Positive psychology draws students in droves.* Boston Globe. Available: http://www.boston.com/news/local/articles/2006/03/10/harvards_crowded_course_to_happiness/.

Goleman, D. (1995). *Emotional intelligence.* New York: Bantam.

Goleman, D. (2009). *Ecological intelligence: Knowing the hidden impacts of what we buy.* London: Allen Lane.

Gomm, R. (2004). *Social research methodology: A critical introduction*. Basingstoke, UK: Palgrave Macmillan.

Gonzalez-Roma, V., Schaufeli, W. B., Bakker, A. B., and Lloret, S. (2006). Burnout and work engagement: Independent factors or opposite poles. *Journal of Vocational Behavior, 68,* 165–174.

Goodlad, S., and McIvor, S. (1998). *Museum volunteers: Good practice in the management of volunteers*. London: Routledge.

Goodwin, C. J. (2005). Reorganizing the experimentalists: The origin of the Society of Experimental Psychologists. *History of Psychology, 8*(4): 347–361.

Gordon, B. (1986) The souvenir: Messenger of the extraordinary. *Journal of Popular Culture, 20*(3): 135–146.

Gould, S. J. (2004). *The hedgehog, the fox and the magister's pox: Mending and minding the misconceived gap between science and the humanities*. London: Vintage.

Goulding, P. J., Baum, T., and Morrison, A. J. (2005). Seasonal trading and lifestyle motivation. *Journal of Quality Assurance in Hospitality and Tourism, 5*(2): 209–238.

Grant, S., and Langan-Fox, J. (2006). Occupational stress, coping and strain: The combined/interactive effects of the Big Five traits. *Personality and Individual Differences, 41,* 719–732.

Grattan, C., and Taylor, P. (1987). Leisure and shopping. *Leisure Management, 7*(3): 29–30.

Grayling, A. C. (2005). *The heart of things: Applying philosophy to the twenty first century*. London: Phoenix.

Green, R. (2005). Community perceptions of environmental and social change and tourism development on the island of Koh Samui, Thailand. *Journal of Environmental Psychology, 25,* 37–56.

Greene, J. O. (1994). What sort of terms ought theories of human action incorporate? *Communication Studies, 45*(2): 187–211.

Greenfield, S. (2000). *The private life of the brain*. London: Penguin.

Greenwood, T., and Moscardo, G. (1999). Australian and North American coastal and marine tourists: What do they want? In N. Saxena (ed.), Recent advances in marine science and technology, 98 (pp. 253–260). Seoul: Korea Ocean Research and Development Institute.

Groff, R. (2004). *Critical realism, post-positivism and the possibility of knowledge*. London: Routledge.

Gump, B., and Matthews, K. (2000). Are vacations good for your health? The 9-year mortality experience after the multiple risk intervention trial. *Psychosomatic Medicine, 62,* 608–612.

Gunn, C. (1994). A perspective on the purpose and nature of tourism research methods. In J. R. B. Ritchie and C. R. Goeldner, *Travel, tourism, and hospitality research* (2nd ed.; pp. 3–11). New York: John Wiley & Sons.

Haley, A. J., Snaith, T., and Miller, G. (2005). The social impacts of tourism: A case study of Bath, UK. *Annals of Tourism Research, 32,* 647–668.

Hall, C. M. (2005). *Introduction to tourism: Dimensions and issues* (4th ed.). Frenchs Forest, NSW: Pearson Education Australia.

Hall, D., and Brown, F. (2006). *Tourism and welfare: Ethics responsibility and sustained well-being*. Wallingford, Oxon, UK: CABI.

Halton, E. (1986). *Meaning and modernity*. Chicago: Chicago University Press.

Han, S. Y., Um, S., and Mills, A. (2005). *The development of on-site experience measurement scale* (pp. 14–22). The 11th APTA Conference—New Tourism for Asia-Pacific, 7–10 July 2005. Pusan, Korea: Dong-A University.

Hanefors, M., and Larsson, L. (1993). Video strategies used by tour operators: What is really communicated? *Tourism Management, 14*(1): 27–33.

Haraway, D. J. (1991). *Simians, cyborgs, and women: The re-invention of nature.* London: Routledge.

Harton, J. J. (1939). An investigation of the influence of success and failure on the estimation of time. *Journal of General Psychology, 21,* 51–62.

Hawkins, B. P., Peng, J., Hsieh, C., and Eklund, S. J. (1999). Leisure constraints: A replication and extension of construct development. *Leisure Sciences, 21,* 179–192.

Hayllar, B., and Griffin, T. (2004). The tourism precinct experience: A phenomenological approach. *Tourism Management, 26*(4): 517–528.

Hegel, G. (1977). *Phenomenology of spirit.* Oxford, UK: Clarendon Press.

Heidegger, M. (1996). *Being and time.* Albany, NY: State University of New York Press.

Henderson, J. (2006). Destination development: Singapore and Dubai compared. *Journal of Travel and Tourism Marketing, 20*(3/4): 33–45.

Henderson, K. A., Stalnaker, D., and Taylor, G. (1988). The relationship between barriers to recreation and gender-role personality traits for women. *Journal of Leisure Research, 20,* 69–80.

Hendrick, S., and Hendrick, C. (2002). Love. In C. R. Snyder and S. J. Lopez (eds.), *Handbook of positive psychology* (pp. 472–485). Oxford, UK: Oxford University Press.

Higgins-Desbiolles, F. (2006). More than an industry: Tourism as a social force. *Tourism Management, 27*(6): 1192–1208.

Higgins-Desbiolles, F. (2008). Justice tourism and alternative globalization. *Journal of Sustainable Tourism, 16*(3): 345–364.

Hirschman, E. C. (1991). Secular morality and the dark side of consumer behavior: Or how semiotics saved my life. In M. Solomon, and R. Holman (eds.), *Advances in consumer research* (pp. 1–4). Urbana, IL: Association for Consumer Research.

Hitlin, S. (2007). Doing good, feeling good: Values and the self's moral centre. *Journal of Positive Psychology, 2,* 249–259.

Hochschild, A. (1983). *The managed heart: Commercialization of human feeling.* London: University of California Press.

Hochschild, A. R. (1983). *The managed heart.* Berkeley: University of California Press.

Holt, D. B. (1998). Does cultural capital structure American consumption? *Journal of Consumer Research, 25*(1): 1–25.

Hom Cary, S. (2004). The tourist moment. *Annals of Tourism Research, 31*(1): 61–77.

Hormuth, S. E. (1986). The sampling of experiences in situ. *Journal of Personality, 54,* 262–293.

Horne, D. (1992). *The intelligent tourist.* McMahons Point, NSW: Margaret Gee.

Houston, T., and Turner, P. (2007). Mindfulness and communicative language teaching. *Academic Exchange Quarterly, 11*(1): 138–142.

Hsu, C. H. C., and Huang, S. (2008). Travel motivation: A critical review of the concept's development. In A. Woodside and D. Martin (eds.), *Tourism management analysis, behaviour and strategy* (pp. 14–27). Wallingford, UK: CABI.

Hu, B., and Yu, H. (2007). Segmentation by craft selection criteria and shopping involvement. *Tourism Management, 28*(4): 1079–1092.

Hudson, S., and Miller, G. (2005). Ethical orientation and awareness of tourism students. *Journal of Business Ethics, 62*(4): 383–396.

Hudson, S., and Shephard, G. W. H. (1998). Destinations: An application of importance-performance analysis to an alpine ski resort. *Journal of Travel and Tourism Marketing, 7*(3): 61–77.

Hughes, K. (1991). Tourist satisfaction: A guided cultural tour in North Queensland. *Australian Psychologist, 26*(3): 166–171.

Hunter, C., and Shaw, J. (2007). The ecological footprint as a key indicator of sustainable tourism. *Tourism Management, 28,* 46–57.

Inglehart, R. (1977). *The silent revolution: Changing values and political styles among Western publics.* Princeton, NJ: Princeton University Press.

Inglehart, R. (1990). *Culture shift in advanced industrial society.* Princeton, NJ: Princeton University Press.

Inglehart, R. (1997). *Modernization and postmodernization: Cultural, economic and political change in 43 societies.* Princeton, NJ: Princeton University Press.

Inui, Y., Wheeler, D., and Lankford, S. (2006). Rethinking tourism education: What should schools teach? *Journal of Hospitality, Leisure, Sport and Tourism Education, 5*(2): 25–35.

Jackson, E. (2006). Workplace stress: What's causing it and what can be done? *In Psych* (June), 16–18.

Jackson, E. L., and Scott, D. (1999). Constraints to leisure. In E. L. Jackson and T. L. Burton (eds.), *Leisure studies: Prospects for the twenty-first century* (pp. 299–321). State College, PA: Venture Publishing.

Jackson, S. A. (1992). Athletes in flow: A qualitative investigation of flow states in elite figure skaters. *Journal of Applied Sport Psychology, 4,* 161–180.

Jackson, S. A. (1996). Toward a conceptual understanding of the flow experience in elite athletes. *Research Quarterly for Exercise and Sport, 67*(1): 76–90.

Jackson, S. A., and Eklund, R. C. (2002). Assessing flow in physical activity: The Flow State Scale-2 and Dispositional Flow Scale-2. *Journal of Sport and Exercise Psychology, 24,* 133–150.

Jackson, S. A., and Eklund, R. C. (2004). The flow scales manual. Morgantown, WV: Fitness Information Technology.

Jackson, S. A., and Marsh, H. W. (1996). Development and validation of a scale to measure optimal experience: The Flow State Scale. *Journal of Sport and Exercise Psychology, 18,* 17–35.

Jafari, J. (1990). Research and scholarship: The basis of tourism education. *Journal of Tourism Studies, 1*(1): 33–41.

Jafari, J. (2005). Bridging out, nesting afield: Powering a new platform. *The Journal of Tourism Studies, 16*(2): 1–5.

Jamal, T. B. (2004). Virtue ethics and sustainable tourism pedagogy: Phronesis, principles and practice. *Journal of Sustainable Tourism, 12*(6): 530–545.

Jamal, T. B., and Menzel, C. (2009). Good actions in tourism. In J. Tribe (ed.), *Philosophical issues in tourism.* Bristol, UK: Channel View.

Jamal, T., and Robinson, M. (eds.). (2009) *The Sage handbook of tourism studies.* London: Sage Publications Ltd.

James, W. (1890). *Principles of psychology.* New York: Holt.

James, W. (1892/1961). *Psychology: The briefer course.* Notre Dame, IN: University of Notre Dame.

Jaspars, J., and Fraser, C. (1984). Attitudes and social representations. In R. M. Farr and S. Moscovici (eds.), *Social representation* (pp. 101–123). Cambridge, UK: Cambridge University Press.

Jones, G. (1987). Elderly people and domestic crime: Reflections on ageism, sexism and victimology. *British Journal of Criminology, 27,* 191–201.

Josiam, B. M., Kinley, T. R., and Kim, Y.-K. (2004). Involvement and the tourist shopper: Using the involvement construct to segment the American tourist shopper at the mall. *Journal of Vacation Marketing, 11*(2): 135–154.

Jurkiewicz, C. L. (2002). The influence of pedagogical style on students' level of ethical reasoning. *Journal of Public Affairs Education, 8*(4): 263–274.

Kabat-Zinn, J. (2003). Mindfulness-based intervention in context: Past, present and future. Clinical Psychology: Science and Practice, *10*(2): 144–156.

Kahneman, D., Diener, E., and Schwarz, N. (eds.). (1999). *Well-being: The foundations of hedonic psychology.* New York: Sage.

Kant, I. (1929). *Critique of pure reason.* New York: Macmillan.

Kaplan, R., and Kaplan, S. (1989). *The experience of nature: A psychological perspective.* Ann Arbor, MI: Ulrich's.

Kaplan, S., Bardwell, L., and Slakter, D. (1993). The museum as a restorative experience. *Environment and Behavior, 25,* 725–742.

Kashdan, T. B., and Breen, W. E. (2007). Materialism and diminished well-being: Experiential avoidance as a mediating mechanism. *Journal of Social and Clinical Psychology, 26*(5): 521–539.

Kasser, T. (2002). *The high price of materialism.* Cambridge, MA: MIT Press.

Kasser, T. (2006). Materialism and its alternatives. In M. Csikszentmihalyi and I. S. Csikszentmihalyi (eds.), *A life worth living: Contributions to positive psychology* (200–214). Oxford, UK: Oxford University Press.

Kasser, T., and Ahuvia, A. (2002). Materialistic values and well-being in business students. *European Journal of Social Psychology, 32*(1): 137–146.

Kasser, T., and Ryan, R. M. (1993). A dark side of the American dream: Correlates of financial success as a central life aspiration. *Journal of Personality and Social Psychology, 65*(5): 410–422.

Kasser, T., and Ryan, R. M. (1996). Further examining the American dream: Differential correlates of intrinsic and extrinsic goals. *Personality and Social Psychology Bulletin, 22*(3): 280–287.

Kasser, T., Ryan, R. M., Couchman, C. E., and Sheldon, K. M. (2004). Materialistic values: Their causes and consequences. In T. Kasser and A. D. Kanner (eds.), *Psychology and consumer culture: The struggle for a good life in a materialistic world* (pp. 11–28). Washington, DC: American Psychological Association.

Kelly, G. A. (1955). *The psychology of personal constructs* (Vols. 1 and 2). New York: Norton.

Keogh, K. A., Zimbardo, P. G., and Boyd, J. N. (1999). Who's smoking, drinking and using drugs? Time perspective as a predictor of substance abuse. *Basic and Applied Psychology, 21,* 149–164.

Kilbourne, W., and Pickett, G. (2008). How materialism affects environmental beliefs, concern, and environmentally responsible behaviour. *Journal of Business Research, 61*(9): 885–893.

Kilbourne, W. E., Dorsch, M. J., McDonagh, P., Urien, B., Prothero, A., Grünhagen, M., et al. (2009). The institutional foundations of materialism in Western societies: A conceptualization and empirical test. *Journal of Macromarketing, 29*(3): 259–278.

Kim, H., and Jamal, T. (2007). Touristic quest for existential authenticity. *Annals of Tourism Research, 34*(1): 181–201.

Kim, S., and Littrell, M. A. (2001). Souvenir buying intentions for self versus others. *Annals of Tourism Research, 28*(3): 638–657.

Kim, Y. J. (Edward), Pearce, P. L., Morrison, A. M., and O'Leary, J. T. (1996). Mature vs. youth travelers: The Korean market. *Asia Pacific Journal of Tourism Research, 1*(1): 102–112.

Kinley, T. R., Josiam, B. M., and Kim, Y. K. (2003). Why and where tourists shop: Motivations of tourist shoppers and their preferred shopping center attributes. *Journal of Shopping Center Research, 10*(1): 7–28.

Klenosky, D. B. (2002). The "Pull" of tourism destinations: A means–end investigation. *Journal of Travel Research, 40*(4): 385–395.

Koester, A. (2004). Relational sequences in workplace genres. *Journal of Pragmatics, 36*(8): 1405–1428.

Kolyesnikova, N. and Dodd, T. H. (2008). Effects of winery visitor group size on gratitude and obligation. *Journal of Travel Research, 47*(1): 104–112.

Kozak, M. (2001). A critical review of approaches to measure satisfaction with tourist destinations. In J. A. Mazanec, G. Crouch, J. R. Brent Ritchie and A. Woodside (eds.), *Consumer psychology of tourism, hospitality and leisure* (pp. 303–320). Wallingford, UK: CABI Publishing.

Kubey, R., Larson, R., and Csikszentmihalyi, M. (1996). Experience sampling method applications to communication research questions. *Journal of Communication, 46*(2): 99–120.

Kubzansky, L. D., Sparrow, D., Vokonas, P., and Kawachi, I. (2001). Is the glass half empty or half full? A prospective study of optimism and coronary heart disease in the normative aging study. Psychosomatic Medicine, *63*, 910–916.

Kubzansky, L. D., and Thurston, R. (2007). Emotional vitality and incident coronary heart disease. Archives of General Psychiatry, *64*, 1393–1401.

Kunzmann, U., and Baltes, P. B. (2003). Wisdom-related knowledge: Affective, motivational and interpersonal correlated. *Personality and Social Psychology Bulletin, 29*, 1104–1119.

Kuyper, J. (1993). *Volunteer program administration: A handbook for museums and other cultural institutions*. Washington, DC: American Council for the Arts.

Lam, T. (2003). Job satisfaction and organizational commitment in the Hong Kong fast food industry. *International Journal of Contemporary Management, 15*, 214–220.

Lambert, N., Fincham, F. D., Stillman, T. L., and Lukas, D. (2009). More gratitude, less materialism: The mediating role of life satisfaction. *Journal of Positive Psychology, 4*(1): 32–42.

Lang, F. R., Staudinger, U. M., and Carstensen, L. L. (1998). Perspectives on socioemotional selectivity in later life: How personality and social context do (and do not) make a difference. *Journal of Gerontology Series B: Psychological and Social Sciences, 53B*, 21–30.

Langer, E. (2009). *Counterclockwise: Mindful health and the power of possibility*. New York: Ballantine Books.

Langer, E. J. (1989). *Mindfulness*. Reading, MA: Addison-Wesley.

Lankford, S. V., and Howard, D. R. (1994). Developing a tourism impact attitude scale. *Annals of Tourism Research, 21*, 121–139.

Larsen, S. (2007). Aspects of a psychology of the tourist experience. *Scandinavian Journal of Hospitality and Tourism, 7*(1): 7–18.

Lashley, C. (1997). On making silk purses: Developing reflective practitioners in hospitality management. *International Journal of Contemporary Hospitality Management, 11*, 180–185.

Lashley, C. (2000). Toward s a theoretical understanding. In. C. Lashley and A. Morrison (eds.), *In search of hospitality: Theoretical perspectives and debates*. Oxford, UK: Butterworth-Heinemann.

Lashley, C. (2002). Learning styles and hospitality management education. *The Hospitality Review* (April), 56–60.

Lashley, C., and Morrison, A. (eds.). (2000). *In search of hospitality: Theoretical perspectives and debates*. Oxford, UK: Butterworth-Heinemann.

Law, J., Pearce, P. L., and Woods, B. A. (1995). Stress and coping in tourist attraction employees. *Tourism Management, 16*(4): 277–284.

Layard, R. (2005). *Happiness—lessons from a new science*. London: Allen Lane/ Penguin.

Leach, W (1993). *Land of desire: Merchants, power, and the rise of a new American culture*. New York: Pantheon.

Lefkowitz, J. (2003). *Ethics and values in industrial-organizational psychology*. Mahwah, NJ: Lawrence Erlbaum Associates.

Lehto, X. Y., Cai, L. A , O'Leary, J. O. and Huan, T. (2004). Tourist shopping preferences and expenditure behaviours: The case of the Taiwanese outbound market. *Journal of Vacation Marketing, 10*(4): 320–332.

Lerner, R. M. (2002). *Concepts and theories of human development*. Mahwah, NJ: Lawrence Erlbaum Associates.

Levett, R. (1998). Footprint: A great step forward, but tread carefully: A response to Mathis Wackernagel. *Local Environment, 3*(1): 67–75.

Levine, R. (1997). *A geography of time: The temporal adventures of a social psychologist, or how every culture keeps time just a little bit differently*. New York: Basic Books.

Lewis, R., Chambers, R., and Chacko, E. (1995). *Marketing: Leadership in hospitality*. New York: Van Nostrand Reinhold.

Linley, P. A., Joseph, S., Harrington, S., and Wood, A. M. (2006). Positive psychology: Past, present and (possible) future. *The Journal of Positive Psychology, 1*(1): 3–16.

Littrell, M. A. (1990). Symbolic significance of textile crafts for tourists. *Annals of Tourism Research, 17*(2): 228–245.

Littrell, M. A. (1996). *Shopping experiences and marketing of culture to tourists*. Paper presented at the conference on tourism and culture: Toward the 21st Century, Northumberland, UK.

Lockenhoff, C., and Carstensen, L. (2004). Socioemotional selectivity theory and health: The increasingly delicate balance between regulating emotions and making tough choices. *Journal of Personality, 72,* 1395–1424.

Lofdahl, C. L. (2002). *Environmental impacts of globalization and trade*. Cambridge, MA: MIT Press.

Lopez, J., and Potter, G. (2001). *After postmodernism: An introduction to critical realism*. London: The Athlone Press.

Lovett, B. J. (2006). The new history of psychology: A review and critique. *History of Psychology, 9*(1): 17–37.

Lowych, E., van Langenhave, L., and Bollaert, L. (1992). Typologies of tourist roles. In P. Johnson and P. Thomas (eds.), *Choice and demand in tourism*. London: Mansell.

Lui, J. C., and Var, T. (1986). Resident attitudes toward tourism development in Hawaii. *Annals of Tourism Research, 14,* 420–429.

Lundin, S., Paul, H., and Christensen, J. B. (2000). *Fish! A remarkable way to boost morale and team results*. New York: Warner Books.

Lyons, E., and Coyle, A. (eds.), (2007). *Analysing qualitative data in psychology*. London: Sage.

Lyubomirsky, S., Sheldon, K. M., and Schkade, D. (2005). Pursuing happiness: The architecture of sustainable change. *Review of General Psychology, 9,* 111–131.

MacCannell, D. (1976). *The tourist: A new theory of the leisure class*. New York: Schocken Books.

MacCannell, D. (2002). Reflections and reviews: The ego factor in tourism. *Journal of Consumer Research, 29*(1): 146–151.

MacCannell, D. (2007). Anthropology for all the wrong reasons. In D. Nash (ed.), *The study of tourism anthropological and sociological beginnings* (pp. 137–153). Amsterdam: Elsevier.

Madrigal, R. (1995). Residents' perceptions and the role of government. *Annals of Tourism Research, 22,* 86–102.

Mak, A., Wong, K., and Chang, R. (2009). Health or self-indulgence? The motivations and characteristics of spa-goers. *International Journal of Tourism Research, 11,* 185–199.

Mannell, R., and Iso-Ahola, S. (1987). Psychological nature of leisure and tourism experience. *Annals of Tourism Research, 14*(3): 314–331.

Marchel, C., and Owens, S. (2007). Qualitative research in psychology: Could William James get a job? *History of Psychology, 10*(4): 301–324.

Marcketti, S., Niehm, L., and Fuloria, R. (2006). An exploratory study of lifestyle entrepreneurship and its relation to life quality. *Family and Consumer Sciences Research Journal, 34*, 241–258.

Marks, G. N. (1997). The formation of materialist and postmaterialist values. *Social Science Research, 26*(1): 52–68.

Martilla, J., and James, J. (1977). Importance-performance analysis. *Journal of Marketing, 41*(1): 77–79.

Martin, R. A., Puhlik-Doris, P., Larsen, G., Gray, J., and Weir, K. (2003). Individual differences in uses of humor and their relation to psychological well-being: Development of the Humor Styles Questionnaire. *Journal of Research in Personality, 37*(1): 48–75.

Marton, F., Hounsell, D., and Entwhistle, N. (eds.). (1984). *The experience of learning.* Edinburgh: Scottish Academic Press.

Maslach, C., and Jackson, S. E. (1986). *Maslach Burnout Inventory manual* (2nd ed.). Palo Alto, CA: Consulting Psychological Press.

Maslow, A. H. (1954). *Motivation and personality.* New York: Harper & Row.

Massimini, F., and Della Fave, A. (2000). Individual development in a bio-cultural perspective. *American Psychologist, 55*, 24–33.

Masten, A. S. (2001). Ordinary magic: Resilience processes in development. *American Psychologist, 56*, 227–239.

Masten, A. S., and Reed, M. J. (2002). Resilience in development. In C.R. Snyder and S. L. Lopez (eds.), *Handbook of positive psychology* (pp. 74–88). New York: OUP.

Mathieson, A., and Wall, G. (1982). *Tourism: Economic, physical and social impacts.* New York: Longman.

Mazursky, D. (1989). Past experience and future tourism decisions. *Annals of Tourism Research, 16*, 333–344.

McAdams, D. P., and de St. Aubin, E. (1992). A theory of generativity and its assessment through self-report, behavioral acts, and narrative themes in autobiography. *Journal of Personality and Social Psychology, 62*(6): 1003–1015.

McCarthy, T. (1981). *The critical theory of Jurgen Habermas.* Cambridge, MA: MIT Press.

McClure, R. F. (1984). The relationship between money attitudes and overall pathology. *Psychology: A Quarterly Journal of Human Behavior, 21*(1): 4–6.

McCool, S., and Lime, D. (2001). Tourism carrying capacity: Tempting fantast or useful reality. *Journal of Sustainable Tourism, 9*(5): 372–388.

McCullough, M. E., and vanOyen Witvliet, C. (2002). The psychology of forgiveness. In C. R. Snyder and S. J. Lopez (eds.), Handbook of positive psychology (pp. 446–458). London: Oxford University Press.

McGehee, N., and Anderlick, K. (2004). Factors predicting rural residents' support of tourism. *Journal of Tourism Research, 43*, 131–142.

McIntosh, R. W. (1992). Early tourism education in the United States. *Journal of Tourism Studies, 3*(1): 2–7.

McRae, R. R., and Costa, P. T., Jr. (1996). Toward a new generation of personality theories: Theoretical contexts for the five-factor model. In J. S. Wiggins (ed.), *The five-factor model of personality: Theoretical perspectives* (pp. 51–87). New York, NY: Guilford.

Medical Tourism Association. (2010). Available: http://www.medicaltourismasso-ciation.com/.

Merton, R. K. (1965). *On the shoulders of giants.* New York: Free Press.

Michalkó, G., Rátz, T., and Irimiás, A. (2008). *The role of tourism in shaping the Hungarian society's sense of happiness.* Available: http://www.mth.gov.hu/main.php?folderID=852andlangchanged=1.

Michalos, A. C. (2008). Education, happiness and well-being. *Social Indicators Research, 87*(3): 347–366.

Miele, M., and Murdoch, J. (2002). The practical aesthetics of traditional cuisines: Slow food in Tuscany. *Sociologia Ruralis, 42*(4): 312–328.

Mitchell, C. J. A. (1998). Entrepreneurialism, commodification and creative destruction: A model of post-modern community development. *Journal of Rural Studies, 14*(3): 273–286.

Mitchell, C. J. A., Atkinson, R. G., and Clark, A. (2001). The creative destruction of Niagara-on-the-Lake. *The Canadian Geographer, 45*(2): 285–299.

Mitchell, C. J. A., and Coghill, C. (2000). The creation of a cultural heritage landscape: Elora, Ontario, Canada. *The Great Lakes Geographer, 7*(2): 88–105.

Morgan, M. (2004). From production line to drama school: Higher education for the future of tourism. *International Journal of Contemporary Hospitality Management, 16*(2): 91–99.

Morrison, A. (2006). A contextualisation of entrepreneurship. *International Journal of Entrepreneurial Behaviour and Research, 12*(4): 192–209.

Morrison, A., and O'Mahony, B. G. (2003). The liberation of hospitality management education. *International Journal of Contemporary Hospitality Management, 15*(1): 38–44.

Morrison, A. M., Yang, C.-H., O'Leary, J. T., and Nadkarni, N. (1996). Comparative profiles of travellers on cruises and land-based resort vacations. *Journal of Tourism Studies, 7*(2): 15–27.

Moscardo, G. (1996). Mindful visitors. *Annals of Tourism Research, 23*(2): 376–397.

Moscardo, G. (2004). Shopping as a destination attraction: An empirical examination of the role of shopping in tourists' destination choice and experience. *Journal of Vacation Marketing, 10*(4): 294–307.

Moscardo, G. (2009a). *Exploring* mindfulness *and stories in tourist experiences*. Paper presented to the 6th CPTHL Symposium, Vienna, Austria: MODUL University Vienna, June 1–3.

Moscardo, G. (2009b). Tourism and quality of life: Towards a more critical approach. *Tourism and Hospitality Research, 9*(2): 159–170.

Moscardo, G., Ballantyne, R., and Hughes, K. (2007). *Designing interpretive signs—principles in practice*. Golden, CO: Fulcrum Publishing.

Moscardo, G., Morrison, A. M., Cai, L., Nadkarni, N., and O'Leary, J. T. (1996). Tourist perspectives on cruising: Multidimensional scaling analyses of cruising and other holiday types. *Journal of Tourism Studies, 7*(2): 54–63.

Moscardo, G., and Woods, B. (1998). Managing tourism in the wet tropics world heritage area: Interpretation and the experience of visitors on Skyrail. In E. Laws, B. Faulkner and G. Moscardo (eds.), *Embracing and managing change in tourism: International case studies* (pp. 285–306). London: Routledge.

Moscovici, S. (1984). The phenomenon of social representations. In R. M. Farr and S. Moscovici (eds.), *Social representations*. Cambridge: Cambridge University Press.

Mowforth, M., and Munt, I. (2003). *Tourism and sustainability: Development and new tourism in the Third World*. London: Routledge.

Murphy, P. (2002). Sea-change: Reinventing rural and regional Australia. *Transformations, 2*, 1–12.

Murphy, P., and Murphy, A. (2004). *Strategic management for tourism communities*. Clevedon, UK: Channel View.

Murray, E. (1908). A qualitative analysis of tickling: Its relation to cutaneous and organic sensation. *The American Journal of Psychology, 19*(3): 289–344.

Myers, D. (2000). *The American paradox: Spiritual hunger in an age of plenty*. New Haven, CT: Yale University Press.

Myers, J. E., Sweeney, T. J., and Witmer, M. (2005). *A holistic model of wellness.* Available: http://www.mindgarden.com/products/wellls.htm Accessed 10.7. 2009.

Nash, D. (2001). On travellers, ethnographers and tourists. *Annals of Tourism Research, 28*(2): 493–495.

Nash, D. (ed.). (2007). *The study of tourism: Anthropological and sociological beginnings.* Amsterdam: Elsevier.

Nash, D. (2009). In the beginning: The making of a book about some beginnings of tourism study. (Dennison J. Nash, Editor, *The study of tourism: Anthropological and sociological beginnings,* 2007). *Tourism Analysis, 14*(1): 29–36.

National Trust, The. (1998). *Volunteering with the National Trust: Summary of the findings of the 1997 survey.* Cirencester, UK: The National Trust.

Nawijn, J. (2009). The holiday happiness curve: A preliminary investigation into mood during a holiday abroad. *International Journal of Tourism Research* (Early View), n/a.

Neal, J. D., Uysal, M. J., and Sirgy, J. (2007). The effect of tourism services on travelers' quality of life. *Journal of Travel Research, 46,* 154–163.

Neuman, S. (2005). *How people trick themselves into overspending.* Available: http://news-info.wustl.edu/news/page/normal/4998.html.

Newbold, K. B., Scott, D. M., Spinney, J. E. L., Kanaroglou, P., and Paez, A. (2005). Travel behavior within Canada's older population: A cohort analysis. *Journal of Transport Geography, 13,* 340–351.

Nickerson, C., Schwarz, N., Diener, E., and Kahneman, D. (2003). Zeroing in on the dark side of the American dream: A closer look at the negative consequences of the goal for financial success. *Psychological Science, 14*(6): 531–536.

Noe, F. P. (1999). *Tourism service satisfaction.* Champaign, IL: Sagamore.

Norman, W. S. (1998). Forming new partnerships: The outlook for US travel and tourism. Keynote speech at annual meeting. Bloomington, MN: Bloomington Convention and Visitors Bureau. Available: http://www.tia.org/Press/wsn020498.asp.

Norrick, N. R. (2006). Humour in language. In K. Brown (ed.), *Encyclopaedia of language and linguistics* (pp. 425–426). Amsterdam: Elsevier.

Norton, D. L. (1976). *Personal destinies.* Princeton, NJ: Princeton University Press.

Oberg, K. (1960). Culture shock: Adjustment to neo-cultural environments. *Practical Anthropology, 17,* 177–182.

Oliver, R. L. (1980). A cognitive model of the antecedents and consequences of satisfaction decisions. *Journal of Marketing Research, 17,* 460–469.

Omondi, R. K. (2003). *Gender and the political economy of sex tourism in Kenya's coastal resorts.* International symposium/doctoral course on feminist perspective on global economic and political systems and women's struggle for global justice, 24–26 September. Tromsø, Norway: Sommoroya Hotel.

Opp, K. D. (1990). Postmaterialism, collective action, and political protest. *American Journal of Political Science, 34*(1): 212–235.

Oropesa , R. S. (1995). Consumer possessions, consumer passions, and subjective well-being. *Sociological Forum, 10*(2): 215–244.

Outhwaite, W. (2000). The philosophy of social science. In B. S. Turner (ed.), *The Blackwell companion to social theory* (2nd ed.; pp. 47–70). Oxford: Blackwell.

Packer, J. (2008). Beyond learning: Exploring visitors' perceptions of the value and benefits of museum experiences. *Curator: The Museum Journal, 55*(1): 33–54.

Panchal, J., and Pearce, P. L. (in press). The integration of health motives into the travel career pattern model. *Proceedings of the Asia Pacific Tourism Association Conference,* Macau.

Parasuraman, A., Zeithaml, V. A., and Berry, L. L. (1988). SERVQUAL: A multiple-item scale for measuring customer perceptions of service quality. *Journal of Retailing,* 64,12–40.

Park, N., Peterson, C., and Seligman M. (2005). *Character strengths in forty nations and fifty states.* Unpublished manuscript, University of Rhode Island.

Pearce, P. L. (1988). *The Ulysses factor: Evaluating visitors in tourist settings.* New York: Springer-Verlag.

Pearce, P. L. (1990). Farm tourism in New Zealand: A social situation analysis. *Annals of Tourism Research,* 17(3): 337–352.

Pearce, P. L. (1993). Fundamentals of tourist motivation. In D. Pearce and R. Butler (eds.), *Tourism research: Critiques and challenges* (pp. 85–105). London: Routledge & Kegan Paul.

Pearce, P. L. (2004). Theoretical innovation in Asia Pacific tourism research. *Asia Pacific Journal of Tourism Research,* 9(1): 57–70.

Pearce, P. L. (2005). *Tourist behaviour: Themes and conceptual schemes.* Clevedon, UK: Channel View.

Pearce, P. L. (2009a). The relationship between positive psychology and tourist behaviour studies. *Tourism Analysis,* 14, 37–48.

Pearce, P. L. (2009b). Now that is funny: Humour in tourism settings. *Annals of Tourism Research,* 36(4): 627–644.

Pearce, P. L., and Caltabiano, M. L. (1983). Inferring travel motivations from travellers' experiences. *Journal of Travel Research,* 22(2): 16–20.

Pearce, P. L., and Foster, F. A. (2007). A "University of Travel": Backpacker learning. *Tourism Management,* 28(3): 720–740.

Pearce, P. L., and Lee, U. I. (2005). Developing the travel career approach to tourist motivation. *Journal of Travel Research,* 43, 226–237.

Pearce, P. L., and Maoz, D. (2008). Novel insights into the identity changes among backpackers. *Tourism, Culture and Communication,* 8, 27–43.

Pearce, P. L., Morrison, A., and Rutledge, J. (1998). *Tourism: Bridges across continents.* Sydney, Australia: McGraw-Hill.

Pearce, P. L., and Moscardo, G. M. (1992). The boutique-specialist accommodation sector: Perceived government needs and policy initiatives. *Queensland Small Business Research Journal,* 34–41.

Pearce, P. L., Moscardo, G. M., and Ross, G. F. (1996). *Understanding and managing the tourism-community relationship.* London: Elsevier.

Pearce, P. L., Murphy, L., and Brymer, E. (2009). *The evolution of backpacking.* Brisbane, QLD: CRC for Sustainable Tourism.

Peterson, C. (2000). The future of optimism. *American Psychologist,* 55(1): 44–55.

Peterson, C., Park, N., and Seligman, M. E. P. (2006). Greater strengths of character and recovery from illness. *Journal of Positive Psychology,* 1, 17–26.

Peterson, C., and Seligman, M. (2004). *Character strengths and virtues: A handbook and classification .* New York: Oxford University Press.

Phillimore, J., and Goodson, L. (eds.). (2004). *Qualitative research in tourism.* London: Routledge.

Phillips, L. L. (2005). *Examining flow states and motivational perspectives of ashtanga yoga practitioners.* Unpublished doctoral dissertation. Lexington, KY: University of Kentucky.

Pickren, W. (2007). Tension and opportunity in post-World War Two American psychology. *History of Psychology,* 10(3): 279–299.

Pine, B. J., and Gilmore, J. H. (1999). The experience economy: Work is theatre and every business a stage. Boston: Harvard Business School Press.

Pinkerton-James, M. (1992). *Trends and issues in crime and criminal justice: The elderly as victims of crime, abuse and neglect.* No. 37. Canberra: Australian Institute of Criminology.

Pizam, A. (2000). Burnout. In J. Jafari (ed.), *Encyclopedia of tourism*. London: Routledge.

Plog, S. C. (1974). Why destinations rise and fall in popularity. *Cornell Hotel and Restaurant Quarterly, 14*(4): 55–58.

Plog, S. C. (2001). Why destinations rise and fall in popularity: An update of a *Cornell Quarterly* classic. *Cornell Hotel and Restaurant Quarterly, 42*(3): 13–24.

Polak, E., and McCullough, M. E. (2006). Is gratitude an alternative to materialism? *Journal of Happiness Studies, 7*, 343–360.

Popcorn, F., and Hanft, A. (2001). *Dictionary of the future*. New York: Hyperion.

Pope, K. S., and Singer, J. L. (eds.). (1978). *The stream of consciousness: Scientific investigations into the flow of human experience*. New York: Plenum.

Porritt, J. (1984). *Seeing green: The politics of ecology explained*. Oxford, UK: Basil Blackwell.

Positive Psychology Centre. (2008). Centre's Web site. Available: http://www.ppc. sas.upenn.edu/.

Prakash, V. (1984). Validity and reliability of the confirmation of expectations paradigm as a determinant of consumer satisfaction. *Journal of the Academy of Marketing Science, 12*(4): 63–76.

Prentice, R. C., Witt, S. F., and Hamer, C. (1998). Tourism as experience: The case of heritage parks. *Annals of Tourism Research, 25*(1): 1–24.

Principles of Responsible Management Education. (2010). Available: http://www. unprme.org/.

Pritchard, M. P., and Havitz, M. E. (2006). Destination appraisal: An analysis of critical incidents. *Annals of Tourism Research, 33*(1): 25–46.

Ramsden, P. (1984). The context of learning. In F. Marton, D. Hounsell and N. Entwistle (eds.), *The experience of learning*. Edinburgh: Scottish Academic Press.

Rashid, T. (2002). *Positive psychology—an experiential course: Lecture schedule outline*. Fairleigh Dickinson University. Available: http://www.ppc.sas.upenn. edu/ppsyllabusrashid.pdf.

Ray, N. M., and Ryder, M. E. (2003). 'Ebilities' tourism: An exploratory discussion of the travel needs and motives of the mobility-disabled. *Tourism Management, 24*, 57–72.

Ray, P., and Anderson, S. R. (2001). *The cultural creatives*. New York: Three Rivers Press.

Rees, W. (1996). Revisiting carrying capacity: Area-based indicators of sustainability. *Population and Environment: A Journal of Interdisciplinary Studies, 17*(3): 195–215.

Reid, K., Flowers, P., and Larkin, M. (2005). Exploring lived experience. *The Psychologist, 18*(1): 20–23.

Richards, G. (ed.). (2001). *Cultural attractions and European tourism*. Wallingford, Oxon, UK: CABI.

Richards, G., and Wilson, J. (2004). The global nomad: Motivations and behaviour of independent travellers worldwide. In G. Richards and J. Wilson (eds.), *The global nomad: Backpacker travel in theory and practice* (pp. 14–42). Clevedon, UK: Channel View.

Richardson, F. C., and Guignon, C. B. (2008). Positive psychology and philosophy of social science. *Theory and Psychology, 18*(5): 605–627.

Richins, M. L. (1994). Special possessions and the expression of material values. *Journal of Consumer Research, 21*(3): 522–533.

Richins, M. R., and Dawson, S. (1992). A Consumer values orientation for materialism and its measurement: Scale development and validation. The Journal of Consumer Research, *19*(3): 303–316.

Richter, L. K., and Richter, W. L. (1999). Ethical challenges: Health, safety and accessibility in international travel and tourism. *Public Personnel Management, 28,* 595–615.

Riley, M., Ladkin, A., and Szivas, E. (2001). *Tourism employment analysis and planning.* Clevedon, UK: Channel View Publications.

Riley, P. (1988). Road culture of international long term budget travellers. *Annals of Tourism Research, 15,* 313–328.

Ring, A., Dickinger, A., and Wöber, K. (2009). Designing the ideal undergraduate program in tourism. *Journal of Travel Research, 48*(1): 106–121.

Ringzone. (2009). Oil and gas conversion calculator. Available: http://www.rigzone.com/calculator/about.asp.

Ritchie, B. W. (2003). *Managing educational tourism.* Clevedon, UK: Channel View.

Ritchie, J. R. B., and Goeldner, C. (eds.). (1994). *Travel, tourism and hospitality research: A handbook for managers and researchers* (2nd ed.). New York: John Wiley & Sons.

Roberts, J. (2006). *A sense of the world: How a blind man became history's greatest traveller.* London: Simon & Schuster.

Robinson, J. P., and Godbey, G. (1997). *Time for life: The surprising ways Americans use their time.* State College, PA: Pennsylvania State University Press.

Robinson, M., and Jamal, T. (2009). *The Sage* handbook *of tourism studies.* London: Sage Publications Ltd.

Rocharungsat, P. (2008). Community-based tourism in Asia. In G. Moscardo (ed.), *Building community capacity for tourism development* (pp. 60–74). Wallingford, Oxon, UK: CABI.

Rojek, C., and Urry, J. (eds.). (1997). *Touring cultures: Transformations of travel and theory.* London: Routledge.

Rolls, E. (1984). *Celebration of the senses.* Ringwood, VIC: Penguin.

Rosenbaum, J. (1972). *Is your Volkswagen a sex symbol?* New York: Hawthorn.

Rosenberg, E. L. (1998). Levels of analysis and the organisation of affect. *Review of General Psychology, 2,* 247–270.

Ross, G. F. (1991). Community impacts of tourism among older and long-term residents. *Australian Journal of Aging, 10,* 17–24.

Ross, G. F. (1992). Resident perceptions of the impact of tourism on an Australian city. *Journal of Travel Research, 30,* 13–17.

Ross, G. F. (2003). Work stress response perceptions among potential employees: The influence of ethics and trust. *Tourist Review, 58,* 25–33.

Ross, G. F. (1995a). Work stress and personality measures among hospitality industry employees. *International Journal of Contemporary Hospitality Management, 7,* 9–13.

Ross, G. F. (1995b). Interpersonal stress reactions and service quality responses among hospitality industry employees. *Service Industries Journal, 15,* 314–331.

Ross, G. F. (1997). Career stress responses among hospitality employees. *Annals of Tourism Research, 21,* 41–49.

Ross, G. F. (1998). *The psychology of tourism* (2nd ed.). Melbourne, VIC: Hospitality Press.

Ross, G. F. (2005a). Senior tourists sociability and travel preparation. *Tourism Review, 60,* 6–15.

Ross, G. F. (2005b). Tourism industry employee work stress—a present and future crisis. *Journal of Travel and Tourism Marketing, 19,* 133–147.

Ross, G. F. (2006). Ethical, career, organizational, and service values as predictors of hospitality traineeship interest. *Tourism, Culture and Communication, 6,* 121–136.

Ross, G. F. (2007). Heritage lost or fortune found: Issues and dilemmas concerning tourist development within host communities. *eTropic: Electronic Journal of Studies in the Tropics, 5*, 1–9.

Ross, G. F. (2008). The poignancy of times past: Heritage travel motivation among seniors. In D. J. Timothy, B. Prideau and K. Chon (eds.), *Heritage and cultural tourism in the Asia-Pacific region.* New York: Hawarth.

Roubini, N. A. (2009). *Global breakdown of the recession in 2009.* Available: http://www.forbes.com/2009/01/14/global-recession-2009-oped-cx_nr_0115roubini.html.

Rowan, J. (1998). Maslow amended. *Journal of Humanistic Psychology, 38*(1): 81–93.

Russo, A. P. (2002). The "vicious circle" of tourism development in heritage cities. *Annals of Tourism Research, 29*, 165–182.

Ryan, C. (1995). *Researching tourist satisfaction: Issues, concepts, problems.* New York: Routledge.

Ryan, C. (1998). The travel career ladder: An appraisal. *Annals of Tourism Research, 25*(4): 936–957.

Ryan, C. (2005). Authors and editors—getting published: Context and policy—an editor's views. *Journal of Tourism Studies, 16*(2): 6–13.

Ryan, C., and Hall, C. M. (2001). *Sex tourism: Marginal people and liminalities.* London: Routledge.

Ryan, R. M., and Deci, E. L. (2000). Self-determination theory and the facilitation of intrinsic motivation, social development and well-being. *American Psychologist, 55*, 68–78.

Ryan, R. M., and Deci, E. L. (2001). On happiness and human potentials: A review of research on hedonic and eudaimonic well-being. *Annual Review of Psychology, 52*, 141–166.

Ryff, C., and Singer, B. (2003). Flourishing under fire: Resilience as a prototype of challenged thinking. In C. Keyes and J. Haidt (eds.), *Flourishing: Positive psychology and the life well-lived* (pp. 15–36). Washington, DC: APA.

Saarinen, J. (2006). Traditions of sustainability in tourism studies. *Annals of Tourism Research, 33*(4): 1121–1140.

Salt, B. (2006). *The big picture.* Melbourne: Hardie Grant Books.

Schabracq, M. J., Winnubst, J. A. M., and Cooper, C. L. (2003). *The handbook of work and health psychology.* Chichester, UK: Wiley.

Scheier, M. F., and Carver, C. S. (1987). Dispositional optimism and physical well-being. The influence of generalized outcome expectancies on health. *Journal of Personality, 55*, 169–210.

Scheier, M. F., and Carver, C. S. (1992). Effects of optimism on psychological and physical wellbeing: Theoretical overview and empirical update. *Cognitive Therapy and Research, 16*, 201–228.

Scheier, M. F., Matthews, K. A., Owens, J. F., Magovern, G. J., Lefebvre, R. C., Abbott, R. A., et al. (1989). Dispositional optimism and recovery from coronary artery bypass surgery: The beneficial effects on positive physical and psychological well-being. Journal of Personality and Social Psychology, 57, 1024–1040.

Schimmack, U. (2003). Affect measurement in experience sampling research. *Journal of Happiness Studies, 4*(1): 79–106.

Schmitt, B. H. (2003). *Customer experience management.* Hoboken, NJ: John Wiley & Sons.

Schor, J. B. (1998). *The overspent American: Upscaling, downshifting, and the new consumer.* New York: Basic Books.

Schutte, H., and Ciarlante, D. (1998). *Consumer behaviour in Asia.* London: Macmillan.

Scollon, C. N., Kim-Prieto, C., and Diener, E. (2003). Experience sampling: Prom-
ises and pitfalls, strengths and weaknesses. *Journal of Happiness Studies, 4*(1):
5–34.

Scott, T. (2007). Expression of humour by emergency personnel involved in sudden
death. *Mortality, 12*(4): 35–364.

Seaton, A. (1994). Tourist maps and the promotion of destination image. In *Proceedings of research and academic papers* (pp. 168–184). Society of Educators
in Travel and Tourism of America.

Seligman, M. E. P. (2000). The positive perspective. *The Gallup Perspective, 3*,
2–7.

Seligman M. E. P. (2002). *Authentic happiness: Using the new positive psychology
to realize your potential for lasting fulfillment*. New York: Free Press.

Seligman, M. E. P. (2008). Positive health. *Applied Psychology: An International
Review, 57*, 3–18.

Seligman, M. E. P., and Csikszentmihalyi, M. (2000). Positive psychology: An
introduction. *American Psychologist, 55*(1): 5–14.

Seligman M. E. P., and Peterson C. (2003). Positive clinical psychology. In L. G.
Aspinwall and U. M. Staudinger (eds.), *A psychology of human strengths: Fundamental questions and future directions for a positive psychology* (pp. 305–
317). Washington, DC: American Psychological Association.

Seligman, M. E. P., Steen, T., Park, N., and Peterson, C. (2005). Positive psychology progress: Empirical validation of interventions. *American Psychologist,
60*(5): 410–421.

Sellars, R. W. (1916). *Critical realism: A study of the nature and conditions of
knowledge*. Chicago: Rand-McNally.

Selwyn, T. (ed.). (1996). *The tourist image: Myths and myth making in tourism*.
West Sussex, UK: Wiley.

Sen, A. (2000). A decade of human development. *Journal of Human Development,
1*(1): 17–23.

Severt, D. E., Tesone, D. V., Bottorff, T. J., and Carpenter, M. L. (2009). A world
ranking of the top 100 hospitality and tourism programs. *Journal of Hospitality
and Tourism Research, 33*(4): 451–470.

Sheldon, K. M., and Lyubomirsky, S. (2004). Achieving sustainable new happiness:
Prospects, practices, and prescriptions. In A. Linley and S. Joseph (eds.), *Positive psychology in practice* (pp. 127–145). Hoboken, NJ: John Wiley & Sons.

Sheldon, P. (2008). *Summary: Towards a framework for values-based tourism curricula*. TEFI II Summit, School of Travel Industry Management, April 11–14.
Hawaii: University of Hawaii.

Sheldon, P., and Bushell, R. (2009). Introduction to wellness and tourism. In R.
Bushell and P. Sheldon (eds.), *Wellness and tourism: Mind, body, spirit, place*
(pp. 3–19). New York: Cognizant Communication Corporation.

Shenhav-Keller, S. (1993). The Israeli souvenir: Its text and context. *Annals of
Tourism Research, 20*(2): 182–195.

Simonton, D. K. (1999). *Origins of genius: Darwinian perspectives on creativity*.
New York: OUP.

Simonton, D. K. (2000). Creativity—cognitive, personal, developmental and social
aspects. *American Psychologist, 55*, 151–158.

Simonton, D. K. (2002a). Creativity. In C. R. Snyder and S. L. Lopez (eds.), *Handbook of positive psychology* (pp. 189–201). New York: OUP.

Simonton, D. K. (2002b). *Great psychologists and their times: Scientific insights
into psychology's history*. Washington, DC: APA.

Simonton, D. K., and Baumeister, R. F. (2005). Positive psychology at the summit.
Review of General Psychology, 9(2): 99–102.

Sin, H. L. (2009). Volunteer tourism: "Involve me and I will learn?" *Annals of Tourism Research, 36*(6): 480–501.

Sindiga, I. (1999). *Tourism and African development: Change and challenge of tourism in Kenya.* Leiden, the Netherlands: African Study Centre.

Singapore Tourism Board. (2005). S1.6 billion to rejuvenate Orchard Road into one of the world's greatest shopping streets. Singapore: Singapore Tourism Board Press Release.

Sirakaya, E., Teye, V., and Sonmez, S. (2002). Understanding residents' support for tourism development in the central region of Ghana. *Journal of Travel Research, 41.* 57–67.

Sirgy, M. J. (2009). Toward a quality-of-life theory of leisure travel satisfaction. *Journal of Travel Research* (Early View), n/a.

Slife, B. D., and Richardson, F. C. (2008). Problematic ontological underpinnings of positive psychology: A strong relational alternative. *Theory and Psychology, 18*(5): 699–723.

Slow Travel Web site. (2008). Available: http://www.slowtrav.com/.

Small, S. (1999). Memory-work: A method for researching women's tourist experiences. *Tourist Management, 20*(1): 25–35.

Smith, J. A. (1996). Beyond the divide between cognition and discourse: Using interpretive phenomenological analysis in health psychology. *Psychology and Health, 11,* 261–271.

Smith, J. A. (2004). Reflecting on the development of interpretive phenomenological analysis and its contribution to qualitative psychology. *Qualitative Research in Psychology, 1, 39–54.*

Smith, M. (2009a). Development and its discontents: Ego-tripping without ethics or idea(l)s. In J. Tribe (ed.), *Philosophical issues in tourism* (pp. 261–277). Bristol, UK: Channel View.

Smith, M. (2009b). Regeneration of an historic spa town: A case study of spa in Belgium. In M. Smith and L. Puczko, *Health and wellness tourism* (pp. 295–300). Amsterdam: Elsevier.

Smith, M., and Kelly, C. (2006). Wellness tourism. *Tourism Recreation Research, 31*(1), 1–4.

Smith, M., and Puczko, L. (2009). *Health and wellness tourism.* Amsterdam: Elsevier.

Smith, M. K. (2005). *Happiness and education—theory, practice and possibility.* Available: http://www.infed.org/biblio/happiness_and_education.htm.

Smith, R. W. (1987). Leisure for disabled tourists: Barriers to participation. *Annals of Tourism Research, 14,* 376–389.

Smith, S. (2000). Satellite account. In J. Jafari (ed.), *Encyclopedia of tourism* (p. 519). London: Routledge.

Snepenger, D., O'Connell, R., and Snepenger, M. (2001). The embrace-withdrawal continuum scale: Operationalizing residents' responses toward tourism development. *Journal of Tourism Research, 40,* 155–161.

Snyder, C. R., and Lopez, S. J. (eds.), (2002). *Handbook of positive psychology.* London: Oxford University Press.

Sondergren, S. C., and Hyland, M. E. (2000). What are the positive consequences of illness? *Psychology and Health, 15,* 85–97.

Sonmez, S., and Apostolopoulos, Y. (2009). Vacation as preventive medicine. In R. Bushell and P. Sheldon (eds.), *Wellness and tourism: Mind, body, spirit, place* (pp. 37–51). New York: Cognizant Communication Corporation.

Stamboulis, Y., and Skayannis, P. (2003). Innovation strategies and technology for experience-based tourism. *Tourism Management, 24*(1): 35–43.

Stebbins, R. (2004). Fun, enjoyable, satisfying, fulfilling: Describing positive leisure experience. *LSA Newsletter, 69,* 8–11.

Stebbins, R. A. (1996). Defusing awkward situations: Comic relief as an interactive strategy for people with disabilities. *Journal of Leisure, 23*(4): 3–38.

Steiner, C. J., and Reisinger, Y. (2006). Understanding existential authenticity. *Annals of Tourism Research, 33*(2): 299–318.

Sternberg, R. (ed.). (1990). *Wisdom: Its nature, origins, and development*. New York: CUP.

Stewart, W. P., and Hull, R. B. (1996). Capturing the moments: Concerns of *in situ* research. *Journal of Travel and Tourism Marketing, 5*, 3–20.

Stiglitz, J. E. (2002).*Globalization and its discontents*. New York: Norton.

Stone, I., and Stubbs, C. (2007). Enterprising expatriates: Lifestyle migration and entrepreneurship in rural southern Europe. *Entrepreneurship and Regional Development, 19*(5): 433–450.

Storey, L. (2007). Doing interpretive phenomenological analysis. In E. Lyons and A. Coyle (eds.,), *Analysing qualitative data in psychology* (pp. 51–64). London: Sage.

Strauss-Blasche, G., Ekmekcioglu, C., and Marktl, W. (2002). Moderating effects of vacation on reactions to work and domestic stress. *Leisure Sciences, 24*(2): 237–249.

Strauss-Blasche, G., Ekmekcioglu, C., and Marktl, W. (2003). Serum lipids responses to a respite from occupational and domestic demands in subjects with varying levels of stress. *Journal of Psychosomatic Medicine, 55*, 521–524.

Strauss-Blasche, G., Muhry, F., Lehofer, M., Moser, M., and Marktl, W. (2004). Time course of well-being after a three week resort based respite from occupational and domestic demands: Carry-over, contrast and situation effects. *Journal of Leisure Research, 36*(3): 293–309.

Strauss-Blasche, G., Reithofer, B., Schobersberger, C., Ekmekcioglu, C., and Marktl, W. (2005). Effect of vacation on health: Moderating factors of vacation outcome. *Journal of Travel Medicine, 12*, 94–101.

Sullivan, O., and Gershuny, J. (2001). Cross-national changes in time-use: Some sociological (hi)stories re-examined. *British Journal of Sociology, 52*, 331–347.

Swanson, E. B., and Ramiller, N. C. (2004). Innovating mindfully with information technology. MIS Quarterly (best paper award for 2004), *28*(4): 553–583.

Swanson, K. K. (2004). Tourists' and retailers' perceptions of souvenirs. *Journal of Vacation Marketing, 10*(4): 363–377.

Swarbrooke, J. (1999). *Sustainable tourism management*. Oxon, UK: CABI.

Sweet, J. D. (1989). Burlesquing: "The other" in Pueblo performance. *Annals of Tourism Research, 16*, 62–75.

Tatzel, M. (2002). Money worlds and well-being: An integration of money dispositions, materialism, and price-related behavior. *Journal of Economic Psychology, 23*(1): 103–126.

Teas, R. K. (1993). Consumer expectations and the measurement of perceived service quality. *Journal of Professional Services Marketing, 8*(2): 33–53.

Tosun, C. (2002). Host perceptions of impacts—a comparative tourism study. *Annals of Tourism Research, 29*, 231–253.

Tosun, C., Pinat-Temizkan, S., Timothy, D., and Fyall, A. (2007). Tourist shopping experiences and satisfaction. International Journal of Tourism Research, 9(2): 87–102.

Tribe, J. (1997). The indiscipline of tourism. *Annals of Tourism Research, 24*(3): 638–657.

Tribe, J. (2002). Education for ethical tourism action. *Journal of Sustainable Tourism, 10*(4), 309–324.

Tribe, J. (2008). Tourism: A critical business. *Journal of Travel Research, 46*(3): 245–255.

Tribe, J. (2009). Philosophical issues in tourism. In J. Tribe (ed.), *Philosophical issues in tourism* (pp. 3–22). Bristol, UK: Channel View.

Tribe, J. (2010). Tribes, Territories and Networks in the Tourist Academy. *Annals of Tourism Research, 37*(1): 7–33.

Tribe, J., and Snaith, T. (1998). From SERVQUAL to HOLSAT: Holiday satisfaction in Varadero, Cuba. *Tourism Management, 19*(1): 125–134.

Truong, T. (1990). *Sex, money and morality: Prostitution and tourism in South-East Asia.* London: Zed Books.

Truong, T. (2005). Assessing holiday satisfaction of Australian travellers in Vietnam: An application of the HOLSAT model. *Asia Pacific Journal of Tourism Research, 10*(3): 227–246.

Truong, T. (2002). Holiday satisfaction of Australian travellers in Vietnam: An application of the HOLSAT model. Master's dissertation, Faculty of Business, RMIT University, Melbourne, Australia.

Turco, D. M., Stumbo, N., and Garncarz, J. (1998). Tourism constraints for people with disabilities. *Parks and Recreation, 33*, 78–84.

Turnbull, D. R., and Uysal, M. (1995). An exploratory study of German visitors to the Caribbean: Push and pull motivations. *Journal of Travel and Tourism Marketing, 4*(2): 85–91.

Turner, A. J., and Coyle, A. (2000). What does it mean to be a donor offspring? The identity experiences of adults conceived by donor insemination and the implications for counselling and therapy. *Human Reproduction, 15*, 2041–2051.

United Nations World Tourism Organisation (UNWTO). (2009). *Tourism statistics.* Madrid: UNWTO.

Uriely, N. (2005). The tourist experience—conceptual developments. *Annals of Tourism Research, 32*(1): 199–216.

Uriely, N., and Belhassen, Y. (2005). Drugs and tourists' experiences. *Journal of Travel Research, 43*(3): 238–246.

Ureily, N., Yonnay, Y., and Simchai, D. (2002). Backpacking experiences—a type and form analysis. *Annals of Tourism Research, 29*, 520–538.

Uswatte, G. (2003). *PY 420/791-2A—Psychology of strengths and virtues: Lecture schedule outline.* The University of Alabama at Birmingham. Available: www.ppc.sas.upenn.edu/strengthssyllabususwatte.pdf.

Vallen, G., and Casado, M. (2000). Ethical principles for the hospitality curriculum. *Cornell Hotel and Restaurant Administration Quarterly, 41*, 44–51.

Van Boven, L. (2005). Experientialism, materialism, and the pursuit of happiness. *Review of General Psychology, 9*(2): 132–142.

Van den Berghe, P. (1994). *The quest for the other: Ethnic tourism in san Cristobal, Mexico.* Seattle: University of Washington Press.

Vansteenkiste, M., Duriez, B., Simons, J., and Soenens, B. (2006). Materialistic values and well-being among business students: Further evidence of their detrimental effect. *Journal of Applied Social Psychology, 36*(12): 2892–2908.

Van Tubergen, A., and van der Linden, S. (2002). Occasional piece: A brief history of spa therapy. *Annals of Rheumatic Disorders, 31*, 273–275.

Veal, A. J. (2005). *Business research methods—a managerial approach.* Frenchs Forest, NSW: Pearson Education Australia.

Veenhoven, R. (1988). The utility of happiness. *Social Indicators Research, 20*, 333–354.

Veenhoven, R. (1991). Is happiness relative? *Social Indicators Research, 24*, 1–34.

Veenhoven, R. (1994). Is happiness a trait? *Social Indicators Research, 32*, 101–160.

Veenhoven, R. (1996). Happy life-expectancy: A comprehensive measure of quality of life in nations. *Social Indictors Research, 39*, 1–58.

Veenhoven, R. (2000). The four quarters of life. *Journal of Happiness Studies, 1*, 1–39.

Veenhoven, R. (2002). Why social policy needs social indicators. *Social Indicators Research, 58*, 33–45.

Verghese, A. (2009). A touch of sense. *Health Affairs, 28*(4): 1177–1182.

Vermuri, A. W., and Costanza, R. (2006). The role of human, social, built and natural capital in explaining life satisfaction at the country level: Towards a national wellbeing index. *Ecological Economics, 58*, 119–133.

Voigt, C. (2010). Understanding wellness tourism: An analysis of benefits sought, health promoting behaviours and positive psychology well-being. Unpublished PhD thesis. Adelaide, SA: University of South Australia.

Wall, G. (2000). Humour in tourism. In: J. Jafari (ed.), *Encyclopedia of tourism* (p. 291). London: Routledge.

Walle, A. (1997). Quantitative versus qualitative tourism research. *Annals of Tourism Research, 24*(3): 524–536.

Waller, N. G., Bouchard, T. J., Jr., Lykken, T. D., Tellegen, A., and Blacker, D. M. (1993). Creativity, heritability, familiarity: Which word does not belong? *Psychological Inquiry, 4*, 235–237.

Wang, N. (1999). Rethinking authenticity in tourism experience. *Annals of Tourism Research, 26*(2): 349–370.

Warr, P. (1987). *Work, unemployment, and mental health.* Oxford, UK: OUP.

Warr, P. (1999). Well-being in the workplace. In D. Kahneman, E. Diener and N. Schwarz (eds.), *Well-being: The foundations of hedonic psychology.* New York: Sage.

Warr, P. (2007). *Work, happiness and unhappiness.* Mahwah, NJ: Lawrence Erlbaum Associates.

Waterman, A. S. (1993). Two conceptions of happiness: Contrasts of personal expressiveness (eudaimonia) and hedonic enjoyment. *Journal of Personality and Social Psychology, 64*(4), 678–691.

Wearing, S., and Lyons, K. (eds.). (2008). *Journeys of discovery: International case studies in volunteer tourism.* Wallingford, Oxon, UK: CABI.

Wearing, S., McDonald, M., and Ponting, J. (2005). Building a decommodified research paradigm in tourism: The contribution of NGOs. *Journal of Sustainable Tourism, 13*(5): 424–439.

Weaver, D. B., and Lawnton, L. J. (2001). Resident perceptions in the urban-rural fringe. *Annals of Tourism Research, 28*, 439–458.

Webster C., and Beatty , R. C. (1997). Nationality, materialism, and possession importance. In M. Brooks and D. J. MacInnis (eds.), *Advances in consumer research* (Vol. 24; pp. 204–210). Provo, UT: Association for Consumer Research.

Westman, M., and Eden, D. (1997). Effects of a respite from work on burnout: Vacation relief and fade-out. *Journal of Applied Psychology, 82*, 516–527.

Westman, M., and Etzion, D. (2001). The impact of vacation and job stress on burnout and absenteeism. *Psychology and Health, 16*(5): 595–606.

Wheeler, T., and Wheeler, M. (2005). *Once while travelling: The Lonely Planet Story.* VIC, Australia: Viking

Wheeller, B. (2003). Alternative tourism—a deceptive ploy. In C. Cooper (ed.), *Classic reviews in tourism* (pp. 227–234). Sydney, NSW: Channel View.

Wheeller, B. (2009).Tourism and the arts. In J. Tribe (ed.), *Philosophical issues in tourism* (pp. 191–208). Bristol, UK: Channel View.

Wickens, E. (2002). The sacred and the profane—a tourist typology. *Annals of Tourism Research, 29*, 834–851.

Wilson, L. (2007). The family farm business? Insights into family, business and ownership dimensions of open-farms. *Leisure Studies, 26*(3): 357–374.

Winchester, S. (1998). *The surgeon of Crowthorne.* Harmondsworth, UK: Penguin.

Wood, K., and House, S. (1991). *The good tourist.* London: Mandarin.

Woods, B., and Moscardo, G. (2003). Enhancing wildlife education through mindfulness. *Australian Journal of Environmental Education, 19*, 97–108.

Woodside, A. G., Cruickshank, B. F., and Dehuang, N. (2007). Stories visitors tell about Italian cities as destination icons. *Tourism Management, 28*, 162–174.

Yardley, L. (2000). Dilemmas in qualitative health research. *Psychology and Health, 15*, 215–228.

Yeung, S., Wong, S., and Chan, B. (2002). Ethical beliefs of hospitality and tourism students toward their school life. *International Journal of Contemporary Hospitality Management, 14*, 183–192.

Yoon, Y., and Uysal, M. (2005). An examination of the effects of motivation and satisfaction on destination loyalty: A structural model. *Tourism Management, 26*(1): 45–56.

Young, G. (1973). *Tourism, blessing or blight?* Harmondsworth, UK: Penguin.

Yu, H., and Littrell, M. (2003). Product and process orientations to tourism shopping. *Journal of Travel Research, 42*(2): 140–150.

Ziaying, Z., Inbakaran, R. J., and Jackson, M. S. (2006). Understanding community attitudes toward tourism and host-guest interaction in the urban-rural border region. *Tourism Geographies, 8*, 182–204.

Zimbardo, P. G. (2001). *Achieving a balanced time perspective as a life goal.* The Positive Psychology Summit, 5–7 October, Washington, DC.

Zimbardo, P. G. (2002). Time to take our time. *Psychology Today* (March/April), 62.

Zimbardo, P. G., and Boyd, J. N. (1999). Putting time in perspective: A valid, reliable, individual-differences metric. *Journal of Personality and Social Psychology, 77*, 1271–1288.

Zimbardo, P. G., Keogh, K. A., and Boyd, J. N. (1997). Present time perspectives as a predictor of risky driving. *Personality and Individual Differences, 23*, 1007–1023.

Zohar, D. (1994). Analysis of job stress profile in the hotel industry. *International Journal of Hospitality Management, 13*, 219–231.

Author Biographies

DR. PHILIP PEARCE

Dr. Philip Pearce is a Foundation Professor of Tourism at James Cook University in Townsville, Australia, and was appointed the First Professor of Tourism in Australia. He holds a doctorate from the University of Oxford (UK), where he completed a doctorate in psychology (DPhil) studying tourists' social and environmental perceptions in Europe. Professor Pearce grew up in Adelaide, South Australia, where he completed a 1st Class Honours degree in Psychology and a Diploma of Education at the University of Adelaide. He has published widely in the psychology and tourism studies areas and is particularly known for his previous works in the tourist behaviour field. Some of his distinctions and awards include: George Murray scholarship to Oxford University; Fulbright scholar to Harvard University; Honorary Professor of Tourism, Xi'an International Studies University, China; Foundation member of the International Academy for the Study of Tourism; Invited Professor: Masters coursework teaching, AILUN, Sardinia, Italy; Pro Vice Chancellors' award for research excellence; Vice Chancellor's award for Excellence in research supervision and recent Keynote Speaker invitations in Japan, Korea, Thailand, Israel, Australia (2005–2010).

DR. SEBASTIAN FILEP

Dr. Sebastian Filep is a Research Fellow in Travel and Well-Being at the Centre for Tourism and Services Research of Victoria University in Melbourne, Australia. At the time of writing sections of this book, he was a doctoral candidate at the School of Business of James Cook University; his PhD degree was later awarded by that institution and his doctoral research was on the topic of tourist happiness and positive psychology. Dr. Filep also holds a bachelor of business and a bachelor of arts in international studies from the University of Technology, Sydney, and a bachelor of management in tourism (honours) from the same university. He is a member of the International Positive Psychology Association, a Young Tourism Professional of the Pacific Asia Travel Association and a member of the Australian Centre on the Quality of Life. He has a record of international publications on the topics of happiness, tourist satisfaction and positive psychology. He is currently engaged in research projects on optimism and community resilience and benefits of nature to tourists.

DR. GLENN ROSS

Dr. Glenn Ross is an Adjunct Professor of Tourism at James Cook University. He is a Fellow of the International Academy for the Study of Tourism, a Member of the Australian Psychological Society (MAPS), a Member of the Division of Research and Teaching within the Australian Psychological Society, an Associate Fellow of the British Psychological Society (AFBPsS), a Member of the Divisions of Teachers and Researchers in Psychology within the British Psychological Society, and he has a Chartered Status within the British Psychological Society (CPsychol). His research interests are primarily tourism ethics, tourist behaviour and senior tourism. Dr. Ross's recent award includes the winner of the 2005 Elsevier/International Journal of Hospitality Management Prize for the Best Paper in 2004.

Author Index

A

Aas, 72, 73
Abdullah, 176
Abeyraine, 91
Ahuvia, 121
Allen, 68
Altman, 142
Amiable, 93
Anderlick, 70
Anderson, 114
Andrew, 123
Andrews, 123
Ap, 68
Apostolopoulos, 159
Applegate, 34
Aramberri, 20, 42, 114
Archer, 18
Argyle, 10, 24, 65, 67, 83, 84, 89, 161
Aristoppos, 5–6
Aristotle, 28, 65, 66, 81, 82, 83, 85,
    100, 115, 164, 167, 172
Arntzen, 123
Asch, 11
Ashoff, 65
Ateljevic, 20, 25, 26, 41, 123, 128–130,
    134, 137, 140, 141, 169
Atkinson, 140

B

Babakus, 33
Baker, 91
Bakkar, 97
Ballantyne, 35–36
Baloglu, 145
Baltes, 85–86
Bandura, 66
Banks, 63
Bao, 112
Baoying, 111–112

Bardwell, 38
Barsky, 34
Bartlett, 8
Bauer, I., 138
Bauer, T., 24
Baum, 123, 124, 140
Baumeister, 121
Baumgarten, 38
Beardsley, 38, 39
Becher, 2
Beeton, 138
Befus, 125
Belhassen, 53
Belk, 105, 106, 107
Benckendorff, 36
Ben-Shahar, 117, 118
Bentham, 6
Berkman, 77
Berry, 32, 166
Birren, 85
Biswas-Diener, xvi, 5, 22
Black, 34
Blacker, 93
Blalock, 21
Blazer, 77
Bollaert, 41
Boller, 33
Boniwell, 68
Borgmann, 106
Boring, 2–3, 15, 146
Botterill, 43, 62
Bouchard, 93
Bowen, 149
Boyd, 66
Branson, 26
Bratec, 37
Breen, 106
Brentano, 16
Bright, 162

Subject Index